George Thomas Bettany

**Mohammedanism And Other Religions of Mediterranean Countries**

George Thomas Bettany

**Mohammedanism And Other Religions of Mediterranean Countries**

ISBN/EAN: 9783744673334

Printed in Europe, USA, Canada, Australia, Japan

Cover: Foto ©Lupo / pixelio.de

More available books at **www.hansebooks.com**

# MOHAMMEDANISM

*AND OTHER RELIGIONS OF MEDITERRANEAN COUNTRIES.*

## "The World's Religions" Series.

1. **Primitive Religions**: An Introduction to the Study of Religions, with an account of the Religious Beliefs of Uncivilised Peoples.

2. **The Great Indian Religions**: An Account of Brahmanism, Hinduism, Buddhism, and Zoroastrianism.

3. **Mohammedanism**, and other Religions of Mediterranean Countries.

4. **History of Judaism and Christianity**, in the light of Modern Research and Criticism.

LONDON: WARD, LOCK, BOWDEN AND CO.

"The World's Religions" Series.

# MOHAMMEDANISM

### AND OTHER

## *RELIGIONS OF MEDITERRANEAN COUNTRIES.*

#### BEING A POPULAR ACCOUNT OF

Mahomet, the Koran, Modern Islam, together with descriptions of the Egyptian, Assyrian, Phœnician, and also the Greek, Roman, Teutonic, and Celtic Religions.

BY

### G. T. BETTANY, M.A., B.Sc.,

*Author of "The World's Inhabitants," "Life of Charles Darwin," etc.*

WITH MANY ILLUSTRATIONS.

WARD, LOCK, BOWDEN AND CO.,
LONDON: WARWICK HOUSE, SALISBURY SQUARE, E.C.
NEW YORK: BOND STREET.
MELBOURNE: ST. JAMES'S STREET. SYDNEY: YORK STREET.
1892
*(All rights reserved.)*

# PREFACE.

THE countries surrounding the Eastern Mediterranean share with India the distinction of being the greatest originative centres of religion. Egypt, with its strange polytheism, animal worship, ancestor and king worship; Mesopotamia, with its worship of powers of the air and sea, its local deities, its sun and star worship and astrology; the early Greek and Roman religions, with their noble ideals of personal gods under a supreme ruler: all these furnish inexhaustible material for the student of religions. But they are surpassed by the interest growing out of the gradual approach to monotheism, and its assertion in Judaism and Mohammedanism, the one an early, the other a later product of Semitic races, both destined to influence a very large part of mankind.

In this volume will be found material of strange suggestiveness, whether studied by itself, or, better, in connexion and comparison with the history of primitive Chinese and Indian religions, on the one hand, or that of Judaism and Christianity, on the other. In the history of Mahomet we see a most remarkable combination of introspection, revolt against prevalent superstition, rapt prophetic trances, statesmanship, and worldliness, variously predominant at different periods of his life. The simplicity of the theology and worship taught and enjoined in the Koran have been most effective towards its propagation, which has been still more powerfully aided by the injunction to appeal to the sword, and to have no toleration for heretics. After more than a thousand years of conversion at the point of the sword, the same fanatic spirit survives in many parts, kept in subjection in India by the strong arm of British power; but Islam also manifests a capacity for advancing by peaceful conquests both in India and Africa, which, while it may be welcomed in so far as it means the superseding of a lower by a higher religion, of polytheism by monotheism, yet has its dark side for believers in Christianity. For it brings with it a fanatic belief in so imperfect a book as the Koran, a stereotyping of formal worship, and a resolute obstruction to the distinctive teachings of Christianity. This book may be specially commended to those who wish to realise what it is that missionaries in districts dominated by Mohammedan influence have to contend with. It is the fanatical belief in the inspired and final revelation of the Koran, combined with the strength of the good points in its teaching, that make it the most serious obstacle and rival influence to Christianity.

# CONTENTS.

| CHAPTER | | PAGE |
|---|---|---|
| I. | THE EGYPTIAN RELIGION | 1 |
| II. | THE BABYLONIAN, ASSYRIAN, AND PHŒNICIAN RELIGIONS | 31 |
| III. | LIFE OF MAHOMET. PART I. | 56 |
| IV. | LIFE OF MAHOMET. PART II. | 78 |
| V. | THE KORAN AND ITS TEACHINGS | 96 |
| VI. | MODERN ISLAM. PART I. | 114 |
| VII. | MODERN ISLAM. PART II. | 153 |
| VIII. | THE ANCIENT GREEK RELIGION: THE GODS | 183 |
| IX. | GREEK SACRIFICES, PRIESTS, TEMPLES AND FESTIVALS, AND MORALS | 211 |
| X. | SOCRATES, PLATO, AND OTHER GREEK PHILOSOPHERS | 236 |
| XI. | THE ROMAN RELIGION | 253 |
| XII. | THE RELIGION OF THE TEUTONS | 284 |
| XIII. | THE RELIGION OF THE SLAVONIANS | 301 |
| XIV. | CELTIC RELIGION | 309 |

## CHAPTER I.

## The Egyptian Religion.

Modern discoveries—Local deities—Tendency to monotheism—Hymn to Amen-ra—The Egyptian a nature-religion—Ra, the sun-god—Shu and Tefnut—The worship at On—Osiris—Apis—Serapis—Isis—Horus—Hathor—Thoth—Ptah—Anubis and Neith—Amun-ra—Animal worship—Animism—Deification of kings—Temples—The priests—Orders of priests—Festivals and processions—Invocation of the Nile—Animal sacrifices—Oracles—Astrology—Life after death—A funeral song—Osiris, the judge of the dead—"The Book of the Dead"—Other Egyptian Books—Proceedings at the sacred lake—Objects buried with the dead—Egyptian morals—High esteem of truth and charity—Singular custom at banquets.

NOT less astonishing than the religions of India, and probably more ancient in its advanced development, is the religion of the early Egyptians[1] as it has been slowly recovered and pieced together in the present century. Many monuments and records have unfortunately perished, many are still buried and unexplored, but those which have been rescued and explained furnish us with undoubted facts sufficient to give rise to ideas of a highly developed form of religion, in many respects worthy to rank beside that revealed in the Vedas. And geological facts show that the human

<sub>Modern discoveries.</sub>

---

[1] See Sir Gardner Wilkinson, "Manners and Customs of the Early Egyptians," Birch's edition (W.); Renouf, "Hibbert Lectures on the Religion of Ancient Egypt" (R.); Tiele's "Egyptian Religion" (T.); "Memoirs of Egypt Exploration Fund"; Murray's "Handbook for Egypt"; "Records of the Past" (R.P).

race has inhabited the Nile valley for a number of centuries far surpassing all ordinary chronology, and abundantly sufficing to account for the growth of the art, architecture, religion, and other evidences of civilisation, which culminated at least two or three thousand years B.C. The religion which grew with this civilisation was in one sense still more polytheistic than the early Vedic, and it was more thoroughly local and tribal. Each locality, each town and village worshipped local deities. But there are extant texts which indicate that at some early date the priests recognised that there was but one God, and that all the various forms of deity that were worshipped were but the manifestations of different aspects of the same Being, which they identified with the universe. We have abundant evidence that the earlier periods of the Egyptian religion were purer, and that its best features were older than the absurdities and inconsistencies which formed so large a part of later worship. This is but like the contrast between ancient Vedism and much of modern Hinduism. But it cannot be proved that anything like a pure monotheism existed primitively, which only developed later into polytheism. It is evident that the belief in one God and in many gods was held by the same men without the thought of inconsistency. Thus we find many expressions in which the almighty Power is referred to as one and supreme. "If thou art a wise man, bring up thy son in the love of God." "God loveth the obedient, and hateth the disobedient." "Praised be God for all His gifts." "The God of the world is in the light above the firmament; His emblems are upon earth; it is to them that worship is rendered daily." And on the walls of the oasis-temple of El-Khargeh is an inscription from which the following recognition of the identity of this supreme God with all the gods is derived: "The gods salute his royal majesty (Amun-ra, the sun-god) as their Lord, who revealeth himself in all that is, and hath names in everything, from mountain to stream. That which persisteth in all things is Amon. This lordly god was from the very beginning. He is Ptah, the greatest of the gods. . . . Each god has assumed thy aspect. . . . To thee all things that are give praise when thou returnest to the nether world at even. Thou raisest up Osiris by the radiance of thy beams. To thee those give praise who lie in their tombs. . . . The gods are in thine hand, and men are at thy feet. What god is like to thee? Thou hast made the double world, as Ptah. Thou hast placed thy throne in the life of the double

EGYPTIAN DEITIES (*a few out of many diverse representations*).

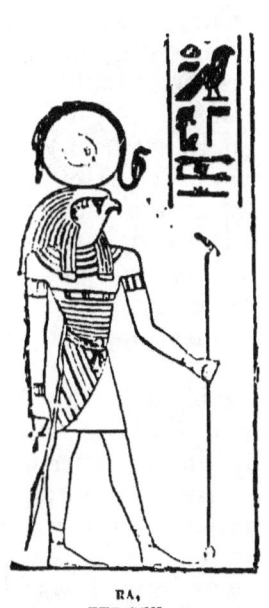

RA, THE SUN.

CHNUM, THE GOD OF THE WATERS.

world, as Amon. . . . Thy form emanated at first whilst thou shinest as Amon, Rā, and Ptah. . . . Thou art Mentu Rā. Thou art Sekar; thy transformations are into the Nile. Thou art Youth and Age. Thou givest life to the earth by thy stream. Thou art heaven, thou art earth, thou art fire, thou art water, thou art air, and whatever is in the midst of them." (R.)

The following extract from a hymn to Amèn-ra still further exemplifies the idea of unity or supremacy among the gods: "The One in his works, single among the gods; the beautiful bull in the cycle of gods, chief of all the gods, Lord of truth, Father of the gods, Maker of men, Creator of beasts, Lord of existences, Creator of fruitful trees, Maker of herbs, Feeder of cattle—good Being, begotten of Ptah, beautiful youth beloved: to whom the gods give honour; Maker of things below and above, Enlightener of the Earth, sailing in heaven in tranquillity," . . . and the hymn continues through a long series of most elevated phrases. In one part Ra is addressed as "Athom, maker of men, supporting their works, giving them life, distinguishing the colour of one from another, listening to the poor in distress, gentle of heart when one cries to him, deliverer of the timid man from the violent, judging the poor, the poor and the oppressed" (R.P., vol. ii.); and one almost imagines he is reading one of the Hebrew Psalms of blessing. Many such splendid compositions have been found; and we must realise that the people who had such conceptions stood at a high level, poetic and spiritual, and that there must have been many besides the composers who reverenced their inspiration, and carefully preserved and valued its products.

<small>Hymn to Amen-ra.</small>

It is evident that this religion is, like the Vedic, at bottom a nature religion. Their mythology concentrated itself mainly upon the daily recurring phenomena, especially of sunrise and sunset, and had a large number of different stories about these events, often mutually inconsistent. Perhaps the oldest form under which the sun was worshipped was Rā, that being the common word for sun. The sky was imagined as a watery expanse, across which the sun-god travelled in a boat. Like the Aryan gods, he had to fight with the demon of darkness, Apap, a serpent, who is pierced by the weapons of the god. He has many names, among which may be mentioned Harmachis as rising sun, and Tum, as the setting sun. He is generally represented as a hawk-headed man, with the solar disc on his head. The sun's disc was termed his emblem, but he was said to journey in it across the sky. The

<small>The Egyptian a nature-religion.</small>

<small>Rā, the sun god.</small>

following quotation from the "Book of the Dead" will give an idea of the worship addressed to him: "Hail, thou who art come as Tum, and who hast been the creator of the gods! Hail, thou who art come as soul of the holy souls in Amenti! Hail, supreme among the gods, who by thy beauties dost illumine the kingdom of the dead! Hail, thou who comest in radiance and travellest in thy disc! Hail, greatest of all the gods, bearing rule in the highest, reigning in the nethermost heaven! . . . Hail, renowned and glorified god! Thy enemies

SECHET, OR PASHT, THE LION-HEADED GODDESS.   SEBEK, THE CROCODILE-HEADED GOD.

fall upon their scaffold! Hail! thou hast slain the guilty, thou hast destroyed Apap." (T.)

Shu, the son of Râ, without a mother, represents the air, and also the principle of heat and light, and as such is called the abode of the sun. But he is also said to be uncreated, the principle of creation, the life-giver, the young old, and by him righteousness and truth reign. Later he was made a sun-god, in union with Râ, and is then represented as a male cat; but his ordinary figure is human. Tefnut, representing dew,

*Shu and Tefnut.*

foam, and ocean, is the wife of Shu, by whom the birth of all things is brought about. She is represented as a lioness.

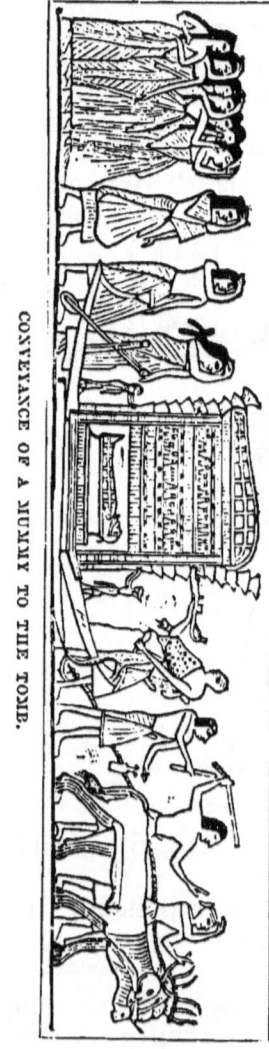

CONVEYANCE OF A MUMMY TO THE TOMB.

**The worship at On.** These three gods formed the central objects of worship at On (known to the Greeks as Heliopolis, the city of the sun). Its priests were notable for their learning; and it was an especial distinction for Joseph to be married to a priest's daughter. This worship continued influential, and was widely spread throughout Egypt to a late period. It was closely associated with the belief in resurrection and immortality.

**Osiris.** Osiris was the chief god worshipped at Thinis and Abydos; his parents were said to be Seb (earth) and Nut (heaven). The myth of Osiris given by Plutarch, describing him as an Egyptian king, is but a late explanation; but it seems that Osiris represents the good principle, and the Creator, always at war with evil, and especially with Seb, the destroyer, his brother, who is darkness. The myth, as given in the "Book of the Dead" in various places, appears to show forth the sun's daily course, as well as the daily round of human life, both combating darkness and evil, continually succumbing and reviving. The aspect in which Osiris was most thought of was that in which he is hidden; and thus the dead were placed under his guardianship, and nearly all the inscriptions on tombs are addressed to him. As typifying the good principle, Osiris also represents Egypt and the Nile.

As his worship spread widely, many local legends were adapted to him, and we find in one chapter of the "Book of the Dead," a hundred names ascribed to him. "It would appear," says Tiele, "that so soon as his worship

PILLARED HALL OF THE TEMPLE AT PHILE, IN EGYPT.

had established itself in any one place, Osiris took the form of the deity whose ancient seat it was, and the sacred animal of that particular town or district was consecrated to him." Thus, at On and at Abydos, he was represented as the migratory bird Bennu, at Memphis as a species of ape and as a lofty pillar, surmounted by his complete headdress and emblems, indicating his abode in the highest heaven.

RESTORATION OF FAÇADE OF ROCK TEMPLE OF HATHOR, ABU SIMBEL, NUBIA.

Apis.

Perhaps the most remarkable of the emblems of Osiris was the living bull, Apis, worshipped as an incarnation of the god in the temple of Ptah at Memphis. His movements and varying appetites were carefully observed, and indeed regarded as giving oracular indications. His life was not to extend beyond twenty-five years; at this age he was put to death, and his successor sought for and recognised by certain markings. Thus the succession of these bulls fixed periods of chronology. When dead he was termed Serapis or Osarapis (Apis who has become Osiris) and lord of the under world. The Mendesian goat, termed the Ram, was an emblem of Rā as well as of Osiris, worshipped at Mendes.

*Serapis.*

AMMON,
THE ALL-CREATING.

PTAH,
THE ALL-ACCOMPLISHING.

Isis, the wife of Osiris, had temples in early Egypt, and had something in common with the Greek Demeter and Persephone. In later Egypt, especially under the Ptolemies, she became elevated to a most prominent position. Originally she represented chiefly festivity, and was mistress of heaven and daughter of Rā. She appears with a cow's head instead of a human one, or with a vulture-headdress, and also in the form of a female hippopotamus. All these symbols show how

*Isis.*

completely the early Egyptians recognised natural phenomena and animals as living manifestations of the gods.

Horus is the son of Osiris and Isis, and his avenger; thus he was identified with the rising sun. His name was associated with a whole group of gods representing the visible sun, and very like Rā in some forms. There are many myths about him which we cannot detail. He is always represented with the head of a hawk.

**Horus.**

Hathor, described both as the mother and wife of Horus, was very like Isis, and was worshipped throughout Egypt, as the female counterpart of Osiris. She was queen of the heavens, both by day and by night, the giver of great gifts to Egypt.

**Hathor.**

Thoth was the Egyptian moon-god, wearing the moon upon his head as crescent or full disc, but often represented with the head of an ibis. From the moon being the measure of time, he becomes patron of all measurement, and hence of all science and letters, and of priestly culture. His influence steadily increased as the kingdom advanced in culture.

**Thoth.**

Phtha, or Ptah, was the chief god of Memphis, representing creative power, but not the sun distinctively. He was worshipped in a human form, and sometimes as a pigmy. The gods were said to have come out of his mouth, and men from his eye. He was the god of justice and of beneficence to man. The frog-headed deity, Ka, is also a form of Ptah.

**Ptah.**

Among other gods whom we can only briefly mention were Anubis, son of Osiris, the god presiding over mummification, with four attendant subordinate divinities; and Neith, or Nit, a goddess worshipped specially at Saïs, described as "the mother who bore the sun, the first-born, but not begotten."

**Anubis and Neith.**

We must also briefly mention the god Amen or Ammon (hidden or unrevealed deity), whose worship assumed such great proportions during later Egyptian history. Amen, his wife, Mut (the mother), and his son, Khonsu, formed the chief triad of gods worshipped at Thebes, especially from the eighteenth to the twentieth

**Amun-ra.**

dynasties. At this period he was identified with Rā, the sun-god, and named Amun-Rā. Later, he was regarded as the god of oracles; and his oracle, in the oasis in the Libyan desert, was consulted by many foreign rulers and nations. Amen was often figured as a man seated on a throne, holding a sceptre in his right hand and a small cross with a handle in his left. His headdress frequently had two huge feathers.

Animal worship became more marked in Egyptian

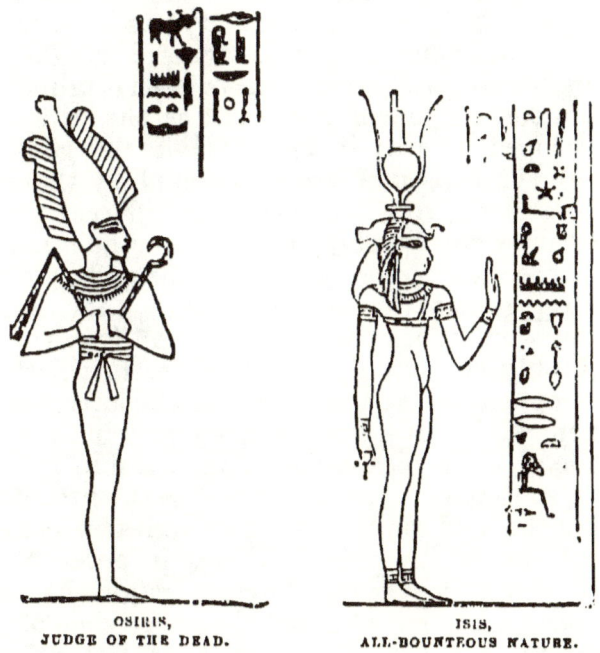

OSIRIS,
JUDGE OF THE DEAD.

ISIS,
ALL-BOUNTEOUS NATURE.

religion than in Indian; and there were fables representing that the spirits of the principal animals were supposed to be embodied in the kings. **Animal worship.**

In later times every important place had its sacred animal; and it was a great part of the local religion to tend it, and to embalm and bury it with honour when dead; and their mummies have been found in many places. The dog-headed ape (cynocephalus) at Thebes, the jackal at Kynopolis, mice and sparrowhawks at Butos, the ibis at

Hermopolis, Memphis, and Thebes, the cat, the ram, the vulture, the ichneumon, the hippopotamus, the crocodile, at other places were waited on with the utmost care. Herodotus relates that the crocodile at Krokodilopolis, on Lake Moeris, had golden earrings, and rings on its forefeet, was fed with meat and meal, and embalmed after death.

No doubt the Egyptian animal worship represents an extreme form of animism. The Egyptians regarded animals, especially those most conspicuous for strength, power, or beauty, as incarnations of spirits, whose favour might be gained or displeasure averted by worship. This may have been originally quite apart from conceptions of gods; but as the latter became more developed, it was imagined that the gods themselves were symbolised or were inhabited by the animals. Later, these ideas grew and varied in different ways, and new animals were worshipped, because their names resembled more or less closely those of the gods.

**Animism.**

As the Egyptians worshipped animals, they also, at an early date, worshipped their kings. At first they were only so worshipped after death, priests being appointed for their service; but later, they were worshipped while alive, and temples were built for them by the side of their pyramids. This worship grew very expensive, so that Una, a high official in the fifth dynasty, boasts that he had built four sanctuaries in connection with great levies for public works, in order that the spirits of the living king, Merenra, might be invoked "more than all the gods"; and the succession of priests of the several kings was kept up till a late date. The divine right of kings was never more zealously believed in or more devoutly expressed than by the Egyptians. What we should term, now-a-days, the most abject servility, was an unquestioned commonplace among them; and it by no means appears to have been first imposed by the kings themselves. Indeed, if an animal was regarded as an incarnation of a god, how much more a king? Thus we find a disgraced servant imploring his king in this fashion: "Let god be gracious to him whom

**Deification of kings.**

he has removed, whom he has banished to another land, let him be mild as Rā." When restored to favour, he cannot sufficiently express his adoration of the king. "The great god, the equal of the sun-god, mocks me! thy majesty is as Horus, the power of thy arm extends over all lands." When admitted once more to his presence, he says: "The god spoke amicably to me. I was like one brought out of the darkness into the light. My tongue was dumb, my limbs refused their office, my heart was no longer in my body, so that I knew not whether

HORUS,
SON OF OSIRIS.

NEBI-HA,
A SUBTERRANEAN DEITY.

I lived or if I was dead." (T.) When such opinions prevailed, even among the common people, it is not surprising that the kings accepted with complacency the adoration offered to them. The China of to-day was outdone by ancient Egypt, and the king alone was fully competent to approach the gods in the temples with the priests. In many an inscription the king claims the empire over all nations and the whole world. Even the gods are represented as worshipping the living king. The god says to Rameses II., "I am thy father; by me are begotten all thy members as divine. . . . Thou

RUINS OF TEMPLE OF AMUN-RĀ, KARNAK, EGYPT.

art lord like the majesty of Rā; the gods and goddesses

are praising thy benefits, adoring and sacrificing before thine image." And the king was said to possess the seven souls and the fourteen Rās, or spirits of Rā. Yet the divinity assigned to the kings did not prevent them from worshipping the gods in the humblest attitudes. Perhaps the kings so utterly flattered really had some notion of their own insignificance before the Divine power.

It would be as impossible to describe within our limits the Egyptian as the Indian or the Greek temples. They were erected, to a large extent, on a uniform plan, though differing considerably in details. Each was built by a king in honour of some god or triad of gods; and the motive was not that the people might worship the gods, but that the king might pay honour to them, and secure their future favours. The temples are always massive stone structures, surrounded by lofty brick walls, with fine entrances, sometimes flanked by huge broad towers sculptured with representations of the king's doings, either in war or peace. Within was an avenue of sphinxes; images wherein the body of a lion was conjoined with a human head, denoting the combined excellence of mind and body of the king; this might be interrupted by one or more portals, flanked by huge side towers. Then came a portico opening into one or more fore-courts, through which a roofed enclosure was reached, adjoining the sacred sanctuary, which was low and comparatively small, and contained a sort of ark or chest, half covered by a veil or curtain, and contained in a boat. Both these were decorated with symbols of life, light and fertility. The ark contained a small image of the god, never seen, and supposed to have never been seen. Everywhere in the temple the deeds of the great king were celebrated in pictures and sculptures of various kinds, and records of them were engraved upon the walls. To the right and left of, or all round the central sanctuary, might be smaller courts in which special kinds of offerings were made. Huge statues of the kings, obelisks, and other special Egyptian features were abundant. As a specimen of the greater temples we may mention

*Temples.*

that that of El-Karnak, Thebes, has a front 360 feet wide; the first court is 275 feet long; the great roofed hall is 170 feet long by 329 feet wide, and its roof is supported by 134 columns, of which the twelve tallest are seventy feet high, and about 40 feet in diameter, and form an avenue through the middle, the smaller columns forming groups on either side. Thus a marvellous effect, as of a forest of columns, is produced. It does not appear that the people performed their worship at any time in the temples; they, if they had any special place of worship, probably had private chapels.

The Egyptian priests were not a definite hereditary order, and were not absolutely confined to their priestly office. "The priest of a god was often a military or naval commander, exercised the office of scribe, and was invested with the supervision of public works or local government. A general in the army could marry the daughter of a priest, and his children could be scribes, priests, or public functionaries." (W.) All this emphasised the power of the king, who was fully initiated as a priest, and was the head of the national religion. In fact, upon great occasions, the king himself offered the sacrifices; he appointed and superintended the great festivals and regulated the sacrifices. But the extent to which the priests were employed in all the great offices of the State, and their function of expounding to the king his moral duties, gave them an aggregate influence transcending that of any other class. In fact, viewing the king as priest also, it must be acknowledged that, as in China, India, Greece, and Rome, the priests of Egypt practically ruled the country.

**The priests.**

The priests were very numerous, and formed many colleges, classed according to the god they specially served, and their various functions. Thus, there were the prophets, who were the chief priests, four being attached to each principal god; the divine fathers, who might become prophets; the purifiers or washers, the incense-bearers, the funeral attendants, the bards, and others. There were also priestesses, divine wives and divine handmaids, singers, etc.; and in the early Empire

**Orders of priests.**

there were prophetesses, and these offices were held by queens, princesses, and members of the noblest families. The priests and their families had great privileges, were free from taxes, and received as a body one-third of the land, besides being provided for out of the public stores. The prophets had the greatest amount of learning about all religious matters, they also managed the priestly revenues, and they had a conspicuous place in religious processions. They kept their mysteries as secret as some of the Greek priesthoods, and only admitted to them those who had satisfied them of their high character and learn-

ANUBIS,
THE ESCORT OF THE DEAD.

THOTH,
THE MOON-GOD.

ing. They paid great attention to the education of their children in all the science of the time, and kept up a strict discipline and severity of outward demeanour. They were strict as to the quantity and quality of their food—fish and the flesh of swine, pulse, etc., being strictly forbidden. They bathed twice in the day and twice in the night; and they shaved the entire body every third day. Fasts of great length, from seven to forty-two days, were observed by them, preceded by a period of purification. They were circumcised at initiation (though this was very general among the people). Their ordinary garments were of linen, but the high priests wore an entire leopard's skin on great occasions; they wore sandals of papyrus and palm leaves, and they lay either on skins on the ground, or on wickerwork beds of palm branches, the head being raised on a semi-cylinder of wood.

The great occasions of Egyptian religion were the festivals and processions; among these were the processions **Festivals and processions.** of shrines, the dedication of temples; the conveyance of the royal offerings to the gods; the king's coronation, and his triumphs on returning from war. The procession of shrines included a variable number of arks and their boats, carried by priests, by means of long staves passed through metal rings at the sides. A shrine of the reigning king might also be included in the procession, as well as the statue of the principal deity, of the king and of his ancestors. The shrine or shrines were brought into the temple, placed on a table, and decked with fresh flowers. Many offerings were made, on several altars, and the king offered incense and made a libation. The anointing of the king at his coronation was performed by the high priest in a similar manner to the anointing of the Jewish high priest; but such anointing was an ordinary expression of welcome in Egypt. Many other ceremonies showed the intimate connection of the kings with the national religion; the king represented the whole nation and was everything in himself.

The annual invocation of the Nile was one of the most important festivals. If this were not duly celebrated, **Invocation of the Nile.** the people believed the Nile would not rise and inundate the land. People assembled in the towns from all the villages around to take part in this festival, which was marked by hymns, music, and dancing, as well as feasting. A wooden statue of the Nile-god was carried through the villages. A remarkable hymn or invocation to the Nile has been preserved, in which it is credited with divine honours. "O inundation of the Nile," it is said, "offerings are made to thee, oxen are slain to thee, great festivals are kept for thee . . . unknown is his Name in heaven, he doth not manifest his forms, vain are all representations." (R.P. iv.) Many other festivals were held in celebration of the various qualities of the gods and of the recurring seasons. The festivals of Isis and Osiris were numerous and magnificent, and so many details are known that it is impossible here to give even an outline of them; but yet Sir Gardner Wilkinson remarks that "the greater part of the fêtes and religious rites of the Egyptians are totally unknown to us." How thoroughly, therefore, the religious element entered into Egyptian as into Indian and Chinese life!

The Egyptians offered animal sacrifices to all their gods, as well as cakes and wine, incense, flowers, and herbs. Oxen were prominent among the victims, which also included gazelles, ibexes, geese, and wild fowl, but not sheep. The right shoulder was generally the part first offered on the altar. The king was present at the daily sacrifices, when the people prayed for him, and the priests praised him and warned him against the faults of other kings, caused by ill advice having been given to them. The king himself inspected the entrails of the victim and performed some of the ceremonies of sacrifice. There is no distinct evidence that human sacrifices were ever made in Egypt within historic times; and indeed, at the earliest time we can clearly read, they seem to have advanced beyond the idea that human victims are required by the gods. *(Animal sacrifices.)*

We have already seen how important a place oracles came to occupy in Greece; but the Greeks themselves confessed that they were of late institution among themselves, and had been derived from Egypt. The most famous oracles were those of Thebes, of Buto, of Heliopolis, and of Ammon, in Libya, the giving of oracles being a function of some gods only. In some temples questions were taken to the temple in writing, and sealed; and answers were given in the same fashion, and supposed to have been inspired or given by the god. The oracle of Ammon was highly celebrated *(Oracles.)*

in foreign countries. In some cases oracles were spontaneously sent, to warn, censure, or command prominent persons or States. Astrology was also largely cultivated in connection with the temples; and future events were predicted by the indications of the stars. These predictions gained high repute in the ancient world through their frequent accuracy.

**Astrology.**

It is in the funeral rites and literature of the Egyptians that we come upon some of the most interesting features of their religion. That they very early had a belief in a continuous life after the death of the body is indubitable. Every human soul being supposed to have a divine part which returned to the deity after death, the good were believed to attain reunion with the deity, and consequently received the name Osiris. The deceased person's body was bound up so as to bear a resemblance to Osiris; and offerings were made to Osiris after the burial, in the deceased's name. Sacrifices and liturgies were offered to Osiris by the priests in the presence of the mourners; and these were repeated on a greater or less scale as long and as frequently as the family were willing to pay for them.

**Life after death.**

Sometimes the special funeral songs composed for a festival or anniversary attained great beauty. Thus, when we read such a song as this of the harper, dating from the eighteenth dynasty, we are irresistibly reminded of passages in the Bible; and this is older than a large proportion if not all of the Hebrew Psalms. "The great one is truly at rest, the good charge is fulfilled. Men pass away since the time of Rā, and the youths come in their stead. Like as Rā reappears every morning, and Tum sets in the horizon, men are begetting and women are conceiving. Every nostril inhaleth once the breezes of dawn, but all born of women go down to their places. . . . No works of buildings in Egypt could avail; his resting-place is all his wealth. Let me return to know what remaineth of him. Not the least moment could be added to his life. Those who have magazines full of bread to spend, even they shall encounter the hour of a last end. . . . Mind thee

**A funeral song.**

of the day when thou too shalt start for the land to which one goeth to return not thence. Good for thee, then, will have been an honest life, therefore be just and hate transgressions. . . . The coward and the bold, neither can fly the grave, the friendless and proud are alike." (R.P. vi.)

The treatment of the deceased after death and the general practices of the Egyptians in regard to death showed that, as Diodorus says, they regarded the tombs as "eternal dwelling-places," and this idea goes very far back in the records. Only the evil are spoken of as actually dead. The greatest importance was attached to the permanence of the religious ceremonies for the dead, just as among the Chinese, and the motive of building the Great Pyramids was to perpetuate the dwelling-place of the dead kings for ever.

The supposed fate of the dead, as related by Herodotus, quite corresponds with the sculptures, pictures, and inscriptions. He describes the principal office of Osiris as being that of judging the dead in the under-world (Amenti); seated on his throne, he received an account of the actions of the dead as recorded by Thoth, his actions having first been weighed in the scales of Truth by Anubis, who, assisted by Horus, placed the heart, as typifying virtuous actions of the deceased, in the balance against the figure of the twofold goddess of Truth and Justice. Sometimes the deceased are represented as wearing round their necks the emblem which appears in the scales, signifying their acceptance. Those who had done evil were supposed to pass in succession into the bodies of different animals, the number and kinds of the animals depending upon their guilt; it is however a disputed point whether this view was really held by the Egyptians.

These views are borne out by the manuscript and inscribed writings found in Egyptian tombs and known as "The Book of the Dead," or the "Ritual of the Dead," containing prayers mostly supposed to be recited by the deceased in the underworld, but always recited in his name by those present at the funeral ceremonies. In many cases, however, there is great difficulty in ascertaining the precise meaning of expressions, owing to the carelessness of copyists, and to different readings. Much of it dates from the early dynasties, and implies a complete knowledge of the early mythology. In it the happy dead are represented as leading a life like that on earth; the gods provide their food and admit them to their tables. Even agricultural employments are attributed to them. But they were believed also to be able to traverse the whole universe in every desired shape and form. Through their identification with Osiris and their utterance of "words of power," they can pass unhurt in any direction. In some chapters of the Ritual the limbs of the deceased are each separately identified with a distinct god. In one chapter it is said that "Whom men know not" (a mode of referring to a god without naming his revered name) is his name. The "yesterday which sees endless years is his name. The deceased is the lord of eternity." (R.) His soul, his Rā or genius, and his shadow are all given back to him; he overcomes in combat crocodiles, serpents, etc., and successfully surmounts all kinds of difficulties and dangers, to which

*"The Book of the Dead."*

evidently those of evil life or not protected by the gods would succumb.

The recitals made by the deceased to the gods indicate the virtues which were highly esteemed. Thus: "I am not a doer of fraud and iniquity against men. I am not

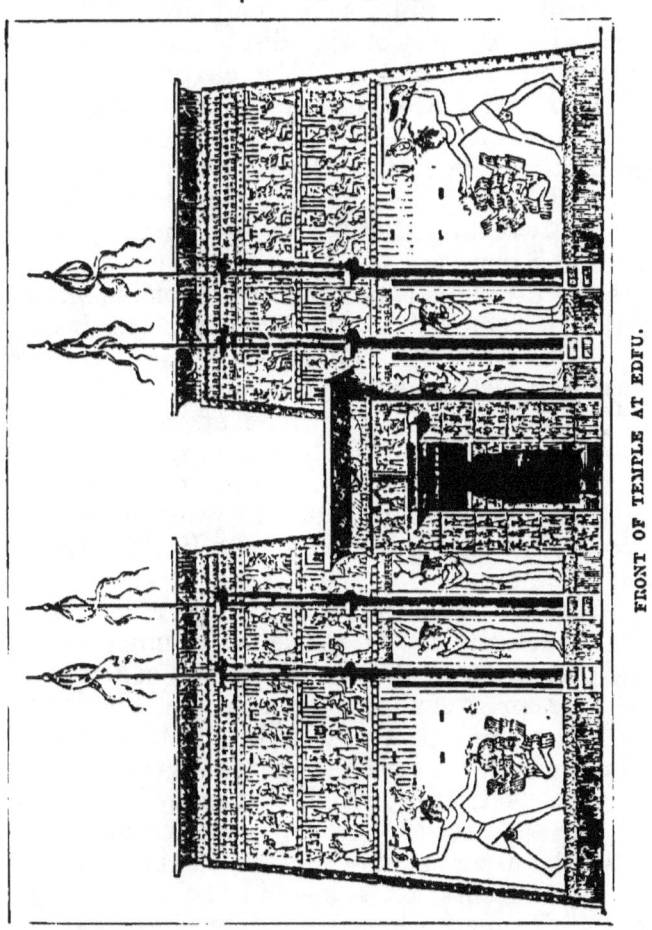

FRONT OF TEMPLE AT EDFU.

a doer of that which is crooked in place of that which is right. . . . I do not force a labouring man to do more than his daily task. . . . I do not calumniate a servant to his master; I do not cause hunger; I do not cause weeping; I am not a murderer; I do not give order to murder privily; I am not guilty of fraud against any one; I am not a falsifier of the measures in the temples." Even inward faults or crimes are referred to in this way by implication, such as causing pain of mind to another, turning a deaf ear to the words of truth and justice; and sins against chastity are included in the list of sins disclaimed. These quotations are contained in the 125th chapter of the "Book of the Dead," and are believed to represent the oldest known code of morals. It is entitled: "Book of entering into the Hall of the twofold Maat: the person parts from his sins that he may see the divine faces." The twofold Maat is the twofold god of Truth and Justice, represented by a double figure.

There are other ancient Egyptian books of great interest, which we cannot detail. Such are the book which *Other Egyptian books.* describes the course of the sun through the night, the twelve divisions of his journey, and the names of the gods of each locality; the Lamentations of Isis and Nephthys, supposed to be recited by the two sisters of Osiris in order to bring about his resurrection, and actually recited by priests over the dead; "the Book of glorifying Osiris," "the Book of the Breaths of Life," etc., etc.

The influence of the Egyptian ideas about the future state was markedly shown in the preliminary proceedings *Proceedings at the sacred lake.* at the sacred lake which was constructed near or in every city or centre. The body of a deceased person was brought to the borders of the lake, and a number of judges were assembled to hear any accusation of evil life that might be brought against the deceased. On sufficient proof, ceremonial burial and transport across the sacred lake were denied; while a false accusation subjected the accuser to heavy penalties. If no accuser appeared, or if accusations were disproved, the relations praised the dead person, enlarging on his virtues, and begging the gods below to receive him as a companion of the pious; and if the family already possessed special tombs, the funeral then proceeded. But the denial of honourable burial was considered an extreme disgrace, foreshadowing the terrible

FUNERAL OF AN EGYPTIAN KING.

fate which overtook the deceased in Hades; and no little

share in this feeling was due to the triumph enjoyed by
the enemies of the family. There appears, however, to
have been a way of escape; crimes might be thus punishable for limited periods; and thus when the priests had
been sufficiently paid to make continuous prayers for
them, and the sorrowing relatives showed sufficient religious devotion, it was believed that the evil destiny could
finally be removed from the deceased. Many persons of
course had no money to go through this ceremony of the
sacred lake at all, or to be embalmed, and such had to
be buried on the shores of the lake, or in the houses of
their relatives. Even kings had to go through the ordeal
of possible accusation and judgment, and in several cases
a public honourable funeral was refused to them.

The descriptions of mummies and embalming, besides
being very well known, would lead us too far from our
main subject. We may note that the tombs
of rich persons had various objects of value
placed in them, such as vases, some with the
heads of the genii of Amen-ti, and small images of the
deceased, papyri with sacred or other writings upon them,
tablets of stone or wood decorated with funeral subjects or
narratives relating to the deceased, and many objects connected with the deceased's profession. Some of the little
figures, in all kinds of materials, had their arms crossed
like Osiris, with whom the dead became identified, and
bearing hieroglyphics containing the deceased's name
and rank and the formulæ of presentation of his soul to
Osiris. These figures, which only commence in the
eighteenth dynasty, were called "respondents" in the
"Ritual of the Dead," being imagined to answer the
deceased's call for aid to do various agricultural work
for him in the other world. One of these has engraved
on it a chapter of the ritual, entitled "Avoiding," or
"How not to do Work in Hades," showing that in that
degenerate period the Egyptians were greatly concerned
to avoid the toils of the future.

In some respects Egyptian morals present a favourable
picture; in others, the kings appear as trying varied ex-
periments in social legislation and regulation; in others,

morals fared but badly. Truth and justice were sought to be attained, but sometimes by primitive methods. False oaths were even punished with death; and a man who slandered the dead was severely punished; whilst a false accuser was condemned to the same punishment as the accused would have deserved if guilty. Wilful murder, even of a slave, was punishable with death; and the witness who did not try to prevent the crime was similarly punished. Parricide was punished with torture before death. Child-murder was visited, not with death, but with the strange punishment of spending three days and nights with the dead body fastened to the neck of the culprit under a public guard. Adultery in a woman was punished by loss of the nose; forgery and falsification of weights and measures by loss of the hands. Many offences which are now visited with imprisonment were visited with the bastinado. Usury was condemned, and interest was never allowed to increase beyond double the original sum. Only goods, not persons, could be seized for debt, the person being the property of the king or of the State. At an early period people were required to give in pledge for borrowed money the mummy of a father or near relative, a deposit certain to be redeemed if at all possible, for if it were not redeemed the debtor could not be buried with the usual ceremonies, or in any honourable place. Luxury and vice had their place in Egypt as in every other rich country; but we do not find evidence that Egypt was worse than other nations, if so bad. Women occupied a considerable place in society and in politics, and were by no means kept as secluded as in modern Oriental life. One wife was the rule, but not the limit; and the kings had as many wives as they pleased; the marriage of brothers and sisters was however allowed. All children, by whatever mother, shared in the inheritance. Sons were required to pay great deference to their parents and to serve them much as in China. Their respect for old age and for elder strangers, reverence for ancestors and for the monarch, remind one of marked features in the Chinese, and suggest that if the Egyptians and the Chinese did not

*Egyptian morals.*

derive their religion from a common source in a far-distant past, they were at least founded on such deeply implanted instincts or such naturally growing perceptions that strikingly similar results appeared in widely different nations. Whether Egypt was the original home or not of the divine right of kings, it was there very early and markedly believed in; and the king's actions, unless flagrantly injurious, were celebrated as great benefits to the nation, and his funeral was marked by extreme magnificence and by prolonged fasting and mourning. The whole country, in fact, belonged to the gods, who regarded it with special affection, and conferred on it all its great institutions. It was not wonderful that the Israelites should have been powerfully influenced by what they saw in Egypt, or that they should cast longing eyes back to its gorgeous forms and objects of worship, and seek to introduce some of them among or in addition to the features more peculiarly their own.

It is noteworthy how frequently the Egyptian inscriptions praise the strictest truthfulness and works of charity. *High esteem of truth and charity.* Thus we read of one man: "Doing that which is right, and hating that which is wrong, I was bread to the hungry, water to the thirsty, clothes to the naked, a refuge to him that was in want; that which I did to him, the great God hath done to me." Again, "I was one who did that which was pleasing to his father and his mother; the joy of his brethren, the friend of his companions, noble-hearted to all those of his city. I gave bread to the hungry; my doors were open to those who came from without, and I gave them wherewith to refresh themselves. And God hath inclined his countenance to me for what I have done; he hath given me old age upon earth, in long and pleasant duration, with many children at my feet." (R.) It must be remembered that these commendations, though put in the mouth of the deceased, were the work of his survivors; even if they are not strictly accurate, they show what features of conduct were considered worthy of praise in view of the eternal world, and therefore they have a wide-reaching significance in our estimate of the character of the ancient Egyptians.

RUINS OF TEMPLE OF RAMESES II. AT THEBES.

It is singular to find, in a song of a king so early as the eleventh dynasty, ideas which are familiar to us in the much later book of Ecclesiastes. Herodotus describes a custom which may be connected with the recitation of some song. He says: "At the entertainments of the rich, just as the company is about to rise from the repast, a small coffin is carried round, containing a perfect representation of a dead body, . . . as it is shown to the guests in rotation, the bearer exclaims, 'Cast your eyes on this figure: after death you yourself will resemble it; drink then, and be happy.'" The song, after reciting that the body passes away, goes on, "After all, what is prosperity? Their fenced walls are dilapidated. Their houses are as that which has never existed. No man comes from thence who tells of their sayings, who tells of their affairs, who encourages their hearts. Ye go to the place whence they return not. Strengthen thy heart to forget how thou hast enjoyed thyself, fulfil thy desire whilst thou livest. . . . The day will come to thee, when one hears not the voice, when the one who is at rest hears not their voices. Lamentations deliver not him who is in the tomb. Feast in tranquillity, seeing that there is no one who carries away his goods with him. Yea, behold, none who goes thither comes back again." (R. P. iv.)

*Singular custom at banquets.*

Altogether, in considering the moral nature of Egyptian religious teaching, we cannot but give it a high place. The standard set up was high, an ideal excellence was aimed at and praised; and if the people failed ultimately to keep up to that level, it was scarcely for want of knowledge or opportunity. All the systems of religion we have yet surveyed seem to have gone through stages of development and degeneracy, as if human religions were in themselves endowed with bodily or mental life which they were compelled to imitate by decay and death, as well as by stages of growth, assimilation, and differentiation.

## CHAPTER II.

## The Babylonian, Assyrian, and Phœnician Religions.

Early magical texts—Exorcists—Heaven and earth as creative powers—Local religions—Ea, the god of the deep—Dav-kina, the lady of the earth—Hymn to Ea—Mul-lil, lord of the ghost-world—The moon-god of Ur—The sun-god Samas or Tammuz—Istar—The fire-god—Nergal—Matu—Bel-Merodach—His temple at Babylon—Nebo—Assur—Rimmon—Hymns to the gods—Penitential hymns—Future existence—Star-worship and astrology—Early cosmogony—Mr. George Smith's discoveries—Bel and the dragon—The tower of Babel—The epic of Izdubar—The Chaldæan deluge—Priests—Festivals and sacred days—Sacrifices—Images—Monotheism—Religious character of people—Phœnician religion—Baal—Melkarth—Ashtoreth—Adonis—Nature-gods—The Kabiri—Human and other sacrifices—Moloch—Chemosh—The Philistine gods—Dagon.

BABYLONIA and Assyria, like Egypt, in varying degrees and through long periods, influenced the Israelites and were influenced by them; and consequently the study of their religious development is of high importance. Though much remains to be known about Mesopotamian religion, much is already known.[1]

In Chaldæa, as in China, we come near to primitive

---

[1] Sayce: "Hibbert Lectures" (Religion of Ancient Babylonians), (S.). Sayce's edition of Smith's Chaldæan Account of Genesis; Rawlinson's "Five Great Monarchies," and "Religions of the Ancient world"; Sayce's "Ancient Empires of the East." St. Chad. Boscawen, in "Religious Systems of the World," 1890. "The Cuneiform Inscriptions of Western Asia." Published by Trustees of British Museum (I.).

animism and its development into an advanced polytheism.

**Early magical texts.** The magical texts which form the earliest Chaldæan sacred literature probably date from a time as early as the earliest Egyptian records, when there was no distinct idea of gods, and when the world around the Accadian was peopled by supernatural powers and spirits of living things. This state of mind was dealt with by shamanists or exorcists who can hardly be called **Exorcists.** priests, but who rank rather with the medicine-men of the American Indians. They undertook to cure or prevent all kinds of diseases, and to cause the spirits of evil things to depart; and this was effected especially by incantations such as the following: "The evil god (or spirit), the evil demon, the demon of the field, the demon of the mountain, the demon of the sea, the demon of the tomb, the evil spirit, the dazzling fiend, the evil wind, the assaulting wind, which strips off the clothing of the body as an evil demon, conjure, O spirit of heaven! conjure, O spirit of earth!" "The painful fever, the potent fever, the fever which quits not a man, the fever-demon who departs not, the fever unremovable, the evil fever, conjure O spirit of heaven! conjure, O spirit of earth!" (I.) These texts which have come down to us, probably do not represent the earliest form of exorcism, but rather the highest level attained by the system; and they show in a most interesting way, that, in connection with these early incantations, the idea of the spirit of heaven and the spirit of earth, as representing the essence of the higher powers, was impressed upon the early Accadians and their successors the Babylonians and Assyrians. The belief in these great powers as beneficent grew stronger as the cures wrought by medicines, by natural recovery, or by mental faith were noted; and the idea of the good powers as antagonistic to and stronger **Heaven and earth as creative powers.** than the evil demons rose into prominence. It was conceived that the heaven and earth, and the deep sea, were the creative powers, and were especially the creators of man, and of all good things. Strangely enough, these powers, Ana or Anu, the sky, Mul-lil, the earth, Ea, the deep, were represented as themselves having a spirit, like all living or moving objects. These gods might assume human forms, and then their spirits corresponded to those of men; they are represented as inhabiting animals, which were worshipped as totems. Thus Ea appeared as antelope, fish, and serpent, and we find divine bulls, storm-birds, dogs, etc. So, according to Prof. Sayce, innumerable spirits were believed in, controlled by creative gods representing the order and law of the universe. In opposition to them were the malevolent spirits of darkness and disease, and there were also spirits neither good nor bad. All these were supposed to be controlled by the sorcerer-priest, using spells and exorcisms, and communicating with, and practically influencing, the gods by his ritual. The forms of worship became enlarged with this higher belief, and true supplication appears in the Penitential Psalms, such as this:—

"Accept the prostration of the face of the living creature. I, thy servant, ask thee for rest. To the heart of him who has sinned thou utterest words of blessing. Thou lookest on the man, and the man lives, O potentate of the world, mistress of mankind! Compassionate one, whose forgiveness is ready, who acceptest the prayer. (*Priest*) O God and mother goddess that art angry with him, he calls upon thee! Turn thy face towards him and take his hand!" (I.) In this prayer, as well as in others, we see an invocation of more gods than one, as being in combination or alliance. Of course while this elevation was proceeding, the incantations and exorcisms remained largely in use among those less enlightened, but were gradually lowered in esteem, like charms in modern days; while the religious development went on to produce the hymns to the gods. But these were due partly no doubt to the early Semitic influence which largely altered the character of Mesopotamian religion.

As in Egypt, the national religion grew upon the basis of local religions, adopting and adapting local gods of cities and tribes. Thus, Ea was originally the local god of the city Eridu, at the then mouth of the Euphrates. Under the name of Oannes, he is said by Berosus, the late Chaldæan historian, to have come out of the water of the gulf, to have passed his days among men, and to have given them insight into letters and sciences, and arts of every kind. "He taught them to <small>Ea, the god of the deep.</small> construct houses, to found temples, to compile laws, and explained to them the principles of geometrical knowledge. He made them distinguish the seeds of the earth, and showed them how to collect the fruits; in short, he instructed them in everything which could tend to soften manners and humanise their lives." Thus he was the god of wisdom of early Babylonia, and was represented as partly man and partly fish.

In conjunction with Ea was worshipped his consort Dav-kina, the lady of the earth, which she personified; <small>Dav-kina, the lady of the earth.</small> and this relationship accords with the old Chaldæan idea of the origin of the world from the deep, upon which the earth lay. Through Davkina the words of Ea were conveyed to men, as heard in the roar of the waves. The attributes of Ea may be gathered from a hymn addressed to him. He is "the god of pure life, who stretches out the bright firmament, <small>Hymn to Ea.</small> the god of good winds, the lord of hearing and obedience, creator of the pure and the impure, establisher of fertility, who brings to greatness him that is of small estate. . . . May he command, may he glorify, may he hearken to his worshippers. . . . May he establish, and never may his word be forgotten in the mouth of the black-headed race, whom his hands created. As god of the pure incantation may he further be invoked, before whose pure approach may the evil trouble be overthrown; by whose pure spell the siege of the foe is removed." A later part of the same hymn is occupied with recognising the identity of the Bel of Northern Babylonia with Ea, showing the process of fusion by which different local deities became amalgamated, and regarded as practically the same. Ea is represented as saying, "Since he (Bel) has made his men strong by his name, let him, like myself, have the name of Ea. May he bear (to them) the bond of all my commands, and may he communicate all my secret knowledge through the fifty names of the great gods." The hymn goes on, "His fifty names he has pronounced, his ways he has restored. . . . May father to son repeat and hand them down." (S.) This emphasis on the

GREAT MOUND ON SITE OF BABYLON.

"name" is intelligible when we remember that the name signified the essential nature of the deity, as in the Old Testament and in Egyptian religion.

We find a son also ascribed to Ea, namely Mardugga,

the holy son, the same name being traceable in Marduk,
**Marduk, or Merodach.** or Merodach. He was supposed to visit mankind as a mediator and healer. Between Ea and Merodach, as good gods, and the powers of evil typified by a serpent with seven heads and seven tails, there was continual warfare. There is doubtless some connection between this belief and that recorded in the early chapters of Genesis.

Another of the gods dating back to Accadian times is Mul-lil, the lord of the ghost-world, of the earth, and of
**Mul-lil, lord of the ghost-world.** the spirits of the earth, originally a local god of Nipur (now Niffer) in northern Babylonia. Here the belief in ghosts and demons and spirits of disease was strong, and hence it spread to other parts. Adar (a name possibly read wrongly) was the son of Mul-lil, a sun-god, represented as issuing from night, as typified by the god of the lower world; and his wife was the lady of the dawn. Adar was especially the meridian sun, the warrior and champion of the gods, the messenger of his father.

It is strange to find the moon-god represented as masculine, and the sun-god as his offspring. There was ap-
**The Moon-god of Ur.** parently a local moon-god in every Babylonian town; Ur seems to have been a great centre of his worship, and the moon-gods of Ur and Nipur were early identified. At Ur the moon-god, known as Nannak or Nannar, became the father of the gods. Part of an old hymn to him runs thus: "Lord and prince of the gods, who in heaven and earth alone is supreme, . . . Father Nannar, lord of heaven, lord of the moon, prince of the gods. Father, long-suffering and full of forgiveness, whose hand upholds the life of all mankind. . . . Father, begetter of gods and men, who causes the shrine to be founded, who establishes the offering, who proclaims dominion, who gives the sceptre, who shall fix destiny unto a distant day; First-born, omnipotent, his heart is far-extended; none shall describe the god. . . . As for thee, thy will is made known in heaven, and the angels bow their faces. . . . As for thee, thy will is done upon the earth, and the herb grows green. . . .

As for thee, thy will is the far-off heaven, the hidden earth which no man hath known. . . . Look with favour on thy temple; look with favour on Ur; let the high-born dame ask rest of thee, O lord; let the free-born man ask rest of thee, O lord! Let the spirits of earth and heaven ask rest of thee, O lord."

When we remember that this Ur in Chaldæa was the place whence Abraham migrated to Harran, we shall see that he already lived in an atmosphere of very considerable development. Local gods were worshipped, not a truly universal god; but already conceptions of no slight elevation had been attained, and Harran, to which he in the first place migrated, was closely connected with Ur in religion. The moon-god of Ur appears to have gained fame and to have taken a predominant position among the Babylonians as the father of gods and men, under the name Sin (the bright). And in conformity with the Chaldæan idea of the sun coming forth and being produced from the night (over which the moon presides), we find the sun-god Samas (Tammuz) described as the son of Sin. Perhaps the most noted sun-god of the Accadians was that of Larsa, not far from Ur, whose temple was famous, having been founded or restored by Ur-bagas, the earliest known king of United Babylonia. He also was noted as the builder or restorer of the temple of the moon-god at Ur, that of Mullil at Nipur, and those of Anu and Istar at Erech. Istar was the goddess of the evening star, assigned as the wife of Samas, later developed into the Ishtar or Ashtoreth of Semitic worship. The sun-god was also worshipped under his name of Samas at Sippara (the Scripture Sepharvaim), where there was a temple believed to have already grown old and decayed in B.C. 3800, which was the centre of a vigorous worship, with many priests, scribes, schools; and most interesting hymns to the god have come down to us apparently from this very early date.

*The sun-god Samas, or Tammuz.*

*Istar.*

*Worship at Sepharvaim.*

There was also a fire-god among the early Accadian gods, celebrated in this fashion in an early hymn: "The Fire-god, the first-born supreme, unto heaven they pur-

sued and no father did he know. O Fire-god, supreme
**The fire-god.** on high, the first-born the mighty supreme, enjoined of the commands of Anu. The Fire-god enthrones with himself the friend that he loves." He is represented as conquering especially seven evil or injurious spirits of earth and heaven. Another god of whom we know little in his early Accadian form is Ana or Anu, the sky, the chief deity of Erech, which city regarded him as a creative god. He became early in the Semitic dominion of Babylonia the chief member of a sort of triad of gods, Anu, Bel or Mul-lil, and Ea, representing the heaven, the earth, and the ghost-
**Nergal.** world, and the water. Nergal, the god of Cutha (now Tel-Ibrahim), the strong one, the god of death, among the Accadians, became rather the champion of the gods among the Semites, destroying especially the wicked. But he passed very considerably out of mind with the advance of Semitic forms of worship. The winds, especially the destructive ones, were also worshipped as
**Matu.** deities; and one of them, Matu, is supposed to have given rise to part of the Semitic conception worshipped under the name of Ramman or Rimmon. Many other spirits or gods were included in the worship of the many separate states or cities of early Babylonia, spirits of heaven, spirits of earth, etc.; and we even meet with such expressions in the Penitential Psalms before mentioned, as "To the god that is known and that is unknown, to the goddess that is known and that is unknown, do I lift my prayer."

When the Semites gained predominance in Mesopotamia, they to a large extent adopted or adapted the religious worship they found already established, in accordance with a general idea that it was necessary, or at least advisable, for the conquerors to establish friendly relations with the gods of a conquered country, while maintaining their own original beliefs.

The Semites were already to a large extent sun-worshippers. We cannot yet unravel this develop-
**Bel-merodach.** ment in its details, but it seems probable that Bel-merodach, the great god of Babylon, represented

a local god of Babylon who was identified by the Semites with their sun-god and elevated to a supreme position above all the gods, though not excluding their worship. The following prayer of Nebuchadnezzar indicates that monarch's attitude toward his god:—

"To Merodach my lord I prayed; I began to him my petition, the word of my heart sought him, and I said: 'O prince that art from everlasting, lord of all that exists, for the king whom thou lovest . . . thou watchest over him in the path of righteousness! I, the prince who obeys thee, am the work of thy hands; thou createst me and hast entrusted to me the sovereignty over multitudes of men, according to thy goodness, O lord, which thou hast made to pass over them all. Let me love thy supreme lordship, let the fear of thy divinity exist in my heart, and give what seemeth good unto thee, since thou maintainest my life.' Then he, the first-born, the glorious, the first-born of the gods, Merodach the

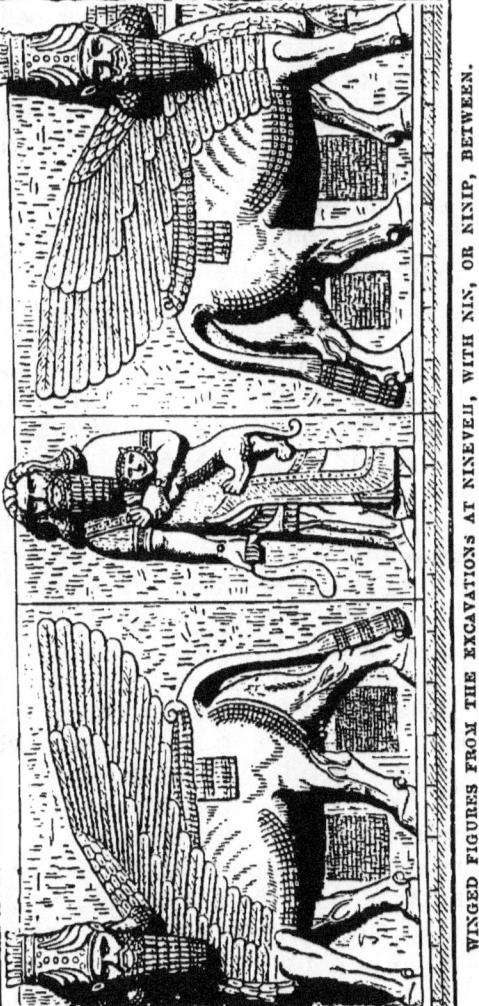

WINGED FIGURES FROM THE EXCAVATIONS AT NINEVEH, WITH NIN, OR NINIP, BETWEEN.

prince, heard my prayer and accepted my petition." It is evident that Merodach was supreme in Babylon; but outside Babylon other gods and creators were acknowledged. He is variously described as merciful, as the intercessor between gods and men, and as interpreter of the will of Ea. Not the least remarkable of the old Chaldæan hymns is one in which he is addressed as " the merciful lord who loves to raise the dead to life," and this is held to show that the Chaldæans had some belief in a resurrection.

To Bel-Merodach a great temple was erected at Babylon, a huge square containing a tower of eight great stages, **Merodach's temple at Babylon.** with a shrine in the topmost, also used as an observatory. The temple at the foot contained a great golden statue of the god, seated; and outside was a golden altar for the sacrifice of special victims, while a larger altar was used for the offering of large numbers of sheep, and for burning large quantities of frankincense at the god's festival. The ceremonies at this temple are said to have presented many resemblances to those of the Jews; they included daily morning and evening sacrifices, meat and drink offerings, the free-will offering, the sin-offering, and the shew-bread. In close association with this temple was a smaller one erected to Nebo, the god of prophecy, called the son of Merodach, the proclaimer of his mind and wishes; and within the shrine of Nebo, Merodach was supposed to descend at his festival and announce his oracles **Nebo.** to his priests. Nebo had a separate grand temple in the suburb Borsippa. He was famed as the creator of peace, the author of the oracle, the creator of the written tablet, the author of writing; he was also the bond of the universe and the overseer of the angel hosts. Thus we can understand the exultation of Isaiah's words: "Bel boweth down, Nebo stoopeth," and those of Jeremiah, " Babylon is taken, Bel is confounded, Merodach is broken in pieces." The conquest of Babylon by Cyrus introduced a wider cult, in which Merodach was recognised as the god of all men; and the Greeks even identified him with Zeus. The Assyrians especially worshipped him, and, in conjunction with him, Beltis his lady.

Now we come into the area of the Semitic tendency to attribute to each god a corresponding goddess. The worship of Nebo passed westward, like that of Bel-merodach, and he was assigned a consort, Tasmitu, "the hearer," who opened the ears of those who received Nebo's inspiration. In addition to Bel and Nebo, a third important god rises to view in Assyria, being the national god of the people, Assur, king of all the gods, enabling the Assyrians to destroy "the enemies of Assur." He was originally the local god of As-

Assur.

NIN, OR NINIP.

sur, the early capital, and became a national god, being transferred to Nineveh when it was made the capital. Assur was still more special among the Semites, as not having a consort. "When a female divinity is invoked along with him, it is the equally independent goddess Istar or Ashtoreth." (S.) With him were worshipped many of the gods of Babylonia; but he is especially named as their creator and father. In many respects the characters ascribed to Assur correspond to those by which Jehovah was worshipped by the Israelites. Thus, to quote Prof. Rawlinson, "He places the monarchs upon their throne, firmly establishes them in the government, lengthens the years of their reigns, preserves their power, protects their forts and armies, makes their name celebrated, and the like. To him they look to give them victory over their enemies, to grant them all the wishes of their heart, and to allow them to be succeeded on their thrones by their sons, and their sons' sons, to a remote posterity. . . . It is to spread his worship that they carry on their wars. They fight, ravage, destroy in his name. Finally, when they subdue a country, they are careful to set up 'the emblems of Assur,' and to teach the people his laws and his worship." He is often represented as a man with a horned cap, and carrying a bow, and his face appears in the middle of a winged circle, shooting an arrow or stretching out his hand; and this emblem is upon everything royal—robes, rock-carvings, obelisks, etc. A probable suggestion is, that Assur represents an early ruler or king; but later he was closely identified with the ruler of heaven and earth.

Among the other gods introduced into Assyria from Chaldæa, Nergal was much worshipped, together with Nin (Ninus) or Ninip. The symbol of the latter, the winged bull, was greatly in vogue throughout Assyria. Nin and Nergal sharpened the king's weapons, and gave him the victory over the fiercest beasts. There was a large temple to Nin (Ninus) at Calah (the modern Nimrod). Nergal was symbolised by the winged lion with a human head.

Another god of interesting history, most especially worshipped in the kingdom of Damascus, by the northern Syrians, was Rimmon, more properly Ramánu, the exalted one, believed to be a literal translation of the name of the Accadian god Muru, representing the air. The Hebrews identified the name with rimmon, a pomegranate, and in that form it became widely known. In Syria, Rimmon was identified with the northern Baal or sun-god Hadad; and there are traces of the worship of Hadad-Rimmon as far south as the plain of Jezreel (Zech. xii. 11). In Babylonia and Assyria he was a god of the air and winds, whose worship incorporated that of many older deities. To some of these only their evil powers remained, while Rimmon exemplified beneficence. .

*Rimmon.*

We must now return again to the religious texts of Babylonia. The hymns to the gods, composed at different dates, and largely Semitic in origin, include forms to be recited at sunrise and sunset, and on special festivals of the gods. There appear to have been separate collections for each temple, but it is doubtful how far they were incorporated into any general collection; at any rate, they have travelled far beyond primitive conceptions, and include many advanced ideas. Many of the penitential hymns show strong resemblances to the Old Testament psalms. For instance: "I sought for help and none took my hand; I wept and none stood at my side; I cried aloud and there was none that heard me. I am in trouble and hiding; I dare not look up. To my god, the merciful one, I turn myself, I utter my prayer. The feet of my goddess I kiss and water with tears. To my god whom I know and whom I know not I utter my prayer. O lord, look upon me; O goddess, look upon me. . . . How long, O goddess whom I know and know not, shall thy heart in its hostility be not appeased? Mankind is made to wander, and there is none that knoweth. Mankind, as many as pronounce a name, what do they know? Whether he shall have good or ill there is none that knoweth. . . . The sins I have sinned turn to a blessing. The transgressions I have committed may the wind

*Hymns to the gods.*

*Penitential hymns.*

carry away. Strip off my manifold wickednesses as a garment. O my god, seven times seven are my transgressions; forgive my sins! . . . Forgive my sins; may thy bane be removed." (I.) This psalm, copied out from the original by direction of Assur-bani-pal (Sardanapalus) in the 7th century B.C., dates back to a much earlier time, when, however, the Semites were in full possession of Babylonia. It is interesting for its view of sin, penitence, and prayer for forgiveness, as well as for its association of the goddess with the god. Instead of evils being due to evil spirits, they were now read as the offspring of man's sinfulness or the punishments inflicted by the gods. Yet there are Accadian ideas clearly distinguishable in it; the gods are not personally named lest they should be offended, and there is no clear idea what is the nature of the sin committed, or how it became an offence.

There is remarkably little reference in the early magical hymns and incantations to ideas of future existence. **Future existence.** Later we find Merodach invoked as raising the dead to life; but it is not certain that future life is meant. Still the description of Mul-lil as god of the ghost-world, implies some kind of belief in the continuance of the dead. Later we find reference to the "land of the silver sky." But there were various inconsistent views of the abodes of the gods produced in Mesopotamia, which we can merely allude to. One of these describes a "mountain of the world," a sort of Chaldæan Oympus, where the gods were born and lived. It was also called "the mighty mountain of Mul-lil, whose head rivals the heavens; and whose foundation is the pure deep." The predominant impression as to the ghosts of the departed was, that they abode in the gloomy underworld, eating dust and mud, and sometimes emerging to drink the blood of the living. It was not a land of punishment, but of darkness and forgetfulness, shadows and spectres. But in the Epic of Gisdhubar we find the ghost of Ea-bani described as rising to heaven and living among the gods, reclining on a couch and drinking pure water, beholding the deeds done on earth. In later Assyrian times, the idea of heaven became somewhat spiritualised as the heaven of Anu, and some notion of future rewards and punishments arose. It was now that prayers began to be offered that they might live for ever in the land of the silver sky. Thus we trace ever and again the similarities which are to be found among the Semitic religions.

Little has yet been said about the star-worship which was formerly supposed to be the main feature of Chaldæan religion. It is true that the Chaldæans very early observed and revered the constellations, and framed a calendar; and we may perhaps see in the names given to the signs of the zodiac evidences of primitive totemism, the names being Accadian, and indicating in an interesting way the thoughts connected with animals at that early period. Prof. Sayce shows good reason, from the first place being given to the "Directing Bull," for concluding that the signs of the zodiac were named long before 2,500 B.C., and probably more than 4,000 years before Christ. It is not till the Semitic period of Sargon's rule over Accad that the ram marked the beginning of the year; and to this period may be credited much of the early astrology which essayed to predict events by the signs of the sky. In later Babylonia the stars were largely identified with the gods; and the whole heavens were parcelled out between the three deities Anu, Bel, and Ea. In the cuneiform characters a deity is indicated by an eight-rayed star. We cannot stay to trace the development of this worship in its later stages, when elaborate offerings and sacrifices were made to the stars, in some cases even taking precedence before Assur. *Star-worship and astrology.*

An early Semitic cosmogony, with traces of Accadian origin, has been discovered in a tablet originally written for the temple of Nergal at Cutha. It refers to a time when the great gods created living creatures of a compound nature, "warriors with the body of a bird of the valley," "men with the faces of ravens," suckled by Tiamat or the dragon of Chaos. The offspring of these became heroes, but were destroyed ultimately by Nerra, the plague-god, identified with Nergal. Possibly *Early cosmogony.*

this view of early monsters may account for some of the strange compound figures found in Assyria. But greater interest attaches to the series of tablets of a later Chaldæan cosmology discovered by Mr. George Smith in 1872, which, though comparatively late in their present form, embody a very early series of legends, of deep interest from their correspondences with the narrative in the first chapter of Genesis. The record is unfortunately in a very fragmentary condition. The first tablet begins thus:

*Mr. George Smith's discoveries.*

1. At that time above, the heaven was unnamed;
2. Below the earth by name was unrecorded;
3. The boundless deep also (was) their generator.
4. The chaos of the sea was she who bore the whole of them.
5. Their waters were collected together in one place, and
6. The flowering reed was not gathered, the marsh-plant was not grown.
7. At that time the gods had not been produced, any one of them;
8. By name they had not been called, destiny was not fixed.

Then follow verses describing the birth of several gods. The first half of the fifth tablet gives an account of the creation of the heavenly bodies:

1. (Bel) prepared the (seven) mansions of the great gods;
2. He fixed the stars, even the twin-stars, to correspond to them;
3. He ordained the year, appointing the signs of the zodiac over it;
4. For each of the twelve months he fixed three stars,
5. From the day when the year issues forth to the close.
6. He found the mansion of the god of the ferry-boat (the sun-god), that they might know their bonds.
7. That they might not err, that they might not go astray in any way.
8. He established the mansion of Mul-lil and Ea along with himself.
9. He opened also the great gates on either side,
10. The bolts he strengthened on the left hand and on the right,
11. And in their midst he made a staircase.
12. He illuminated the moon-god that he might watch over the night,
13. And ordained for him the ending of the night that the day may be known.

In similar style another tablet relates the creation of animals.

But while there is great interest in finding a Chaldæan legend agreeing in some features with that of Genesis, there is no warrant for saying that either of the accounts has given rise to the other; but that they have some connection is very possible. They are of special importance, however, in anthropology as examples of the ways in which the human mind has explained creation. The Chaldæan account adds a very striking narrative in one tablet, of the contest between the god Bel and the dragon of Chaos, which is too complex to describe here. <small>Bel and the dragon.</small>

Among other early Chaldæan fragments is one which appears to describe a parallel incident to the confusion of tongues at Babel. Bel, the father of the gods, is said to have been angry at the sin of the builders of Babylon, and especially of the "Illustrious mound," and the builders were punished, and the mound destroyed at night by the winds; but nothing is said of the confusion of tongues. It is probable that the tower of Babel is represented by the great mound of Nimroud, with its succession of diminishing stages, forming a great temple or "gate of the gods." In the time of Nebuchadnezzar it was incomplete, and had long been ruinous, when he undertook its restoration and completion. It has been suggested that during its long period of decay the legend arose which described it as a monument of human folly and presumption, and that the variety of languages spoken in Babylonia gave good cause for attributing the diversity to divine punishment. <small>The tower of Babel.</small>

In the great Epic of Izdubar or Gisdhubar, also discovered by Mr. Smith in 1872, we have a Semitic translation of the exploits of an early Accadian king or primitive Hercules, arranged on a solar plan, which accords with the representation of the hero as sun-god. In many ways the events recorded in the epic correspond to the twelve labours of Hercules; and it may be that the Izdubar legend is one of the early forms from which Phœnicia and then Greece derived the famous myth. The most perfect tablet is that which describes a deluge, which has been very generally identified with <small>The epic of Izdubar.</small>

that of Noah. The character of Izdubar corresponds exactly to that of Nimrod in Genesis; and it is not certain that the names may not be identical, for Izdubar is but a provisional rendering.

The deluge, according to the Chaldæan epic, was due to the judgment of the gods Anu, Bel, and Ninip, and **The Chaldæan** Ea told the "man of Surippak," Samas-Napiati **deluge.** (the living sun), to build a ship to preserve plants and living beings; it was to be 600 cubits long, and 60 broad and high. Numerous details of the building and construction are given; and when Xisuthrus with his people, and animals, and plants, and food had entered the ship, "the waters of dawn arose at daybreak, a black cloud from the horizon of heaven. Rimmon in the midst of it thundered, and Nebo and the wind-god went in front." The earth was covered, and all living things destroyed. Even the gods were afraid at the whirlwind, and took refuge in the heaven of Anu. After six days and nights the storm abated, and the rain ceased, and the wind and deluge ended. "I watched the sea making a noise, and the whole of mankind were turned to clay, like reeds the corpses floated. . . . In the country of Nizir (east of Assyria) rested the ship; the mountain of Nizir stopped the ship, and to pass over it it was not able. . . . On the seventh day I sent forth a dove, and it left. The dove went, it returned, and a resting-place it did not find, and it came back." Later a raven was sent forth, and it did not return. Then the ship was opened, the animals came forth, sacrifice was offered to the gods, and Xisuthrus became the father of Izdubar, himself being afterwards translated to live as a god. We cannot attempt a detailed comparison of the Chaldæan and Noachian floods, for which reference must be made to Professor Sayce's edition of Mr. Smith's "Chaldæan Account of Genesis;" but we may remark that this deluge narrative, perhaps more than anything else, shows how closely the narratives in Genesis are related to Chaldæan traditions or sources of information.

In various Assyrian records we find the king himself offering sacrifices, as in Egypt and Palestine; but there were also high priests, and several orders of inferior priests. One of the most important of these was the anointer, who purified persons and things with oil and water; others were the soothsayers and the elders, or "great ones." The movable symbols or images of the gods were carried about in procession in little arks or "ships," at least in Babylon; and this custom can be traced back to the early Accadian times of the city of Eridu. Festivals were numerous; in fact, it seems that almost every day could be celebrated as a festival. We have a complete list of festivals assigned to the intercalary month Elul; and we find, for example, that on the second day "the king makes his farewell offering to the Sun, the mistress of the world, and the Moon, the supreme god: sacrifices he offers." The third day, a fast day, is dedicated to Merodach and Zarpaint, the fourth to Nebo, the fifth to the Lord of the Lower Firmament and the Lady of the Lower Firmament, the sixth to Rimmon and Nin-lil, and so on, the king offering sacrifices on every day. On the seventh day we have an interesting record of what was lawful or unlawful on the Babylonian Sabbath, or day of rest. "The shepherd of mighty nations must not eat flesh cooked at the fire in the smoke. His clothes he must not change. White garments he must not put on. He must not offer sacrifice. The king must not drive a chariot. He must not

TEMPLE AT AMRITH, PHŒNICIA.

issue royal decrees. In a secret place the augur must not mutter. Medicine for the sickness of his body he must not apply. For making a curse it is not fit." (S.) These prohibitions are repeated on the 14th, 19th, 21st, and 28th days. These Sabbath days go back to the times of the Accadians, who called them "unlawful days." It was also customary to observe special days of thanksgiving or humiliation, as when Esarhaddon II. prayed to the sun-god to remove the sin of his people, and when Assur ani-pal purified the shrines and cleansed the temples and restored the daily sacrifices.

In early Accadian times human sacrifice was practised; and a text is extant which declares "that the father must give the life of his child for the sin of his own soul, the child's head for his head, the child's neck for his neck, the child's breast for his breast"; and later, in "the observations of Bel," an astronomical record, it is stated that, "on the high places the son is burnt." But there are no accounts of human sacrifices in the historical tablets. Oxen, sheep, and gazelles, corn and wine, are the chief kinds of offerings we read of, accompanied by the offering of prayers and repeating of hymns. A distinction was made between different animals, the flesh of some being declared unlawful to eat; and the pig is not even mentioned in the inscriptions. In one inscription the flesh of men, gazelles, dogs, wild boars, asses, horses, and dragons is mentioned as unlawful.

*Sacrifices.*

The early Babylonians used much religious symbolism, both by mystic numbers and by emblematic signs. Many of these are not yet understood. The Assyrians had many images representing their gods, and some of these have been obtained from the ruins. Nebo is represented as a man standing, heavy and solid-looking. These images were of metal, sometimes of silver or gold, but usually of stone or baked clay. The latter are often of small size, as if intended for private use. Feasts were set out before the images, and it was currently believed that the god really ate and drank. The inner shrine of the temple of Bel, at Babylon, had a grand couch and a golden table for the god. We hear some-

*Images.*

times of riotous excesses in connection with the festivals; and in the worship of the goddess Beltis there was a regular system of immorality prescribed to women.

There are traces of a monotheistic school or teaching in Chaldæa, and hymns have been found addressed to "the one god." Another phenomenon, still more marked, is the attribution of universal power to the particular deity addressed, though another god might be addressed in similar terms. We cannot enlarge on the contrasting system of magic and augury which was elaborately developed, apart from the State religion, and had a very powerful influence on the mass of the people. *Monotheism.*

We must allow that the Mesopotamian peoples show a marked religious character. Everything the kings did or gained was attributed to the favour of their gods; and their records begin and end with praises, prayers, and invocations to them. The kings show their devotion by much expenditure on temples, offerings, and religious sculpture; and we cannot but acknowledge that in their religious devotion they are parallel with the kings of Israel. Still, the sensuous had a large share in their religion, which did not diminish their ferocity and treachery towards their enemies; and they are described in no moderate terms by the Hebrew prophets. As to the moral condition of the people generally, it is difficult to say anything with certainty; we have no reason to think it exceptionally high. Harsh and cruel punishments were undoubtedly inflicted on offenders and on enemies; and if the Babylonian nobles had cause to tremble at the slightest displeasure or caprice of their king, it is only likely that the same rule applied through lower grades of society. Pride and luxury developed wherever possible, and yet we must couple with their prominent religiousness a considerable degree of honesty and calmness of demeanour. *Religious character of people.*

The religion of the Phœnicians, the nearest Semitic neighbours of the Israelites, is but too scantily known to us, and yet is of great interest, owing to the influence it had on them. We have neither sacred books nor

extensive sculptural remains to guide us; but we can
discern clearly that the Phœnicians, more than
the Chaldæans, worshipped the power or powers
which moved in and through the principal natural phenomena. Their principal divinity was undoubtedly Baal,
"lord," originally a sun-god, worshipped now in his
beneficent aspects, and now as the fierce god of fire and
summer heat. He was early worshipped on the tops of
mountains, where his presence was indicated by upright
conical stones. There was a marked tendency in the
Phœnicians to give separate names to separate aspects
of the deity; whether these worships gradually became
united, and the common term Baal was prefixed, or whether
they gradually separated from a common origin,
cannot be determined. Thus we find such
names as Baal-Tsur, "Lord of Tyre," Baal-Tsidon, "Lord
of Zidon," Baal-Peor, "Lord of Peor," Baal-Zebub, "Lord
of flies," etc. Moloch, or Melek, "king," represents Baal
in his fierce aspect, and was a god who required his worshipper to sacrifice his best or dearest possession to him,
often his only or his eldest son. In later times a ram
was substituted. The special god of Tyre, Baal-Melkarth,
united the two aspects of the god; and it is
this god who appears in the Greek "Melicertes,"
or the Tyrian Hercules. The temple of Melkarth was
said to be the oldest building in Tyre, but it was destitute
of images, the altar-fire burning continually being his
symbol. No women, dogs, or swine were permitted to
enter his temples, which were erected in many towns of
Phœnicia, as well as in Carthage, Cadiz, and Malta.

Perhaps an earlier name under which the sun was
worshipped was El, "the exalted one," also known as El
Shaddai, the thunderer, and Adonai, "Master," but much
about their worship is obscure. There are numerous
references to these divinities in the Old Testament;
which can be understood now that Semitic religions are
better known; thus, Melchizedek was priest of El Eliun,
"the most high God."

Ashtoreth, or Ashtaroth, the chief goddess of the Phœnicians (Astarte of the Greeks), represented both the productive female power and the moon; her name is really derived from the Accadian Istar, the subject of the Semitic Babylonian myth which "recounts the descent of the goddess Istar into Hades in search of the healing waters which should restore to life her bridegroom Tammuz, the young and beautiful Sun-god, slain by the cruel hand of night and winter." (S.) At Gebal, or Byblos, eight miles north of Beyrout, the death of Adonis, or Tammuz, was yearly commemorated, when the river Adonis (Nahr Ibrahim) became red with mountain mud in the flood season, by a funeral festival of seven days. "Gardens of Adonis, as they were called, were planted,—pots filled with earth and cut herbs, which soon withered away in the fierce heat of the summer sun, —fitting emblems of the lost Adonis himself. Meanwhile, the streets and gates of the temples were filled with throngs of wailing women. They tore their hair, they disfigured the face, they cut the breast with sharp knives, in token of the agony of their grief. Their cry of lamentation went up to heaven mingled with that of the Galli, the emasculated priests of Ashtoreth, who shared with them their festival of woe over her murdered bridegroom." (Sayce: "Hibbert Lectures," p. 229.) Ezekiel (viii. 14) was indignant at finding women weeping for Tammuz (Adonis) at the very gate of the Lord's house in Jerusalem. In Phœnician worship, Istar, or Ashtoreth, came into such general favour as to serve as the generic name for a goddess; and by the side of the Baalim were the Ashtoreth, their consorts. The reproductive aspect of

THE PHŒNICIAN ASTARTE.

Ashtoreth led to the connection with her worship of much licentiousness. Under the title "Queen of Heaven," and under her own name, she appears as an abomination to the Hebrew historians and prophets, having often led the people astray into idolatry (Jer. vii. 18; xliv. 25). In Gen. xiv. 5, she is called Ashtoreth Karnaim, Astarte of the two horns, in allusion to one of her symbols, the head of a heifer, with crescent horns.

But the Phœnician worship extended widely through the field of nature. There were gods or Baalim of the **Nature gods.** rivers, of the mountains, etc.; but on the whole there was a tendency to regard all deities as identical at bottom, so that Baal worship may be regarded as the predominant Phœnician religion. The Kabiri were **The Kabiri.** eight special divinities, the patrons of manual arts and civilisation, the inventors of ships and medicine. Trees are accounted specially sacred, and certain wonderful stones, especially aërolites, were reverenced and consecrated as signs of the presence of the deity.

Whatever tendency there was in Phœnicia to worship the unity of the godhead was neutralised as a moral **Human and other sacrifices.** force by the sensuality of the worship offered. Human sacrifices were offered on exceptional occasions; and children, especially firstborn sons, were the principal victims. Usually, however, oxen and male animals, or birds, were sacrificed. The purity of women was also violated in the groves of the queen of heaven, as part of the worship at certain feasts. Although idols were few and simple and scarcely ever in human form, the worship of dwarf or distorted images, two-headed, or winged, or horned, had no superior efficacy in making the worship of a higher character; and thus there was full reason for the strength of the opposition of Elijah and other Israelitish leaders to the whole system of Phœnician religion.

There probably was more religious affinity between the Ammonites and Moabites and the Israelites, for each pro- **Moloch.** fessed the exclusive worship of one god; Moloch being the god of the former, and Chemosh of the Moabites. But the service of Moloch was sharply differentiated from that of Jehovah, especially by the practice of sacrificing children by fire to Moloch. In 2 Kings iii. 27, we read how the king of Moab sacrificed his eldest son as a burnt-offering upon the wall of his city, as a last resort when threatened with destruction by the Israelites; and that afterwards the invaders raised the siege and returned home. Such examples had an influence over more than one king of Judah, who acted similarly (2 Kings xvi. 3, xxi. 6), and the people followed in their wake; and "high places" were built, where they slew and then burnt their sons and daughters. So general and open became the practice that the Israelites went direct from slaying their children, on the same day, into the temple to worship. In fact, in recognising Baal or Moloch as the equivalent of their own Jehovah, the Israelites gave way to all the cruel and evil practices associated with the alien gods. There is no clear distinction to be made between Chemosh and Moloch; and on the celebrated Moabite stone, the Moabite king, Mesha, attributes the victories of the Israelites over him to the wrath of Chemosh, and his deliverance to his aid. *Chemosh.*

The worship of the Philistines appears to have been of a general Semitic type, with local deities and special types, as the Baalzebub (or god of flies), of Ekron and Dagon the fish-god, whose image was partly human, partly fish-like. The Philistines carried the image of their god into battle, and used oracles and divination; and their ceremonies appear to have been much like those of the Phœnicians, though we know very little about the details. It is conjectured that Dagon is derived from the Assyrian Dorgan or Daken, figured as half-man, half-fish. *The Philistine gods.* *Dagon.*

Of the Hittite religion too little is known to make it desirable to discuss it here.

# CHAPTER III.
## Life of Mahomet. Part I.

The latest great religion—Early Arab religious ideas—Tribal deities—Importance of kinship—Pilgrimages—The Jinn, or genies—Abodes of the gods—Sacred trees, wells, pillars, etc.—Sacrifices—Hair offerings—Idols—Notion of a supreme God—Prevalent profane spirit in Arabia—Jewish and Christian influence—Mahomet's family—His birth—Early life—His marriage to Khadijah—State of morals in Arabia—Rebuilding of the Kaaba—Mahomet's solitude and reveries—His high ideal—Dawn of prophetic mission—The vision of Gabriel—Command to preach—Apparent break in revelation—Nervous disorder and agitation—His early adherents—Opposition at Mecca—Attempts to silence him—Flight of adherents to Abyssinia—A proposed compromise—Withdrawal by Mahomet—Return of fugitives, and second flight—Hamza and Omar converted—Hostility of the Koreish—Mahomet's alliance with Jews—Boycotting—Seclusion—Mahomet preaches to strangers—Death of Khadijah—Mahomet's despondency—Re-marriage—The pilgrims from Medina—First pledge of Acaba—Adherents won at Medina—The visions of Jerusalem and of heaven—The Emperor Heraclius—Famine at Mecca—Mahomet's high claims—Commencement of the flight to Medina—Mahomet leaves Mecca—Takes refuge in a cave—Arrives at Medina, A.D. 622.

AFTER the successful foundation and wide propagation of Christianity, few could have predicted the rise and establishment of a new religion; and, inasmuch as practically no other great religion has been founded since Christianity, it may be granted that Mohammedanism rested upon or gratified some important and deeply seated factors in humanity. What these were, and how far they were due to the founder himself, it must be our aim to discover. It is

*The latest great religion.*

desirable to have in mind, when considering Mohammedanism, the history of Judaism and the early history of Christianity; but these will be dealt with later in this volume, in continuity with the later history of the Christian Churches.

Situated between the great populations of Asia and Africa, the Arabs, as might be expected, had numerous religious elements in common with the adjacent peoples. Fetishism, animal-worship, nature-worship, especially of the sun and heavenly bodies, as well as ancestor-worship, undoubtedly existed among the Arabs before Mahomet's time. And the founder of Mohammedanism had to build upon the state of things he found deeply ingrained in his people. How powerful his influence and that of his successors was, may be gathered from the facts, that they elevated an obscure dialect into a language as widespread as Latin in the days of the Roman empire; and that to this day new conquests are being made by Islam and the Arabs. *Early Arab religious ideas.*

The study of the early religion of the Arabs is of intense interest, from its necessary relation to that of the early Hebrews. It is to be regretted that it is still obscure, although much important work has been done, especially by Wellhausen and Robertson Smith. No doubt the type and forms of early Arab religion were influenced by their separation into small tribes; and this caused or allowed a certain variety, as well as a certain smallness of conception to prevail. Each tribe, or group of tribes, had its particular god or gods, with which it was in peculiar relation, which fought for it and against the gods of hostile peoples, which were believed to be equally real. Then, when two or more tribes became amalgamated, a commencement was made of a polytheistic system, in which several gods were worshipped side by side. Very generally, if not always, the tribal god was an ancestor-god, either an actual or a fabled deified ancestor. Something of the same idea is seen in the Genesis narrative that the sons of God took wives of the daughters of men. Many Arab tribes bore the names of their gods, or of celestial bodies worshipped *Tribal deities.*

as gods; but in later times, before Mahomet, these relationships were forgotten, and "the later Arabs worshipped gods that were not the gods of their fathers, and tribes of alien blood were often found gathered together on festival occasions at the great pilgrim shrines." (Robertson Smith.) But the idea of kinship in blood to the god was a predominant factor in early Arabia; and this made the blood of a kinsman holy and inviolable, and sanctioned the extremes of blood revenge. Inasmuch as the connection by kinship suggests motherhood as well as fatherhood, it is not surprising to learn that numerous early Arab deities were goddesses; and it is believed that in later times the goddesses became changed to gods, in accordance with a change in the predominant idea of kinship. One of the goddesses was Al-Lat, worshipped by the Nabatæans as mother of the gods; another was Al-Uzza, who has been named Venus by Latin writers. As is so often the case in goddess-worship, sensualism largely existed.

*Importance of kinship.*

The nomad life of the Arabs was not favourable to the growth and permanence of ideas of the godhead suited to agricultural peoples. We do not find that they gave fixed annual offerings to the gods, or offered stated sacrifices at set seasons. They, however, early became accustomed to the idea of pilgrimages to towns (when such arose), which were the seat of some specially sacred object or worship; and thus it was that gradually the religion of the townspeople gained great importance, and threw that of the nomads into the shade. There were temples of some kind in these towns; and even when they did not exist, sanctuaries were formed in caves, and priests guarded the abode of the gods. Gifts to the gods were offered by being brought to the sacred place, hung on a sacred tree, or if the offering were one of blood or other liquid, by being poured over a sacred stone.

*Pilgrimages.*

We may refer here briefly to the primitive Arab belief (associated with animism) that nature is full of superhuman beings, the *Jinn* (Djinn), or demons, corporeal beings with hairy skins, and capable of assuming varied shapes: and Mohammedanism has degraded all the heathen gods into *jinn*. They were feared and avoided, living as they did in uninhabited wastes, occupying the mysterious mountains that were believed to encompass the earth, and also invading baths, ovens, wells, the junctions of roads, etc. Many injuries were supposed to have been inflicted by them on human beings. There were many orders of them, and the belief in them was so profound that it has been perpetuated among modern Arabs. *(The Jinn, or genies.)*

The early Arabs recognised abodes or haunts of the gods, which they clearly marked out, such as a tract of pasture land marked off by pillars or cairns, or a whole valley or town, within which bloodshed was forbidden and no tree was to be cut down, and numerous other things were forbidden. *(Abodes of the gods.)* Within these was to be found some special place or altar at which the blood of sacrifices was smeared on sacred stones, or some tree upon which gifts were hung. Fountains or wells, trees, pillars, and heaps of stones were very general symbols or centres of worship. Sometimes all were combined in one sacred place. *(Sacred stones, trees, wells, pillars, etc.)* At Mecca the holy well Zamzam was holy long before Mahomet's time. At Nejran a sacred date-palm was worshipped; and at its annual feast it was hung with fine garments and female adornments. The people of Mecca used to hang weapons, garments, ostrich eggs, etc., upon a similar tree. Even the modern Arabs revere sacred trees as places where the *jinn* or genii descend, and may be heard dancing and singing. They regard it as a deadly danger to pluck a bough from these trees; they make sacrifices to them, hanging parts of the flesh of the victims upon them, as well as calico, beads, etc. Sick men, when brought to sleep under them, have dreams which restore them to health.

Except in the case of human victims, sacrifice by fire was little practised, the pouring of the blood over a rude altar of stones being regarded as sufficient. *(Sacrifices.)* In some cases the flesh of the slaughtered animals was left to be devoured by wild beasts, but usually it was eaten by the worshippers. There was a customary offering of firstlings as well as firstfruits among many Arab tribes. Sometimes gifts of food, meal, etc., were cast at the foot of the idol, mingled with the giver's hair, and milk was poured over the sacred stones. Libations were very prominent among the Arabs. It appears to have been a very early Arab usage to sacrifice the hair of youths as a sign of admission into the adult religious status; and a hair-offering formed part of every Arab pilgrimage. The people of Taïf shaved their heads at their holy place every time they returned from a journey. In Mahomet's time the ordinary worship of household gods among the Arabs consisted in stroking them with the hand in going in or out of the house or tent.

*Hair offerings.*

Ten idols of the ancient Arabs are mentioned in the Koran, viz., Al-Jibl and Al-Taghut, Al-Lat, Al-Uzza, Manat, Wadd, Suwa, Yaghus, Yaug, and Nasr. The first two were idols of the Koreish, Al-Lat was the idol at Taïf, Al-Uzza was identified with Venus, but was worshipped under the form of an acacia-tree; Manat was a large sacrificial stone. The five succeeding names represent deified ancestors; but several were worshipped under animal forms, as the Lion-god (Yaghus), the Vulture-god (Nasr), the Horse-god (Yaug). Habhah was a large sacred stone on which camels were sacrificed; and the remarkable Black Stone of Mecca was another object of intense reverence. In the Kaaba at Mecca there were images representing Abraham and Ishmael, each carrying divining arrows in his hand.

*Idols.*

But in the midst of the old idolatry there had arisen some perception of a supreme God, who was known as Allah, the other gods being termed children of Allah. The word Allah may be connected with the Babylonian and Semitic El; it is doubtful whether it should be regarded as a contraction of Al-ilah, the Strong One, or should be read Al-lah, the Secret One. "By him," according to Wellhausen, "the holiest oaths were sworn; in his name treaties and covenants were sealed. The enemy was reminded of Allah

*Notion of a supreme God.*

to deter him from inhuman outrage; enemy of Allah was the name of opprobrium for a villain. But, since

ARABS PRAYING

Allah ruled over all, and imposed duties on all, it was not thought that one could enter into special relations with him. In worship he had the last place, those gods being preferred who represented the interests of a specific circle, and fulfilled the private desires of their worshippers. Neither the fear of Allah, however, nor reverence for the gods, had much influence. The chief practical consequence of the great feasts was the observance of a truce in the holy months; and this in time had become mainly an affair of pure practical convenience. In general, the disposition of the heathen Arabs, if it is at all truly reflected in their poetry, was profane in an unusual degree. . . . The ancient inhabitants of Mecca practised piety essentially as a trade, just as they do now; their trade depended on the feast, and its fair on the inviolability of the Haram and on the truce of the holy months." Just at Mahomet's time, some few individuals in Taïf, Mecca, and Medina, who worshipped Allah, had gained the name of Hanifs, probably meaning "penitents," rejecting polytheism, seeking freedom from sin, resignation to God's will, and feeling a sense of human responsibility and judgment to come. It is doubtful how far their ideas were derived from Jews and Christians. Jews were very numerous both in Hejaz and in Yemen, and a certain amount of their lore and peculiar tenets was no doubt current among the more intelligent Arabs. There does not appear to have been any considerable development of Christianity in Arabia, though the travelled Arabs knew something of Greek, Syrian, and Abyssinian Christians. The Sabians and anchorites of the northern deserts of Arabia are more likely to have had an influence on the Arabs preceding Mahomet; and in the Koran Mahomet notes that they believed in God and in the day of resurrection and judgment. They were not the same as the people who later took the name of Harranians, who were star-worshippers (Sabæans) and polytheists descended from the early people of Mesopotamia. The ascetic anchorites of the desert undoubtedly impressed the Arabs by their earnestness, their consecration to a holy life, and their steadfast preparation for a life to come. Thus the seed was, to some extent, prepared for the prophet of Islam.

Mecca was the strongest centre of Arab worship, however superstitious it might be; and out of Mecca, and the tribe of the Koreish who dominated it, came the family of Mahomet. His grandfather, Abd-al-Muttalib, was chief of a family of the Koreish in the middle of the sixth century, A.D. His youngest son, Abdallah, married Amina, the daughter of Wahb, but did not live to see his son Mahomet, who also lost his mother when he was still a child. Mahomet was born in A.D. 570; his name is more precisely Muhammad, "the Praised"; but the rendering "Mahomet" has so long enjoyed vogue in this country that it is retained in this book. He was put out to nurse in the desert with a Bedouin woman. At five years of age he visited Medina with his mother, who died on the return journey. After his grandfather's death he was cared for by his uncle, Abu-Talib, and with him he went on a journey with a caravan to Syria about 582 A.D. A few years later he was perforce engaged in the so-called sacrilegious war between the Koreish and the Hawazin, which occurred within the sacred months and was carried into the sacred territory. In this war, says Mahomet, "I discharged arrows at the enemy, and I do not regret it." The chief remaining incident of interest in his early life is his taking part in a league of several families of the Koreish, who swore by the avenging Deity to take the part of the oppressed and see his claim fulfilled, so long as a drop of water remained in the ocean, or that they would satisfy it from their own resources. At one time he was occupied as a shepherd. At the age of twenty-five he was recommended by his uncle to take charge of a trading caravan belonging to a wealthy Koreishite widow named Khadijah. In charge of this he travelled to Bostra, sixty miles east of Jordan on the road to Damascus. Being successful, and attracting the regard of Khadijah, she conveyed to him her desire to marry him; and this marriage, though the wife was fifteen years the husband's senior, was a very happy one. Khadijah bore him two sons, who died young, and four daughters, of whom the most famous was Fatima.

Mahomet's life, previous to his announcement of his mission, was passed among a people with whom revenge was a religious duty, and blood feuds were common, whole tribes being involved in them. Drunkenness and gambling prevailed largely. Female children were often buried alive as soon as born. Women were in general mere chattels; polygamy and divorce were frequent. Idolatry, divination, bloody sacrifices (not unfrequently of sons by fathers), sensualism, were prevalent. We have no record as to how far Mahomet himself conformed to the customary worship and beliefs; but it may well be conceived, judging from his later life, that his inward self gradually revolted from them, and that he pondered over the different ideas he had received from surrounding religious systems—chiefly by word of mouth and by sight, for there is no probability that Mahomet could read or write.

*State of morals in Arabia.*

When Mahomet was about 35 years old, the Kaaba, or shrine of the sacred stone at Mecca, was rendered insecure by a flood, and it was decided to rebuild the walls and cover them with a roof. During a dispute as to who should place the black stone in its position in the wall, Mahomet was chosen to decide the question, and he took off his mantle and placed the stone on it and said, "Now let one from each of your four divisions come forward and raise a corner of this mantle." This was done, and Mahomet with his own hand guided it to its place; and this decision increased his influence among his fellow-tribesmen. Other incidents are recorded, showing his capacity for forming warm friendships, for showing gratitude and kindness, and for exercising paternal judgment.

*Rebuilding of the Kaaba.*

About his fortieth year Mahomet became more and more contemplative, and frequently retired into solitary valleys and among rocks near Mecca. His favourite resort was a cave at the foot of Mount Hira, north of Mecca; and here, in dark and wild surroundings, his mind was wrought up to rhapsodic enthusiasm; and it may well be that some few of the earliest chapters in the Koran date from this time, such as :—

*Mahomet's solitude and reveries.*

> "By the declining day I swear!
>   Verily man is in the way of ruin;
>   Excepting such as possess faith,
>   And do the things which be right,
>   And stir up one another to truth and steadfastness."

In others of the early chapters we find Mahomet possessed by an ideal of truth and righteousness, and a stern reprobation of evil, injustice, and lying, and their certain punishment; together with visions of his own people as designated by Providence to overthrow evil and to preserve true worship at Mecca. He points out as the lofty path: *His high ideal.*

> "Freeing the captive,
>   And giving food in the day of want
>   To the orphan that is near of kin,
>   Or to the poor that lieth in the dust."

Further, the righteous must be of those that believe and stir up one another unto steadfastness and compassion:

> "These are the heirs of blessedness."

Apparently some of his thoughts and his rhapsodic utterances were communicated to his family and friends, who regarded him as one almost beside himself. When he enlarged on the purer ideas that he had heard were possessed by the Jews and Christians, they said: "If a prophet had been sent unto us, we should no doubt have followed his directions, and been as devout and spiritual in our worship as the Jews and Christians." His meditations led him more and more to the belief that a preacher or prophet was needed by his people, and that he might be the destined prophet. After long mental struggle, during which he fell into deep depression and often meditated suicide, he became encouraged and confident, and looked for a period when the sway of his preaching should extend over all Arabia, and lead to the destruction of idols and the conquest of other peoples. The tradition is, that one night, while he was in Mount Hira, during the month of Ramadan, engaged in pious exercises, the angel Gabriel came to him as he slept, and held a silken scroll *Dawn of prophetic mission.* *The vision of Gabriel.*

F

before him, and compelled him to recite what was written on it; and it is asserted that this is part of the ninety-sixth sura,[1] beginning: "Recite! in the name of thy Lord, who created man from congealed blood! Recite! for thy Lord is the most High, who hath taught the pen, hath taught man what he knew not. Nay, truly man walketh in delusion when he deems that he suffices for himself" [otherwise translated: "Man is indeed outrageous at seeing himself get rich"]; "to thy Lord is the return." When the angel left him, continues the tradition, Mahomet came to his wife and told her what had happened; and she comforted him and confirmed him in the belief that this was a revelation from God. But no others would listen to him, and he was thrown back upon his meditations.

One day, while stretched upon his carpet and covered with his garments, it is related that the angel Gabriel again appeared to him, and said:

*Command to preach.* "O thou that art covered, arise and preach [or warn], and magnify thy Lord; and purify thy garments, and depart from uncleanness; and grant not favour to gain increase; and wait for thy Lord."

Revelations now began to follow one another frequently; but, after a certain time there was a break, during which the inspiration was suspended, and Mahomet's thoughts turned towards suicide. How *Apparent break in revelation.* far during this time he was overpowered by hysterical hallucinations it would be idle to attempt to determine; but it is related that from youth he had suffered from a nervous disorder which has been termed epilepsy; and that this tendency was increased during his spiritual struggles by his mental excitement, *Nervous disorder.* night-watchings, and fastings is most probable. But this does not detract from the genuineness of his belief in his Divine inspiration. On one occasion, when about to commit suicide, it is related that he was suddenly arrested by a voice from heaven, and saw the angel on a throne between the heavens and the earth,

---

[1] The name given to the chapters of the Koran, meaning, "reading."

who said: "O Mahomet, thou art in truth the prophet of Allah, and I am Gabriel." It is said that in moments of inspiration his anxiety of countenance was painfully evident; he would fall to the ground like one intoxicated or overcome by sleep, and in the coldest day his forehead would be bedewed with sweat. These periods were unexpected even by Mahomet himself. He himself said later: "Inspiration descendeth upon me in one of two ways: sometimes Gabriel cometh and communicateth the revelation unto me as one man unto another, and this is easy; at other times it affecteth me like the ringing of a bell, penetrating my very heart, and rending me as it were in pieces, and this it is which grievously afflicteth me."

Mahomet now preached his doctrines privately among his friends. His wife's freedman, Zaid; his cousin Ali; his intimate friend Abu-bekr, a ready believer, a steadfast friend, a rich merchant, generous in purchasing slaves who had become believers; Othman, Zobair, and others soon formed a little community. He was in accord too with the Hanifs. Gradually his appeal extended to the whole of the Koreish and their slaves, who, being foreigners, had often some knowledge of Judaism and Christianity, and were somewhat predisposed to accept a new doctrine that elevated them; but the Meccans in general paid him little heed. They were already familiar with the essence of his teaching about the one God, and the necessity of truth and righteousness. He was not preaching to them a really new and attractive doctrine; it was one which, if followed out, demanded painful changes in their life, a true obedience to the all-powerful Judge of man, accompanied by prayer, almsgiving, and temperance of life. If the slaves, the children of the lower classes, heard him gladly, that was an additional reason why the haughty Koreish would not listen to him. *His early adherents.* *Opposition at Mecca.*

Repulsed very considerably, Mahomet proceeded to denounce more vigorously the false gods and the false ideas of the Koreish, and to threaten them with judgments of God if they did not listen to His *Attempts to silence him.*

prophet. They were constrained at one time to beg Abu Talib, Mahomet's uncle, to silence him or to withdraw his protection from him. When Abu Talib discussed matters with his nephew, the latter was sturdy in upholding the paramount imperiousness of his convictions. "Though they gave me the sun in my right hand and the moon in my left," said Mahomet, "to bring me back from my undertaking, yet will I not pause till the Lord carry my cause to victory, or till I die for it." So saying, he burst into tears, and turned to go away. "Go in peace," said his uncle, "and say what thou wilt, for, by God, I will on no condition abandon thee."

At this time Mahomet was holding his meetings in the house of Arkun, one of his converts, close by the sanctuary of the Kaaba; but petty insults were heaped on Mahomet, and grosser indignities and cruelties on the humbler converts, so that while Abu-bekr purchased the freedom of some slaves, others fled to Abyssinia, where they were kindly received by the Christians.

*Flight of adherents to Abyssinia.*

After this, Mahomet, depressed by apparent failure, was in a mood for compromise. One day he sat down among the chief men of Mecca beside the Kaaba, and recited to them the fifty-third sura, including an account of the first visit of the angel to him, and also of a later vision, containing "What think ye of Al-Lat and Al-Ozza, and Manat the third with them?" At this verse, so the story runs, the devil suggested to Mahomet words of reconciliation. "These are the sublime Females" [otherwise "cranes"], "whose intercession may be hoped for;" whereupon the Koreish were delighted at this recognition of their deities, and when Mahomet concluded, "Wherefore bow down before Allah and serve Him," they all prostrated themselves and worshipped; and professed themselves ready to recognise the prophet, since he had granted them part of their idolatry. But Mahomet went home disquieted, and in the evening was visited by Gabriel, who said to him, "What hast thou done? thou hast repeated before the people words that I never gave unto thee." Then Mahomet grieved

*A proposed compromise.*

sorely and said, "I have spoken of God that which He hath not said." Then he was comforted, and Allah erased part of the sura, making it read, after "Manat the third," "What? shall there be male offspring for them, and female for you? That were an unfair division. They are naught but names, which ye and your fathers have invented." When the Meccans heard of this, their hostility broke out with renewed violence. Withdrawal by Mahomet.

There can be little doubt that this story indicates a period of attempted compromise, which failed, owing to the unreality of any change produced in the Meccans. A profession which was no conversion was useless in establishing a reformation. The news of it brought back the Abyssinian refugees; but finding enmity again in full activity, they returned in added numbers, including Mahomet's daughter Rokkaya and her husband Othman. The Koreish were very scornful after this change of front, and said, "Ah, is this he whom Allah sent as an Apostle; verily, he had nearly seduced us from our gods, unless we had patiently persevered therein." "Verily thou plainly art a fabricator." Return of fugitives, and second flight.

In the midst of these discouragements, Mahomet made two notable converts, his uncle Hamza, and Omar, a young man who had till then been strongly hostile to the new faith. Omar was twenty-six years old, tall and commanding in figure, with a strong and impetuous temper, and he had great personal influence, though neither rich nor of a principal family. He was converted owing to his discovery that his sister Fatima and her husband Said had believed in the new faith, and he was welcomed cordially by Mahomet. From this time people were not afraid to profess the new faith openly. Omar first offered his prayers publicly at the Kaaba, and performed the accustomed walks round its precincts, and other adherents of Mahomet soon followed his example. The Koreish were alarmed, and became still more hostile to the prophet and all his family, the Hashimites. Meanwhile he attacked them more fiercely by his reve- Hamza and Omar converted. Hostility of the Koreish.

MAHOMET, PROPHET OF ISLAM.

lations, many of them at this time being alleged to be confirmed by the Jewish scriptures. Not a few of the chapters of the Koran which date from this period contain narratives distorted evidently from the Old Testament narratives, or from Jewish traditions. Again and again he refers to his own revelation as confirming and attesting the Book of Moses or the Jewish Scriptures. In fact, he claimed, that "the learned men of the children of Israel" recognised this; and there is very strong reason to believe that some of the Jews to whom he was known gained the idea that he might be "the Prophet whom the Lord would raise up." There is no proof that Mahomet ever studied from an actual copy of the Old Testament. But his utterances became more and more intermingled with Jewish stories, and he even claimed the revelation of these as proof of his mission. His enemies said: "They are fables of the ancients which he hath had written down; they are dictated to him morning and evening;" and Mahomet's only answer was, "He hath revealed it who knoweth that which is hidden in heaven and in earth." *Mahomet's alliance with Jews.*

The Meccans were not likely to relish the plain denunciations of Mahomet, threatening them with a terrible overthrow; but these threatenings were so often repeated that the people at last expressed a wish that the day might arrive; and they termed his revelations tedious. Finally, they resolved to adopt a very severe form of boycotting Mahomet and the Hashimites. They would not intermarry with them; they would neither sell to nor buy from them; in fact, dealings of all kinds should cease. This ban was put into writing and sealed with three seals; then it was hung up in the Kaaba, as a sign of its religiously binding nature. So severe a measure naturally frightened those at whom it was aimed, and they withdrew strictly within the quarter of Abu Talib, separated by cliffs, buildings, and a gateway from the rest of Mecca (A.D. 616-7). Not being strong enough to send out a caravan of their own, they soon began to suffer from scarcity. No one ventured outside, except during *Boycotting of Mahomet and his followers.* *Seclusion.*

the sacred months. Yet the Hashimites maintained themselves thus for two or three years, a few of the other Meccans now and then venturing to help them. Mahomet devoted himself to preaching to those of his clan who were unconverted, and to strengthening the believers. "Conduct thyself gently unto the believers that are with thee," says his revelation about this time, "and put thy trust in Him that is glorious and merciful."

During the sacred pilgrimages, however, he preached to the strangers who flocked to Mecca, warning them against idolatry, proclaiming the worship of the One God, and promising them dominion on earth and Paradise hereafter, if they would only believe. But he was generally repulsed with the words, "Thine own kindred and people should know thee best, wherefore do they not believe and follow thee?"

*Mahomet preaches to strangers.*

At last the ban was removed, after events of which there is more than one traditional account. It had been discovered that insects had eaten up the parchment record in the Kaaba: and five chief men of the Koreish went to the quarter of Abu Talib, and commanded all the refugees to return to their respective homes in safety. Yet this apparent victory was the prelude of worse losses: Khadijah died (A.D. 619–620), and then the venerable Abu Talib. Protection of his party became more difficult, and Mahomet began to turn his thoughts towards other places. He went and preached at Taïf (sixty miles east of Mecca), but failed; he was hooted and stoned out of the place, and was sunk in the deepest despondency. His prayer at this time has been handed down. In it he bewails his feebleness and insignificance. "Oh, Thou most merciful, Thou art the Lord of the weak, and Thou art my Lord. Into whose hands wilt Thou abandon me? Into the hands of the strangers that beset me round, or of the enemy to whom Thou hast given the mastery over me? . . . I seek for refuge in the light of Thy gracious countenance by which the darkness is dispersed, and peace ariseth both for this world and the next, that Thy wrath light not upon me, nor Thine indignation. It is

*Death of Khadijah.*

*Mahomet's despondency.*

Thine to show anger until Thou art pleased; and there is not any power or resource but in Thee." On his way home during one night, while in prayer or while dreaming, he saw a company of the jinn, or genii, listening to the Koran, and eager to embrace the faith.

Returning to Mecca, Mahomet married again,—two months after Khadijah's death—Sauda, the widow of Sakran, an early convert; and was betrothed to Ayesha, the young daughter (only seven years of age) of his bosom friend Abu-bekr. *Re-marriage.* Thus he first gave way to that polygamy which has been one of the great features of Mohammedanism. When the time of pilgrimage came round again, Mahomet preached earnestly to the pilgrims; and met with a little band of persons from Medina, 250 miles north of Mecca, who showed an unusual readiness to hear him. *The pilgrims from Medina.* He found that they had close connections with the numerous Jews of Medina, and asked them whether he could find protection and a hearing in their city. They promised to let him know the next year. In the meantime they made known the doctrines he had taught them. They learnt how the Jews were expecting another prophet to arise, and they identified Mahomet with this prophet; so that when the pilgrims from Medina again met Mahomet, twelve men pledged themselves to him in the following terms: "We will not worship any but the One God; we will not steal, neither will we commit adultery, nor kill our children; we will not slander in any wise; and we will not disobey him (*i.e.* the Prophet) in anything that is right." *First pledge of Acaba.* This is called the First Pledge of Acaba, from the locality where it was taken; and also the Pledge of Women, because it does not include any vow to defend the Prophet, and thus was afterwards the pledge required of women. Mahomet's reply was, "If ye fulfil the pledge, Paradise shall be your reward. He that shall fail in any part thereof, to God belongeth this concern, either to punish or forgive."

The twelve returned to Medina as missionaries of the new faith, and at once zealously spread it, and with such

success that they sent to Mahomet for a teacher versed in
the Koran, who could give fuller instruction.
Musab, a great-grandson of Hashim, was sent
and received with general assent, and Mahomet
from this time had visions of a journey to Medina. To
this period apparently belongs his vision of being carried
by Gabriel on a winged horse past Medina to the temple
at Jerusalem, where he was welcomed by the Prophets.
Thence he appeared to mount from one heaven
to another, appearing at last in the presence of
Allah, from whom he received the command
that His people were to pray five times in the day. When
he awoke and told his vision, some of his followers were
staggered and drew back, others believed and accepted it.
However, the only mention of this wonderful vision in
the Koran is in the seventeenth Sura; "Celebrated be the
praises of Him who took his servant a journey by night
from the Sacred Mosque (the Kaaba) to the remote Mosque
(the Temple at Jerusalem), the precinct of which we have
blessed, to show him of our signs. Verily He both hears
and looks."

*Adherents won at Medina.*

*The vision of Jerusalem and of heaven.*

At this time there was a great struggle going on
between the Byzantine empire and the Persians, who for
some years were encroaching everywhere, but
in 621 were driven back by the emperor Heraclius. Before his victories Mahomet, whose sympathies
were with the Greek empire, prophesied his success.
Finding his efforts at Mecca fruitless, he retired from his
endeavour—with a revelation to justify him—"We have
not made thee a keeper over them, neither art thou
unto them a guardian." His resource was in calmness
and confidence of future success. "Verily we will destroy the unjust; and we will make you to dwell in the
land after them" (K. xiv. 17). A famine came upon
Mecca—a punishment from Allah; relief came,
—it was Allah's goodness, to give the Meccans
yet another chance. Meanwhile the Koran said to the
unbelievers, "Work ye in your place,—wait ye in expectation; we too in expectancy will wait." Mahomet's
claims rose higher still, and he taught, "Whosoever

*The Emperor Heraclius.*

*Famine at Mecca.*

MECCA, WITH THE KAABA IN THE FOREGROUND.

rebels against God and His prophet, verily for him is the fire of hell; they shall be therein alway, for ever."

**Mahomet's high claims.** He asseverated about his mission with the strongest language, putting into the mouth of Allah the most dire threats against Mahomet if he had fabricated anything concerning Him. In temporal want he was thus reassured: "Do not strain after what We have provided a few of them with—the show of this life—to try them by; but the provision of thy Lord is better and more lasting. Bid thy people pray, and persevere in it; We do not ask thee to provide, We will provide, and the issue shall be to piety."

In March, 622, when the pilgrimage again brought his adherents from Medina, Mahomet learnt at a meeting by **Second pledge of Acaba.** night, that they had increased to a large number. At this meeting more than seventy persons from Medina pledged themselves to defend Mahomet at the risk of their lives, and took an oath which has been called the second pledge of Acaba; and he expressed himself ready to go with them to Medina. Mahomet named twelve of the chief men, saying, "Moses chose from amongst his people twelve leaders. Ye shall be sureties for the rest, even as were the apostles of Jesus; and I am the surety for my people." The meeting was suddenly broken up by a noise, and next day the chiefs of the Koreish sought to discover what had taken place, under threats of hostility. When they found out the true nature of the meeting, they pursued the Medina pilgrims, but could not come up with them. This was followed by a renewed persecution of the Mohammedans at Mecca; and a few days afterwards Mahomet commanded them to depart to Medina, since Allah had given them brethren and a refuge in that city. It was in April, 622, that the flight began, from which the Moslem chronology begins.

**Commencement of the flight to Medina.** The emigration went on secretly for the most part, house after house at Mecca being found abandoned. Within two months about 150 emigrants had reached Medina. The Koreish looked on helpless and amazed, having no precedent for forcibly detaining them. Finally only Mahomet, Abu Bekr, and their families, including Ali, were left in Mecca; and the Koreish plotted how they might detain, expel, or kill Mahomet. Hearing of their arrangement to visit his house, Mahomet left it secretly, took Abu Bekr with him, and both crept through a back window and escaped unnoticed from the southern suburb of the city, and took refuge in a cave of Mount Thaur, where they hid for two or three days. The Prophet in the Koran (ix. 42) thus describes the situation: "And God did help him, when those who disbelieved drove him forth the second of two [*i.e.* with only one companion]." When they two were in the cave alone, he said to his companion: "Be not cast down, for verily God is with us. And God sent down His Shechinah upon him, and aided him with hosts ye could not see, and made the word of the unbelievers to be abased, and the word of God to be exalted, for God is mighty and wise." Meanwhile, seeing the daylight through a crevice in the cave, Abu Bekr said, "What if one of them were to look beneath him; he might see us under his very feet." "Think not this, Abu Bekr," said the Prophet, in perhaps his sublimest utterance, "We are two, but God is in the midst, a third." They were fed by friends secretly and not discovered; at last, they set out towards Medina, where they arrived, it is believed, on the 28th of June, 622. Thus the Hegira (or flight) was completed. Mahomet's and Abu Bekr's families remained behind at Mecca for a time.

[Wellhausen, "Life of Mohammed," *Encyclopædia Britannica*; Robertson Smith, "Religion of the Semites;" Muir, "Life of Mahomet"; Bosworth Smith, "Mohammed and Mohammedanism"; Hughes, "Dictionary of Islam."]

## CHAPTER IV.

### Life of Mahomet. Part II.

Mahomet at Medina—He enters the city on a camel—Brotherhood of refugees and citizens—The first mosque—Its fame—Mahomet and the Jews—Jewish "witnesses"—Changed direction of prayer—The Ramadan fast—Day of sacrifice—The call to prayer—Mahomet's pulpit—Mode of conducting service—War and politics—Incentives to war—Promised rewards—Battle of Badr—War against kin—Compulsion and cruelty towards Jews—Mahomet's new wives—Battle of Ohod—War of the ditch—Pledge of the Tree—Treaty with the Koreish—The Jews of Khaibar—Mahomet's messages to great powers—Mahomet visits Mecca, 629—Mahomet marches on Mecca, 630—Destroys the idols—All Mecca submits to him—Battle of Honein—The Coptic maid and Mahomet—His growing dominion—Taif submits—Ban proclaimed against unbelievers—Mahomet's last pilgrimage, 632—His illness and death—Funeral—Personal appearance—Character—Moral influence.

THE beautiful oasis of Medina, crowded with date-palms and other fruit-trees, and inhabited by two tribes of Arabs,—of whom the more powerful, the Khazraj, included Mahomet's adherents,—as well as by many Jews, was far more inviting and favourable to the Prophet than Mecca. He was received with a joyful welcome by his converts, whom he bade to show their joy by good-will to their neighbours, by sending portions to the poor, by increased family unity, and by prayer at night. "Thus," he said, "shall ye enter Paradise in peace."

<small>Mahomet at Medina.</small>

After a short stay in Coba, one of the suburbs of

Medina, Mahomet entered the city on a Friday, seated on a camel, with Abu Bekr behind him. He halted at a place of prayer on the way, and performed his first Friday service, giving a sermon on the new faith. *He enters the city on a camel.* From that day to this, Friday has been the Mahometan Sunday. The after-journey was a grand triumphal procession; and so numerous and pressing became the invitations to the Prophet to take up his abode with particular persons, that he announced that the camel must decide. She entered the eastern quarter, and sat down in a large open courtyard, near Abu Ayoub's house; in his house, therefore, Mahomet lived, until a house of prayer, with houses for his wives, had been built in the courtyard, which Mahomet bought. Meanwhile, the change from the dry climate of Mecca to the damp and cold of Medina were very trying to his followers, most of whom suffered from fever. Mahomet hit upon an excellent plan for raising their spirits and attaching them to their new home. He enjoined them to form a peculiar brotherhood, each stranger taking a man of Medina as his brother, and the pair undertaking a degree of mutual devotion even beyond the claims of blood. *Brotherhood of refugees and citizens.* After a time this proved unnecessary or inconvenient, and in about a year and a half it was abolished.

The new mosque was on the site now occupied by the great mosque of Medina; and though less capacious than the latter, it was very large, being about one hundred cubits (say 150 feet) square; and the roof was of palm-tree trunks, covered in with palm-wood rafters. *The first mosque.* The worshippers directed their faces towards the north, while Mahomet, when in prayer, stood near the north wall and looked towards the north-west, to Jerusalem, with the people at his back; when preaching he faced them. On the eastern side rooms were built for the Prophet's wives and daughters, his marriage with his child-wife Ayesha being now completed. To the north was a shelter for poor adherents who had no homes, and who slept in the mosque.

"Though rude in material," says Muir, "and compara-

tively insignificant in extent, the mosque of Mahomet is
**Its fame.** glorious in the history of Islam. Here the prophet and his companions spent the greater portion of their time; here the daily service, with its oft-recurring prayers, was first publicly established; here the great congregation assembled every week, and trembled often while they listened to the orations of the Prophet and the messages from heaven. Here he planned his victories. From this spot he sent forth envoys to kings and emperors with the summons to embrace Islam. Here he received the embassies of contrite and believing tribes; and from hence issued commands which carried consternation amongst the rebellious to the very ends of the Peninsula. Hard by, in the room of Ayesha, he yielded up the ghost; and there he lies buried."

Mahomet's attitude to the Jews gradually changed. At first he was most anxious to conciliate them, professed his **Mahomet and** approval of them, laid emphasis upon the points **the Jews.** of agreement between them, and even framed a sort of treaty, agreeing to aid and succour and defend them, and permitting them the full maintenance of their religion. But as his claims grew, as he began to emphasise his position as the "greater Prophet" spoken of by their scriptures, the Jews of Medina felt that they could not accept him as their lawgiver in place of or in addition to Moses, since he was not of Jewish blood. A few **Jewish** joined him entirely, becoming practically Maho-**"witnesses."** metans, and these were carefully utilised as "witnesses" to the Prophet's claims, asserting that their brethren merely denied them through jealousy. The portions of the Koran now issued were full of attacks upon the Jews, reciting their old idolatry and disobedience to God. At first Jerusalem was the chief sacred place, as we have seen, towards which Mahomet turned in prayer. Before he had been eighteen months in Medina, one day Mahomet, having already, it is related, desired permission **Changed** of God to turn towards the Kaaba at Mecca, **direction of** suddenly received it in the midst of service, **prayer.** and turned round to the south, towards Mecca. From this time the Jews were hostile to the Mahometans.

Previously, Mahomet had adopted the Fast Day of the Atonement from the Jews; he now established his own peculiar fast, and extended it over the month of Ramadan —as a day-fast from meat, drink, and all enjoy-ments, which however were lawful at night. *The Ramadan fast.*

At the end of the month a festival was held, called "the breaking of the fast," marked by abundant alms to the poor. He also established a day of sacrifice, which was celebrated on the concluding day of the pilgrimage to Mecca. After a solemn service, two fat kids were sacrificed by the prophet, the first for the whole people, the second for himself and his family. *Day of sacrifice.*

After the direction of prayer was changed, a special call to prayer was established, to which a supernatural origin was ascribed. Bilal, Mahomet's negro servant, ascending a lofty wall near the mosque before daybreak, on its first glimmer proclaimed, "Great is Allah! great is Allah! I bear witness that there is no God but Allah. I bear witness that Mahomet is the Prophet of Allah! Come unto Prayer! Come unto Happiness! Great is Allah! Great is Allah! There is no God but Allah, Prayer is better than sleep, Prayer is better than sleep!" And the same call was repeated at each of the five hours of prayer. *The call to prayer.*

Mahomet's dignity and convenience were further promoted by the construction of a pulpit, the platform of which was raised three steps above the floor, and placed near the southern wall of the mosque. It became an object of great sanctity to Mahometans, oaths being taken close to it, and a false swearer being condemned to hell. *Mahomet's pulpit.*

We may here quote from Muir the traditional account of Mahomet's mode of first conducting service in his pulpit. "As he mounted the pulpit, turning towards the Kaaba, he uttered a loud *Takbir*, 'Great is the Lord!' and the whole assembly from behind burst forth into the same exclamation. Then he bowed himself in prayer, still standing in the pulpit with his face averted from the people; after which he descended, walking backwards, and at the foot of the pulpit prostrated himself towards the Kaaba. This he *Mode of conducting service.*

did twice, and having ended the prayers, he turned towards the congregation, and told them he had done this that they might know and imitate his manner of prayer." His mode of conducting the Friday service was as follows: "As the Prophet mounted the steps of the pulpit he greeted the assembly with the salutation of peace. Then he sat down, and Bilal sounded forth the call to prayer. After the prescribed prostrations and reciting of the Koran, he delivered two discourses, twice sitting down; and he would point with his fingers, enforcing his instructions: the people raised their faces towards him, listening attentively, and fixing their eyes upon him; when he ended, they joined in a universal Amen. As he discoursed he leant upon a staff. His dress on these occasions was a mantle of striped Yemen stuff, six cubits in length, thrown over his shoulders; the lower garment was a girdle of fine cloth from Oman, but of smaller dimensions than the other. These robes were worn only on Friday, and on the two great festivals; at the conclusion of each service they were folded up and put carefully away."

The later life of Mahomet may be considered as a period of war and politics even more than of religion; or rather, his religion became identified with war and politics. From the time of his flight to Medina, though the Meccans abstained from active hostilities, he had threatened divine vengeance against them, and events proved that he only bided his time. We cannot detail the marauding expeditions which were sent out by Mahomet or led by him against Meccan caravans, with varying success. One of these attacked a caravan during the sacred month of Rajab; one of the Koreish was killed and two were taken prisoners. After a period of discouragement, Mahomet declared a revelation that "war during the sacred month was grievous, yet to obstruct the way of God and to hinder men from the Holy Temple was worse." The warlike spirit, so temptingly combining religious incentives with those of plunder, grew apace, and Mahomet produced a revelation in favour of war against unbelievers, until all opposition ceased and there was no religion but Allah's. "Kill them wheresoever ye find them; and expel them from that out of which they have expelled you. . . . Yet fight not against them beside the Holy Temple, until they fight with you thereat." "An excellent provision in Paradise" was promised to those who fell in battle. Contributions were solicited towards war, and a higher place was to be granted to those who contributed before the victory. "Who is he that lendeth unto the Lord a goodly loan? He shall double the same, and he shall have an honourable recompense."

*Promised rewards.*

The first important battle for the new faith was that of Badr, fought in December, 623, when Mahomet with 308 followers attacked the Koreish 950 strong, and put them to flight, after many of their principal men had been slain. Two prisoners whom he hated personally Mahomet put to death, and others were set free on payment of heavy ransoms. Thus was started that career of bloodshed and conquest which has distinguished Mohammedanism more than any other religion, even remembering the Crusades and other wars of Christians. No religion has ever made extension by war so important an element. In the matter of dissolving old relationships and ties, Islam was but like numerous other religions; still this was a new attitude in Arabia, which struck the Koreish with consternation. Brother was ready even to slay brother at the bidding of the Prophet. The new brotherhood superseded everything, and no toleration was allowable towards unbelievers. Active natures found full scope for their energies; and no man could hope for distinction in Islam by a life of contemplation such as the Buddhists favoured. The new religion showed that it was to be founded upon human passion, upon pride of domination, upon fanaticism, quite as much as upon simplification of truth, and remodelling of belief about God, and new principles and fashions in personal conduct. The very process of winning the first victory became in the hands of Mahomet and his principal followers a method of strengthening their convictions and their hold upon their followers at the same time. The men of Medina extended their pledge to defend

*Battle of Badr.*

*War against kin.*

Mahomet in Medina in these words, "Prophet of the Lord, march whither thou listest, encamp wherever thou mayest choose, make war or conclude peace with whom thou wilt. For I swear by Him who hath sent thee with the Truth, that if thou wast to march till our camels fell down dead, we should go forward with thee to the world's end." The distribution of the spoils too was made the occasion of a revelation claiming one-fifth for God and the prophet and his kin, together with the orphans and the poor. In numerous other ways this victory was skilfully used to deepen the convictions of the believers, and the influence of Mahomet as a Divine teacher.

*Loyalty of men of Medina.*

*Division of spoils of war.*

Bloodshed leads to bloodshed. Mahomet could now brook no opposition. Jews and Jewesses, who attacked him or spread defamatory verses about him and his doings, were assassinated one after another by his followers, either by his direct instigation or with his subsequent approval. Tribe after tribe of Jews were either compelled to submit to Islam and profess its faith, or were expelled, or attacked and exterminated.

*Compulsion and cruelty towards Jews.*

And sensuality followed hard on bloodshed. New wives were added to Mahomet's harem; and from this time (624) there was scarcely a year of his life in which he did not take a new wife.

*Mahomet's new wives.*

The Meccans, after long mourning, decided to take active steps against Mahomet; and early in 625 the two met outside Medina at Mount Ohod, and after a partial victory for the Mohammedans, they were taken in the rear, Mahomet was wounded, and his uncle Hamza slain; but the Meccans retired after their victory, and Mahomet retained his influence at Mecca. He executed a capital sentence on a follower who in the battle had slain an enemy of his own side, and those who had been killed at Ohod were regarded as martyrs. Passages in the Koran (ii. and iii.) represent God as causing alternations of success as tests, and encourage the believers to perseverance, even if Mahomet himself should be killed; and no soul died without the permission of God.

*Battle of Ohod.*

In March, 627, the expelled Jews, allied with the Koreish

and two great Bedouin tribes, in all 10,000 strong, attacked Mahomet at Medina. He entrenched himself behind a wide ditch or foss which he dug across the exposed side of the city; and his followers defended it so well that the attacking army, after fourteen days' siege, broke up and returned home. After this Mahomet massacred the men of the last remaining independent Jewish tribe in Medina, 600 or 700 in number, who had had some negotiations with the enemy but had broken them off, and who now refused to join his ranks; their women and children being sold into slavery. *War of the ditch.*

Mahomet now prepared to attack Mecca itself. He first attempted to visit Mecca (in March, 628) with 1500 men, but was forced to halt at Hodaibya, just outside the sacred territory, the Koreish refusing to let him perform the circuit of the Kaaba. On this occasion, when in a state of alarm and suspecting treachery, Mahomet made all the pilgrims give a pledge to serve him faithfully till death (this is called the Pledge of the Tree, from the acacia-tree under which it was sworn). The Koreish, realising the devotion of Mahomet's followers, offered him a compromise, by which he was to withdraw for that year, and in the next return and remain three days within the sacred territory and offer the sacrifices he desired. Mahomet, willing to accept this, did not even demur to his being described in the treaty as "Mohammed the son of Abdallah," instead of by his title "Apostle of God," and he allowed the Koreish to use that name of God which they chose. The treaty provided for a truce of ten years, with freedom for all to join either Mahomet or the Koreish. Mahomet, although his people were somewhat disappointed at his agreeing to these terms, realised that he had gained much in being recognised as an independent political power, and in being allowed to enter Mecca undisturbed the next year. He produced a new revelation describing the result as a victory; and his later followers echo this view, showing that the treaty had been won without fighting, and that it led very many to join Islam. Strengthened by this result, Mahomet turned his arms against the rich *Pledge of the Tree.* *Treaty with the Koreish.*

Jews of Khaibar, north of Medina (628) and subdued them in detail with no little cruelty. In the same year he sent a message to the victorious Byzantine emperor Heraclius, demanding that he should acknowledge him as Apostle, lay aside the worship of Jesus, and return to that of the One God. A similar message was sent to the Persian king Siroes, without result. An embassy to the Roman governor of Egypt was received with honour, though without submission; but presents were sent to Mahomet, including two Coptic girls, one of whom he added to his harem. About the same time the Abyssinian prince is reported to have signified his acceptance of Islam. These and other incidents testify to the rapid growth of Mahomet's influence. This reacted upon the Arab mind, susceptible to motives of power and booty; and Mecca was now to drop into Mahomet's mouth, like a ripe plum.

*Mahomet's messages to great powers.*

In March, 629, Mahomet, according to the compromise, visited Mecca with 2,000 men, performed the sevenfold circuit of the Kaaba, reciting, "There is no God but Allah alone. It is He that hath holden His servant and exalted his army. Alone hath He discomfited the confederated hosts." Then he sacrificed the appropriate animals on the rising ground of Marwa, and finally shaved his head. On the second day Mahomet entered the Kaaba, Bilal sounded the call to prayer at midday from the top of the building, and the Moslems responded and performed their accustomed devotions. Thus was the Kaaba reclaimed for Islam. As a diversion from more serious matters, Mahomet arranged yet another marriage, with Meimuna, a bride of over fifty years old—this being his last marriage. Some leading men of Mecca joined him. During 629 some further victories over various Arab tribes, and the conquest of Syrian border tribes to the south of the Dead Sea added to his prestige.

*Mahomet visits Mecca, 629.*

At the end of 629, some alleged infractions of the treaty of Hodaibya led Mahomet to march secretly on Mecca with nearly 10,000 men, in January, 630. Suddenly all their tent fires were lighted

*Mahomet marches on Mecca, 630.*

within view of the city, and the sight spread consternation among the Koreish. Abbas, Mahomet's uncle, had joined him just before, and he now became a medium by

MEDINA: THE MODERN CITY.

which a leader of the Koreish, named Abu Sofyan, approached Mahomet and tendered his submission. At once Mahomet and his army entered the city, with scarcely any opposition. He went to the Kaaba, saluted the sacred stone, and made the seven circuits of the temple; then one by one, by his orders, the idols of **Destroys the idols.** Mecca were destroyed, including the great image of Hobal in front of the Kaaba. He next worshipped outside and inside the temple; had the pictures of Abraham and the angels, which decorated the Kaaba, destroyed, and ordered all believers in Allah throughout Mecca to destroy all images in their houses. At the same time he had the pillars marking the boundaries of the sacred territory repaired, showing his intention to keep up the sanctity of Mecca; but while expressing his intense attachment to Mecca, he comforted the people of Medina by declaring that he should live and die in the city which had first hospitably received him. Four persons, renegades or criminals, were put to death after this peaceful conquest. The rest of the people unanimously submitted to the Prophet, many, no doubt, **Mecca submits to him.** being influenced by fear, by seeing that his was the winning side, by the attractions of war, power, and probable plunder. Various images and shrines of idols in the neighbourhood of Mecca were soon destroyed.

The next important event in Mahomet's history was the battle of Honein, against the powerful Hawazin tribe, in **Battle of Honein.** which Mahomet's forces at first wavered, and were only encouraged to make a firm stand by his reminding the men of Medina of their oath of Hodaibya; their valour turned the day in his favour. Then Mahomet ascribed the victory to the aid of great unseen angelic hosts. Taïf was then besieged, but its defenders were valiant and skilful, and the siege was raised. The distribution of the booty from Honein caused much dissatisfaction among the Medina men, because great favour was shown to the Meccans, especially to Abu Sofyan; but Mahomet again appeased them by expressing his unchangeable gratitude to them, and his determination to stick to them as against all the world.

His relations with one of the beautiful Coptic maids, Mary, sent from Egypt, now caused much vexation among

his wives, owing to his evident preference for her. She
gave birth to a son, Ibrahim, the only one born
to Mahomet at Medina; and his death at about
sixteen months caused the prophet great grief.
Mahomet, in the manner characteristic of his later life,
produced a "revelation" to suit the particular case, to
approve what he had done and what he wished to do,
and cautioning his wives against the consequences of
murmuring against him. *(The Coptic maid and Mahomet.)*

Mahomet's dominion now began to assume the proportions of an empire; those who adopted the faith submitted to his secular rule, and paid annual tithes to consecrate their wealth, these being applied towards the charities and other expenses of the Prophet. Those who refused to pay were compelled. A noted Arab poet, Kab, yielded his submission in a notable poem; when he had recited the lines:— *(His growing dominion.)*

> "Verily the Prophet is a light illuminating the world,
> A naked sword from the armoury of God,"

Mahomet was so delighted that he took his mantle from his shoulders and threw it upon the poet, as a gift. From this incident, the poem was known as "The Poem of the Mantle"; later the mantle became the property of the Caliphs, till the fall of Bagdad. Embassies were received from all parts of Arabia, and even beyond, acknowledging Mahomet's chiefship and office, and receiving presents, confirmations of authority, special privileges, etc. (A.D. 630, 631). Of the Christian tribes which submitted, some were allowed to continue in their religion as before, others were bidden not to baptize their children, though they might maintain their worship. Instructors in the faith of Islam were often sent back with the embassies. In 630 an expedition headed by Mahomet received the submission of numerous Christian and Jewish tribes to the south of Palestine. Some of his adherents who had held back from this expedition were rebuked in severe terms in the latest revealed chapter of the Koran (ix.). Those who had no pretext to offer, were put under a strict boycott, but pardoned on their abject submission.

The people of Taïf had not yet submitted, but still continued in idolatry. Orwa, one of their chiefs, embraced the new faith at Medina, and returned to preach it to his people. After he had announced his conversion at Taïf, and shouted the call to prayer from the top of his house, *Taïf submits.* he was shot at with arrows and mortally wounded. Hence he was accounted a martyr. The Taïfites continued their idolatry, and suffered from the predatory attacks of the Moslems, which compelled them to keep within their walls. At last they sent an embassy to the Prophet, who gave them instructions, and refused to grant them permission to continue in several sinful habits, or to maintain their idol Al-Lat for three years longer, as they desired. After abating their demand to one year, or even a month, the only concession they could get from Mahomet was, that they should not be compelled to destroy the idol with their own hands. A follower of Mahomet was sent to do this; and it was done amid the loud laments of the women and children.

Abu Bekr and 300 pilgrims were deputed to perform the pilgrimage to Mecca in 631, Mahomet not sharing in *Ban proclaimed against unbelievers.* it because a vast number of heathen tribes still went to Mecca and performed idolatrous rites. It was announced that every pilgrimage hereafter would be forcibly limited to worshippers of the One God, after which time all unbelievers should be fought against. This decree was promulgated to all the pilgrims and thus spread throughout Arabia. Christians and Jews were to be subjugated and made to pay tribute. Christian churches were to be destroyed and mosques built on the sites. Various officers were sent out to heathen and to submissive tribes, charged not only with their religious instruction, but also with their judicial and social regulation, according to the Koran and Mahomet's other instructions.

Early in 632 Mahomet prepared for the great pilgrimage, *Mahomet's last pilgrimage, 632.* and set out for Mecca with a vast company, including all his wives, and with a hundred camels destined for sacrifice. He now found mosques to pray in at the several stages of the journey; and in them he led public worship. When he arrived in sight of the Kaaba, he raised his hands to heaven and said: "O Lord, add unto this house in the dignity and glory, the honour and the reverence which already Thou hast bestowed on it. And they that for the greater pilgrimage and the lesser frequent the same, increase them much in honour and dignity, in piety, goodness, and glory." Then he completed the circuits and the rites of the lesser pilgrimage, and ordered those who had brought no victims to put off their pilgrim's garb. The first day of the greater pilgrimage he preached in the Kaaba, and passed the night in a tent at Mina. Next day, proceeding to the height of Arafat, he consecrated it as a pilgrimage station, recited several parts of the Koran relating to the pilgrimage, and concluded, " 'This day have I perfected your religion unto you, and fulfilled my mercy upon you, and appointed Islam for you to be your religion." He returned by moonlight to Mozdalifa, and said the sunset and the evening prayers together; and all his recorded behaviour is imitated by pilgrims to this day. Then returning to Mina, shouting the pilgrims' cry:—

> "Labbeik (Here am I, O Lord!) Labbeik
> There is no other God but Thee. Labbeik!
> Praise, blessing, and dominion be to Thee. Labbeik!
> No one may share with Thee therein. Labbeik, Labbeik!

At Mina he cast stones at Acaba, according to ancient custom, slew the victims brought for sacrifice, and shaved his head and part of his beard, pared his nails, etc., and put off the pilgrim's dress. The flesh of the victims and other animals was distributed for food, and a feast was held. Next day he gave a celebrated parting discourse in the Mina valley, repeating some of his principal injunctions. "Know that every Moslem is the brother of every other Moslem. All of you are on the same equality. Ye are one brotherhood." After inquiring, "Know ye what month this is, what territory this is?" and receiving the answer, "The sacred month, the sacred territory," he said, "Even thus sacred and inviolable hath God made the life and the property of each of you unto the other until you meet your Lord." At the same time he proclaimed the rectification of the calendar by which the month of pilgrimage was to be fixed in future. He subsequently completed the ceremonies of the greater pilgrimage and then returned to Medina.

Fresh "prophets" arose in several regions of Arabia, some of whom were indignantly denounced by Mahomet. Aswad, who had raised the standard of rebellion, was assassinated just before Mahomet's own death. The Prophet had planned an expedition against the Syrian border of the Byzantine empire. About this time he became ill, having previously shown signs of old age. One night he visited the burial-ground, and remained there long in meditation, then prayed for those buried there. On the way home he said to his attendant: "The choice hath verily been offered me of continuance in this life, with Paradise hereafter, or to meet my Lord at once; and I have chosen to meet my Lord." He rapidly grew worse, and betook himself to the apartment of Ayesha, who attended him devotedly. For seven or eight days his fever permitted him to attend the mosque and feebly lead the public prayers. On a final day he publicly intimated his approaching death; and on Abu Bekr bursting into tears, he begged him not to weep, and said to the people: "Verily, the chiefest among you all for love and devotion to me is Abu Bekr. If I were to choose a bosom friend, it would be he; but Islam hath made a closer brotherhood amongst us all." Next day Abu Bekr was deputed to lead prayers. Mahomet suffered greatly, and gave utterance to expressions symbolising his belief that sins were expiated by physical sufferings. He was, however, not too distracted to be able to reprove the desire to make the tombs of prophets objects of worship, and to say, "O Lord, let not my tomb be an object of worship." One of his ejaculations during his sufferings was, "O my soul, why seekest thou for refuge elsewhere than in God alone?" Recovering a little, Mahomet again entered the mosque, saying, with a joyful smile on his face, "The Lord verily hath granted unto me refreshment

*His last illness.*

in prayer." Afterwards he spoke to the people, saying, "As for myself, verily, no man can lay hold of me in any matter; I have not made lawful anything but what God hath made lawful; nor have I prohibited aught but that which God in his book hath prohibited." After this exertion he grew much weaker, praying for aid in the agonies of death. One of his last ejaculations was, "Lord, grant me pardon, and join me to the companionship on high." He died soon after noon, only an hour or two after his visit to the mosque, on Monday, the 8th of June, 632. His death.

It was immediately necessary to choose a chief or deputy (Caliph) to represent Mahomet; for the men of Medina desired to appoint a chief for themselves. But Omar and Abu Bekr gained the adhesion of all the leaders at Medina to the appointment of the latter, who had been "the second of the two in the cave," and had been deputed by Mahomet himself to lead public worship. The Prophet's corpse was visited by all Medina, and then buried in a vault dug out under the place where he died. Abu Bekr and Omar's farewell to him expressly made mention of his having sought no recompense for delivering the Faith to the people, and having never sold it for a price at any time. A red mantle which he had worn was placed beneath his body, which was enclosed in white cloth and striped Yemen stuff, without a coffin. The vault was covered over with unbaked bricks and the grave filled up. Abu Bekr elected Caliph.<br>Mahomet's burial.

In person Mahomet was a little above the middle height, of a handsome and commanding figure; he had a large head with broad open brow, jet black longish hair, deep black piercing eyes, and a long black bushy beard. His face had something very winning in its expression, and his smile was gracious and condescending; but his frown or angry look was such that men quailed before it. His gait was quick and decided, though stooping in later years; and he never turned round in walking. In conversing, he turned his full face and whole body towards the speaker. "In shaking hands, he was not the first to withdraw his own; nor was he the His person and character.

first to break off in converse with a stranger, nor to turn away his ear." He treated the most insignificant of his followers with consideration, visited the meanest, made each man in company think himself the most favoured guest, sympathised with both joys and griefs, was gentle to little children, and ministered to every one's personal comfort. His warm attachment to Abu Bekr, Ali, Zeid, Othman, and Omar was intensely reciprocated by them. He never assumed lordly airs nor demanded personal services, he would do everything for himself, even mend his own sandals and clothes. He greatly enjoyed food, yet could readily live as plainly as his followers; but, a true Oriental, he enjoyed perfumes and the society and charms of women extremely. Whatever he may have been in his earlier days, when Khadijah was alive, in his later years, the attractions of women proved his human frailty perhaps more than anything, and led to the deplorable abrogation of his laws in his own favour. The extreme instance of this was seen when he longed for the wife of his adopted son and friend Zeid, and produced a "revelation" commanding him to marry her. Yet he was devoted to all his wives.

In his conduct to enemies, Mahomet showed both good and bad qualities; politic mercy, to gain them over, **Was he sincere?** but also cruelty in numerous executions, and craft in planning or allowing assassinations, in attacks during the sacred months, and in the use made of Jews and Christians. That he was an erring mortal, in no sense an infallible model of conduct, must be the verdict on Mahomet. Who shall pronounce on his sincerity all through? In many ways, especially before the Flight, he showed marks of entire sincerity; but to believe that he was self-deceived in every act at Medina, is to stretch self-deception to an extreme. The fact that he produced successive revelations to enjoin things he desired to do, may possibly be read in two ways: either he deliberately invented the revelations to suit the emergency, or, being of an excitable, susceptible nature, his broodings on a subject brought about the state of mental exaltation in which he genuinely heard, or imagined that he heard, the appropriate "revelation." As regards both his assassinations and his marriages, they show a very great but not an incredible degree of moral warp or of moral infancy, or else a degree of self-delusion which is scarcely compatible with the practical wisdom of very many of his actions. We find him, after his early struggles and the commencement of his preaching, constantly imbued with a belief in special providence, extending almost to fatalism. He certainly believed that everything was predestined; but events were, he believed, capable of being influenced by prayer. With all this, he had several superstitious beliefs, and was guided by omens and prognostications. We may perhaps explain much of his character by the view that his own inward struggles, his moral debates, and his aspirations seemed to him the very voice of God speaking to him. He lacked the physical courage to face bodily danger in battle. At Mecca, however, he showed true bravery in preaching so long amid hostile surroundings, and in remaining behind when nearly all his adherents had departed for Medina. His denunciation of idolatry, and his preaching of the one God and of the equality of man before God, must ever distinguish him honourably as a great religious teacher. He had a style of delivery, an evident earnestness of belief, which carried home his statements of truth and his eloquent and imaginative poetic outbursts.

At Medina sensuality, deception, cruelty, and intolerance stained the prophet's life. Ceremonial routine, material assistance, became more important, outwardly, than inward conviction and purity. But there was enough good in the faith as Mahomet left it, enough that was influential on mankind, to make Islam the second among the great faiths of the world (counting Judaism and Christianity together as the first); and there was enough mingled good and exclusiveness to make it the most difficult of all for Christianity to contend against.

# CHAPTER V.
## The Koran and its Teachings.

Formation of the text—The general prayer—Teaching about God—Names of God—Righteousness defined—Nature of God—Account of creation—Angels—Iblis, or the Devil—The Moslem paradise—Hell—Intermediate state—The day of judgment—Prophets—Attitude towards Jesus—Predestination—Idolatry and Idolaters—Islam—The creed—Prayer—The fast of Ramadan—Alms giving—The holy pilgrimage—Parents and children—Murder and theft—Divorce and concubinage—Marriage—Position of wives—Rhetorical passages—Structure of Koran—Delineation of old prophets—Chronological sequence—Miracles—Reverence for Koran—Versions—Commentaries.

THE Koran (more precisely Qur'án, a reading), which as a whole is not so long as the New Testament, was not in existence as a complete book in the lifetime of Mahomet; but it was settled in its present form within twenty years of his death. Separate chapters or smaller **Formation of** fragments were written down by followers who **the text.** happened to be present when he first recited them, upon palm-leaves, leather, stones, or anything else that was at hand. Abdallah and Zeid the son of Thabit were among his amanuenses. Copies were afterwards made, and many Moslems learnt to recite large portions by heart; but no completed collection of them, apparently, was kept by Mahomet. After his death, when many who knew much of the Koran had fallen in battle, Omar feared that the whole might be forgotten, and induced Abu Bekr to have a collection of copies made. Zeid was charged with this duty, and he made a fair copy of all he could obtain, which passed through the first two caliphs to Haphsa, one of Mahomet's widows, Omar's daughter. But disputes arose as to the true text, and Othman in 650–1 ordered Zeid with three others to make an authoritative text; they took care to accomplish this, burning all discordant texts besides their own and that which Haphsa possessed. The latter however was soon destroyed, and thus we have not to consider conflicting versions of the Koran. That the chapters as we now have them are substantially authentic is suggested by the language, and by the mixture of subjects in the chapters, no designed order being discernible in them. There are but a few passages existing which purport to have been originally in the Koran and rejected by Zeid. Four copies were made of the Koran, one of which was kept at Medina, and one sent to each of the three (at that time) important Moslem cities of Damascus, Basra, and Cufa. At present there is no likelihood that any one of them exists; but copies probably dating from the first century after the flight are known.

We will first endeavour to set forth the chief doctrines about God and divine things, and then the chief moral precepts of the Koran. It opens with the famous short chapter which for the Moslem answers to the Lord's Prayer. It runs thus:

"In the name of God, the Compassionate, the Merciful. Praise belongs to God, the Lord of the worlds, the Merciful, the Compassionate, the Ruler of the day of judgment. Thee we worship and Thee we ask for aid. Direct us in the right way, the way of those to whom Thou art gracious, not of those Thou art angry with, nor of those who err." *The general prayer.*

It cannot be said that Mahomet here expresses ideas unknown before his time, or which he is not likely to have heard from others, especially the Jews. The term "the Merciful" is directly a Jewish word. The chapter (112) on unity directly resembles *Teaching about God.*

the Christian statement of the doctrine: "Say, He is God alone, God the Eternal. He begets and is not begotten; nor is there like unto Him any one." According to the Koran, "Allah is eternal and everlasting, one and indivisible, not endued with form, nor circumscribed by limit or measure; comprehending all things, but comprehended of nothing": here again thoroughly agreeing with Jewish and Christian belief. There are ninety-nine principal **Names of God.** epithets or names applied to God, expressing most of His attributes, as the Merciful, the Compassionate, the Holy, the Faithful, the Creator, the Forgiver, the Provider, the Knowing, the Judge, the Seer, the Strengthener, the Wise, the Answerer of Prayer, the Loving, the Living, the One, the First, the Last, the Avenger, etc.: here again furnishing nothing new to Christians, however new they may have been to the Arabs to whom Mahomet made them known.

A concise summary of the teaching of the Koran is found in ii. 172. "Righteousness is not that ye turn **Righteousness defined.** your faces towards the east or the west; but righteousness is, one who believes in God, and the last day, and the angels, and the Book, and the prophets; and who gives wealth for the love of God to kindred, and orphans, and the poor, and the wayfarer, and beggars, and those in captivity, and who is steadfast in prayer, and gives alms; and those who are sure of their covenant when they make a covenant; and the patient in poverty, and in distress, and in time of violence."

It is expressly stated (vi. 101) that God has no offspring, because He has no consort. Many passages describe Him **Nature of God.** as all-seeing and knowing, and omnipotent and omnipresent. "No vision taketh in Him, but He taketh in all vision; He is the subtle, the all-informed. He has created men, in order that they should worship Him." God is represented sometimes as creating both evil and good, and as creating evil spirits and men for hell; but again men are assured that the evil that befalls them is of themselves. "God misleadeth whom He will, and guideth whom He will" (xxxv. 9).

The creation is in l. 37, as in Genesis, related to have

been accomplished in six days, but in xli. 7, two days is the period assigned. There is no attempt at a detailed history of it, but as to the creation of man it is said, "God created you from earth (or dust,) then from a clod, then He made pairs." In ii. 29 God is said to have taught Adam the names of all things and to have ordered the angels to worship Adam; and they all did so except Eblis (Satan). A brief account of the temptation and fall is given, after which it is said that God relented towards Adam. This account is evidently an imperfect version of the account in Genesis. {*Account of creation.*}

The Koran represents God as attended by angels, pure beings created from fire, neither eating nor drinking, nor having sexes. They ask forgiveness for the dwellers upon earth. Two angels are assigned to each human being, standing on his right and on his left, and recording all his actions. One angel, Rhazwan (goodwill), presides over paradise, and another, Malik (compare Moloch), over hell. Two others perform the examination of persons immediately after burial, allowing them to rest in peace if they confess that there is but one God, and that Mahomet is His prophet; but if not, beating them very severely, and leaving them to be torn by dragons and serpents till the resurrection. Several archangels are named: Gabriel, Michael, Israfel (who is to sound the last trumpet), and Azrael, the angel of death. Much of the teaching about angels is evidently based on Jewish ideas. The idea of the devil, Iblis or Shaitan, is plainly an adaptation from Jewish-Christian sources; and the lack of any originality on the subject is made up for by giving many repetitions of the story that Iblis fell because he refused to worship Adam. The belief in the ginn or genii,—the evil kinds being termed "efreet,"—has been sufficiently referred to. Mahomet is believed to have converted a tribe of them by his preaching, when returning from Taïf. {*Angels.*} {*Iblis, or the Devil.*}

The descriptions of the Moslem paradise or heaven are famous for the sensual delights depicted; but they are not so elaborate and sensual in the Koran as in the traditional sayings of the Prophet. It {*The Moslem Paradise.*}

100 THE KORAN AND ITS TEACHINGS.

is commonly said that there are eight different heavens; namely, the Garden of Eternity, the Abode of Peace, the Abode of Rest, the Gardens of Eden, the Gardens of Refuge, the Gardens of Delight, the

INTERIOR OF THE MOSQUE OF THE HOLY PROPHET AT MEDINA.

Gardens of the Most High, and the Gardens of Paradise; but they are nowhere mentioned at once, and may be taken as different descriptions of the same place. The following are some passages from the Koran relating to heaven: "Their reward for their patience shall be paradise and silken robes, reclining therein on bridal couches; naught shall they know of sun or piercing cold; its shades shall close over them, and low shall its fruits hang down; and vessels of silver and goblets like flagons shall be borne round among them" (lxxvi. 12). "Theirs shall be the houris with large, dark eyes, like pearls hidden in their shells, in recompense for their labours past. . . . Unfailing, unforbidden, and on soft couches and of a rare creation have we made the houris; and we have made them ever virgins, dear to their spouses, and of equal age" (lvi. 22-35). "Therein are rivers of water which corrupt not; rivers of milk, whose taste changeth not; and rivers of wine, delicious to those who drink it; and rivers of clarified honey; and therein are all kinds of fruit for them from their Lord" (xlvii. 16, 17). It is very noteworthy that the sensual descriptions of Paradise, and especially the passages referring to women, were nearly all included in the earlier series revealed at Mecca, when as yet Mahomet had only one wife, much senior to him; while only two or three simple passages, describing the believers as having "four wives," were promulgated at Medina. As regards the other promised delights, Professor Palmer well describes them as "an intense realisation of all that a dweller in a hot, parched, and barren land could desire; namely, shade, water, fruit, rest, and pleasant companionship and service."

Hell is most frequently termed in the Koran "the Fire," also Gehennum (the Jewish Gehenna). It is said to have seven portals and seven divisions: Gehenna, the purgatory for all Mahometans (xix. 72); Laza, the flaming fire; Hutamah, the raging fire that splits everything to pieces; Sair, the broiling fire; Sagar, the scorching fire; Jahim, the fierce fire; and Hawiyeh, the abyss. The second has been by the Moslem commentators assigned to Christians, the third to Jews, etc., without any

*Hell.*

authority from the Koran. The latter describes hell fire as "leaving naught, sparing naught, blackening the skin"; over it preside nineteen angels. In Gehenna transgressors shall have no coolness nor any drink, save boiling water and running sores" (lxxviii. 24, 25). We need not quote the details of torment which the Traditions attribute to the Prophet.

The Koran teaches nothing very definite about the intermediate state between death and judgment, except as regards unbelievers; but the good are supposed to rest in blissful unconsciousness.

*Intermediate state.*

The "Last Day" is variously termed in the Koran the day of standing up, of separation, of reckoning, of awakening, of judgment, the encompassing day, and the hour. This event is the subject of some of the most poetical passages in the Koran. Thus: "Thinketh man that we shall not reunite his bones? Ay, his very finger tips are we able evenly to replace . . . . When the eye shall be dazzled, when the moon shall be darkened, and the sun and the moon shall be together,

*The Day of Judgment.*

"On that day man shall cry, Where is there a place to flee to? But in vain; there is no refuge; with thy Lord on that day shall be the sole asylum.

"On that day shall man be told of all that he hath done first and last: yea, a man shall be the eye-witness against himself" (lxxv.).

Again: "Surely among delights shall the righteous dwell, but verily the impure in hell-fire. They shall be burned at it on the day of doom, and they shall not be able to hide themselves from it. Who shall teach thee what the day of doom is? It is a day when one soul shall be powerless for another soul: all sovereignty on that day shall be with God" (lxxxii.) Further details will be given in dealing with present-day beliefs of the Mahometans.

The prophets recognised in the Koran are, in addition to Jesus and Mahomet, all Jewish; namely, Adam, the Chosen of God; Noah, the Preacher of God; Abraham, the Friend of God; Moses, the Converser with God;

Jacob, Joseph, and Job. A number of others are mentioned. All these are said to have received inspired books, but they are superseded by the Koran. A very much adapted account of Moses and his doings occupies considerable portions of the Koran. *Prophets.*

Jesus, a "Spirit from God," the "Prophet of God," the "Servant of God," the Word of Truth, is presented in the Koran as a Divine being, but not the Son of God, for "God could not take to Himself a Son." Yet the miraculous conception of Jesus, the annunciation of the Virgin Mary, and the sinlessness of Jesus are taught. Jesus is described as the greatest miracle-worker of all the prophets, and there is an account of His calling a furnished table down from heaven, to become a recurring festival and sign. This may be really a notion derived from the Communion as celebrated by the early Christians. The mission of Jesus is thus mentioned, the speaker being supposed to be God Himself: "We gave Him the evangel, and we put into the hearts of those who followed Him kindness and compassion." His crucifixion, and His return to God are mentioned, with this singularity, that the Jews did not crucify Him in reality, but only "His likeness," God having taken Him up to Himself: this being the belief of not a few early Christians. Jesus is represented in the Koran as denying His own divinity, and threatening with hell-fire those who associate aught with God. The doctrine of the Trinity is specifically denied; but it would appear that Mahomet imagined that the Christian Trinity consisted of the Father, the Son, and the Virgin. The Koran does not refer specifically to the second coming of Jesus, but the traditions about the Prophet speak of him as describing this event as a very material affair; they also represent Jesus as now existing in one of the heavens. *Attitude towards Jesus.*

Predestination is one of the primary teachings of the Koran—a doctrine that has become a most disastrous and paralysing fatalism for very many Mahometans. Nothing can happen to us but what God has fixed. God misleads whom He will. None can die except by His decree. Many are decreed to err and to enter hell. *Predestination.*

These doctrines are still more freely set forth in the traditions about Mahomet.

Idols and idolatry naturally form a prominent subject of denunciation in the Koran. The nothingness of idols **Idolatry and idolaters.** is brought out in passages reminding us of well-known passages in the Psalms and prophets, though much inferior to the Old Testament gems. In iv. 51, after the destruction of the Meccan idols, we read, "Verily God will not forgive the union of other gods with Himself. . . . And he who uniteth gods with God hath devised a great wickedness." Idolaters were then strictly forbidden to enter the sacred temple at Mecca. The forgiveness of idolaters might not be prayed for, even by their kin, and the example of Abraham was alleged in support of this. With all this denunciation of idolatry, Mahomet retained the black stone as an object of reverence, and also several rites, such as the "runnings to and fro," and "stonings of pillars," which were connected with previous idolatrous worship.

Unbelievers who deny a future life and judgment are admonished that they are destined for torment. "Lost now are they who deny a meeting with God, until, when the hour cometh suddenly upon them, they say, 'Oh, woe to us for past negligence of this hour!' And they shall bear their burdens on their back. Will not that be evil which they shall carry?" They will abide in fire for ever. Believers are exhorted not to form intimacies among unbelievers, for they long to corrupt them. Those who become infidels after having believed are denounced as unpardonable offenders.

Coming now to the practical duties of Moslem believers, they may be summed up in the one word which most fitly **Islām.** represents Mahometanism,—Islām, resignation to the will of God, "To God are we resigned." Islām is said to have been the religion of all the prophets before Mahomet. Those who profess this religion are Muslims or Moslems, Musalmans being the Persian form of the original Arabic word.

The five principal elements of Islām as enjoined in the Koran are : (1) Belief in the one God, and in Mahomet as

His prophet; (2) Reciting the daily prayers; (3) Giving the legal alms; (4) Observing the fast of Ramadan; (5) Making a pilgrimage to Mecca once during life. *The creed.* The creed (Kelimah) as such does not occur in the Koran; but the first part of it, "There is no god but God," is in xlvii. 21; and the second part, "Mahomet is the apostle of God," is in xlviii. 29; but the whole often occurs in the Traditions about Mahomet.

Prayer is often enjoined in the Koran, but the five daily prayer-times are not mentioned in any one passage. Thus: "Glorify God when it is evening, and *Prayer.* at morning,—and to Him be praise in the heavens and earth,—and at afternoon and at noontide." The evening prayer is regarded as including both that before sunset and after sunset. The traditions relate that Mahomet received instructions during his ascent to heaven to recite prayers five times a day, having by prayer reduced the requirement from fifty to five. The details of modern Moslem prayers we shall describe later.

The fast of Ramadan (or Ramazan), the ninth month of the Mahometan year, is expressly enjoined in ii. 179–184. The fast is prescribed "that ye may fear God *The fast of* for certain days." It is not to be kept by those *Ramadan.* who are ill or on a journey, but they must fast the same number of other days. The fast is to be kept by day only; and eating and drinking are allowed after dark until the earliest dawn. The first observation of the new moon of the month is to be the beginning of the fast. Tradition ascribes to Mahomet the saying, that during Ramadan "the gates of paradise are open and the gates of hell are shut, and the devils are chained by the leg, and that only those who observe it will be permitted to enter at the gate of heaven called Raiyan." On one particular night in this month, believed to be the twenty-seventh, the Koran is said to have been revealed, and to have come down in one volume to the lowest heaven, from whence it was revealed to Mahomet in portions by the archangel Gabriel. This is called the night of power: "Herein descend the angels and the spirit by permission of their Lord in every matter, and all is peace till the breaking of the morn" (xcvii.). Two sayings in the Tradition are worthy of note: "If a keeper of fast does not abandon lying, God cares not about his leaving off eating and drinking"; "There are many keepers of fast who gain nothing by fasting but thirst, and there are many risers up at night and performers of prayers who gain nothing by their rising but wakefulness."

The duty of almsgiving is often enjoined in the Koran. "Zakat," or the legal alms, literally purification, expresses a portion of property given as a sanctification of the rest. {Almsgiving.} It is paid separately upon different kinds of property that have been at least one year in possession of an adult; but not upon the necessaries of life, slaves employed in service, books, craftmen's tools, etc. These alms may be paid to an appointed collector, or given independently to the poor and needy, to slaves and debtors, for the service of God in religious warfare, or to travellers. Alms beyond this are called Sadaqah, that which manifests righteousness. Cheerful givers of well-gotten wealth are highly praised, and promised repayment by God. Among the traditional sayings attributed to Mahomet are these: "The upper hand is better than the lower one. The upper hand is the giver of alms and the lower hand is the poor beggar"; "The best of alms are those given by a man of small means, who gives of that which he has earned by labour, and gives as much as he is able"; "Doing justice between two people is alms; assisting a man on his beast is alms; good words are alms."

The holy pilgrimage (*hajj* or *hadj*) to Mecca is thus commanded (xxii. 28): "Proclaim to the peoples a pilgrimage. {The holy pilgrimage.} Let them come to thee on foot and on every fleet camel, arriving by every deep defile: that they may bear witness of its benefits to them, and make mention of God's name on the appointed days over the brute beasts with which He hath supplied them for sustenance: and let them pay their vows and circuit the ancient house." Numerous regulations are given as to the time and conduct of the pilgrimage. The actual mode of its observance we will give in a later chapter.

## MARRIAGE.

As regards general moral duties, the Koran is explicit. Parents are to be kindly treated, especially in old age, spoken to respectfully, deferred to humbly. **Parents and children.** Only if they desire to draw their children away to idolatry, they must not be obeyed. A murderer is accounted worthy of hell. "Whosoever slayeth a believer purposely, his reward is hell" (iv. 95); further, "It is incumbent on you to exercise vengeance for murder" (ii. 173), but the heir or next of kin may pardon **Murder and theft.** or compound the offence. Theft, when property is taken out of proper custody in a secret manner, is punishable by the amputation of a hand, according to v. 42, "If a man or woman steal, cut off their hands." As to offences against chastity, the Koran is severe; immoral persons whose guilt is proved are to receive a hundred stripes; guilty persons, if married, were at first shut up in their houses (iv. 19); later they were stoned to death, according to a tradition that Mahomet ordained it. But a practically unlimited right of concu- **Divorce and concubinage.** binage was permitted, both by Mahomet's example and by Koranic precept. Thus, "Unlawful to you are married women, except such as your right hand possesses," *i.e.* those taken in war, or slaves (iv. 28); but free Mahometan women might not be taken as concubines. While not allowing to men generally the same licence as to the Prophet himself, the Koran **Marriage.** permits marriage with four wives: "If women seem good in your eyes, marry two, or three, or four"; and a verse can even be produced (iv. 27) apparently sanctioning merely temporary marriages. Marriage was enjoined on every Moslem. Some of the sayings on marriage attributed to Mahomet are: "Marry women who will love their husbands and be very prolific, for I wish you to be more numerous than any other people." "When a Moslem marries, he perfects half his religion; and he should practise abstinence for the remaining half." "When any of you wishes to demand a woman in marriage, if he can arrange it, let him see her first." "A woman ripe in years shall have her consent asked in marriage; and if she remain silent her silence is her consent, and if she refuse she shall not be married by force." No definite religious ceremony of marriage is prescribed. The Koran prohibits marriage between near relatives, including cousins, between foster-relatives, between parents and step-children; and a man may not marry his wife's sister during her lifetime, unless the first married be divorced.

Severe subjection is the position assigned to wives in the Koran. Thus we read: "Chide those whose refrac-
*Position of wives.* toriness ye have cause to fear. Remove them into sleeping chambers apart, and beat them." "When a man calls his wife, she must come, though she be at an oven." But there are numerous passages enjoining that wives should be treated with kindness, and extolling the happiness of marriage with an amiable and beautiful wife. And it must be admitted that the Koran elevates woman considerably beyond her previous position in Arabia, which was that of a mere chattel, passing with the estate of husband and father, so that a son frequently married the wives of his deceased father as of right. A number of passages in the Koran speak of men and women as equal in regard to their religious duties and ultimate blessedness. They are to be treated with equity; but men are acknowledged to be superior to women on account of various natural gifts.

The Koran allows divorce on grounds of aversion; the divorced woman must be generously treated and must not remarry till four months are past.

Our previous quotations have given comparatively little indication of the elevated, rhetorical, and impassioned
*Rhetorical passages.* style of much of the Koran. The following quotations will illustrate this:—

"When the heaven is cleft asunder, and when the stars are scattered, when the seas gush together, and when the tombs are turned upside down, the soul shall know what it has sent on or kept back.

"O man, what has seduced thee concerning thy generous Lord, who created thee and fashioned thee and gave thee symmetry, and in what form He pleased composed thee? Verily the righteous are in pleasure and the wicked are in hell; they shall broil therein upon the judgment day, nor shall they be absent therefrom (lxxxii.).

"Blessed be He in whose hand is the kingdom, for He is mighty over all: Who created death and life, to try you, which of you does best; for He is the mighty, the forgiving! who created seven heavens in storeys: thou canst not see any discordance in the creation of the Merciful."

There is a singular analogy between the following and Christ's parable of the ten virgins. "On the day when the hypocrites, men and women, shall say to those who believe, 'Wait for us that we may kindle at your light,' it will be said, 'Get ye back and beg a light.' And there shall be struck out between them a wall with a door; within it shall be mercy, and outside before it torment. They shall cry out to them, 'We were not with you!' They shall say, 'Yea, but ye did tempt yourselves, and did wait, and did doubt; and your vain hopes beguiled you; and the beguiler beguiled you about God. Wherefore to-day there shall not be taken from you a ransom, nor from those who misbelieved. Your resort is the fire; it is your sovereign, and an ill journey will it be." Those who desire further quotations of this kind must be referred to translations of the Koran.

It is singular how few aphoristic sentences, proverbs, or gems of moral truth are to be found in the book. Apart from its claim of inspiration, it ranks by no means high as to literary form. It is a mixture of longer and shorter chapters, some including a great many subjects, almost unconnected in many cases. Mahomet does not appear to have written anything down himself; and some at least of his passages seem to have been the outpouring of uncontrollable excitement, giving the greatest show of probable "inspiration." Dr. Noldeke, one of the best authorities on the Koran, says (*Encyclopædia Britannica*, xvi. 598), 'We must bear in mind that he (Mahomet) was no cold systematic thinker, but an Oriental visionary, brought up in crass superstition, and without intellectual discipline; a man whose nervous temperament had been powerfully worked on by ascetic austerities, and who was all the more irritated by the opposition he encountered, because he had little of the heroic in his nature. Filled with his religious ideas and visions, he might well fancy he heard the angel bidding him recite what was said to him. There may have been many a revelation of this kind which no one ever heard but himself, as he repeated it to himself in the silence of the night (lxxiii. 4). Indeed, the Koran itself admits that he forgot some revelations (lxxxvii. 7). But by far the greatest part of the book is undoubtedly the result of deliberation, touched more or less with emotion, and animated by a certain rhetorical rather than poetical glow." With the exception of the word "undoubtedly," the foregoing passage is perhaps near the truth. It is quite evident in reading the Koran that numerous passages contradict or repeat one another; and the abrogation of certain passages or the alteration of their effect by subsequent revelations may be taken as proof of the lack of justification for the idea of infallible inspiration of the Koran; but of course this presents no difficulty to the Moslem, for to him God is a being who can and does change His edicts at pleasure, and who might prescribe opposite things in succession if it pleased Him.

One of the most singular evidences of Mahomet's lack of literary perception is furnished by his delineation of *Delineation of old prophets.* the old prophets, who are in effect duplicates of Mahomet himself. "They preach exactly like him, they have to bring the very same charges against their opponents, who on their part behave exactly like the unbelieving inhabitants of Mecca" (N.). Mahomet further shows his ignorance of the Jewish scriptures by his mistakes, such as naming Haman minister of Pharaoh, making the fertility of Egypt depend on rain, and not on the Nile. We will not further pursue the literary analysis of the Koran, being concerned here chiefly with its religious import.

Although it is by no means arranged in chronological order, it is very possible to mark out most of the chapters of the Koran, according as they were delivered at Mecca before the flight or at Medina; and they have still further been subdivided into six sets characterising different periods.

In the earliest, while the Prophet was still meditating on evil and the terrors of the Last Day, his style is more poetic, fragmentary, and impassioned, with brief sentences and rapidly changing rhymes. To this period belongs the Moslem prayer which opens the Koran. With these are some most vivid pictures of hell and the judgment. A second series marks the opening phases of the Prophet's ministry; in one chapter, when Mahomet has been bidding his clan accept the truth, Abu Laheb exclaims, "Perdition to you!" and in answer the Prophet curses him and his wife (cxi.). The later Meccan chapters deal largely with the same subjects which had been dealt with more briefly in earlier ones, with the addition of many narratives from the Jewish Scriptures and Rabbinical and Arab legends. "A sermonising tone predominates. The suras are very edifying for one who is already reconciled to their import; but to us at least they do not seem well fitted to carry conviction to the minds of unbelievers. . . . In reality these longer Meccan suras appear to have been peculiarly influential for the propagation of Islam" (N.). The Medina chapters are mostly connected with some definite historical event, or some circumstance which called forth the particular revelation. "At one time it is a summons to do battle for the faith; at another, a series of reflections on recently-experienced success or misfortune, or a rebuke for their weak faith, or an exhortation to virtue. He often addresses himself to the doubters, some of whom vacillate between faith and unbelief; others make a pretence of faith, while others scarcely take the trouble even to do that. . . . A part of the Medina pieces consists of formal laws belonging to the ceremonial, civil, and criminal codes, or directions about certain temporary complications. The most objectionable parts of the whole Koran are those which treat of Mahomet's relations with women" (N.). We must not omit to state that the Koran bears testimony to itself in more than one emphatic passage; thus, "If men and genii were assembled together that they might produce a book like the Koran, they must fail" (xvii. 90).

As regards miracles, the Koran does not assert that Mahomet worked them, and only a few which are incredible have been attributed to him by his followers. In xxix. 49, we read, "They say, Why are not signs sent down to him from his Lord? Say, signs are in the power of God alone, and I am only an open warner." In xvii. 92-97, where the unbelievers are represented as asking for miracles, Mahomet is directed to say, "Praise be to my Lord. Am I more than a man, and an apostle?" Mahometan commentators refer to the cleaving of the moon (liv.), the assistance of angels at the battle of Bedr (iii.), the night-journey to heaven (xvii.), and the revelation of the Koran itself as miracles recorded in the Koran. And indeed the reverence with which Mohammedans regard the Koran corresponds with this belief. "They dare not touch it without being first washed and purified, and they read it with the greatest care and respect, never holding it below their girdles. They swear by it, consult it on all occasions, carry it with them to war, write sentences of it on their banners, suspend it from their necks as a charm, and always place it on the highest shelf or some place of honour in their houses." Whatever defects we find in the Koran, it made Arabic a literary language, it has influenced the belief and conduct of countless millions of men, and it is at this day reverenced and obeyed by an increasing number of persons.[1]

*Miracles.*

*Reverence for Koran.*

The Koran was first printed in Arabic at Rome in 1530, but was either burned or remained unpublished. In 1649 an edition was published at Hamburg, and there have been several subsequent editions. The Mahometans themselves have issued versions, interlinear with the original, in Persian, Pushto, Urdu, Turkish, and numerous other languages. A translation of the Koran into Latin was made in 1143 for Peter, the Abbot of Cluny, but was not published till 1543 at Basle. This

*Versions.*

---

[1] Rodwell's Koran; Palmer's Koran ("Sacred Books of the East," vols. 6, 9). Hughes, "Dictionary of Islam,"—*Encyclopædia Britannica*, vol. 17, Art. "Mohammedanism." section, "Koran," by Dr. Noldeke. "Islam," *Quarterly Review*, vol. 127, by E. Deutsch.

version was afterwards further translated into Italian, German, and Dutch. The first French translation was done in 1547; this was translated into English in 1649–1688. The well-known English translation by Sale appeared in 1734. The Rev. J. M. Rodwell published a translation into English in 1861, distinguished by the arrangement of the chapters in their supposed chronological order. Palmer's translation (1880) is more literal and less elegant.

Commentaries in Arabic upon the Koran were made very early, and probably the Commentary of Tabari (839–923) contains much of their substance. Thousands of commentaries have since been written, and many of them are most important aids to understanding obscure passages. There are many other Arabic works connected with the Koran, its spelling and pronunciation, its beauties, the number of its verses and letters, etc. The devotion of Moslems to their sacred book is natural when we consider that they believe it to have been eternally existent and uncreated in the Divine thought. <small>Commentaries.</small>

# CHAPTER VI.

## Modern Islam. Part I.

The First Caliphs—The Ommyads—The death of Hosain—The Abbaside caliphs—Harun-al-Raschid—The Fatimite dynasty—Caliphs in Spain—Saladin—Fall of Bagdad—Various Sultanates—Sunnites and Shiites—Distribution and numbers — Various Sects — Motazilites — Jabarites—Kharijites — Malikites—Hanifites—Shafiites—Hanbalites—The Ulema—Imams—Extra-Koranic beliefs—The exalted name of God—The essence of the Deity—Sins—Mahometan oaths—Abstinence—Restrictions on eating—Ablution—Public prayer—The sermon—Circumcision—Marriage—Divorce — Concubinage—Slaves—Death—Burial—Funeral processions—The immediate fate of the soul—Mosques—Endowment and government—The Sacred Mosque at Mecca—The Sacred Hajj, or pilgrimage—The Prophet's Mosque at Medina—The Mosque of Omar—The Dome of the Rock—Great mosque at Damascus—The Mosque of Cordova—Mosques and tombs at Cairo—St. Sophia at Constantinople—Indian mosques and tombs—The Jummoo Musjid at Delhi—The Taj Mehal.

INASMUCH as the religion of Mahomet speedily became inextricably mingled with political history, in accordance with the injunctions frequently repeated in the chapters of the Koran revealed at Medina, to spread Islam by the sword, we shall but briefly refer to its historical advance, both because it is better dealt with in works of general history, and because we are principally concerned with marked developments in its religious aspect.

Islam was consolidated in Arabia by means of the wars which at once arose after Mahomet's death, to secure the **The First Caliphs.** predominance of the Caliphate, and the wars of extension by which it was successively or simultaneously carried into Syria, Persia, and Egypt. The

Gospel of Christ was in these lands for a time overwhelmed; and the people, who had but slightly assimilated it, readily threw it off at the bidding of their conquerors. The names of Abu-bekr (632-634), Omar (634-644), Othman (644-656), and Ali (656-661), the first four caliphs, are mainly associated with this rapid career of conquest, Omar especially having consolidated the Arabian State at Medina. At the beginning of his reign he uttered a sentence which has become famous: "By God, he that is weakest among you shall be in my sight the strongest, until I have vindicated for him his rights; but him that is strongest will I treat as the weakest, until he complies with the laws."

By a strange stroke of fate, the family of the Koreish which furnished the leader, Omayya, in the battle of Ohod, and to which one of Mahomet's most violent opponents, Abu Sofyan, belonged, gave rise to the great Ommyad line of Caliphs, which lasted from Othman's murder in 661 to the death of Merwan II. in 750. Moawiya, the first of the line, made Damascus his capital; his religion, like that of most of his successors, became largely subservient to his political aims. Long war raged between them and the adherents of Ali's descendants, the cousin of Mahomet and husband of Fatima, the only child who survived him. The Ommyads plundered Medina, took Mecca, and burnt the Kaaba, which, however, was soon rebuilt. The slaughter of Hosain, the son of Ali, on the 10th Moharram (Oct.) 680, at Kerbela, has given rise to one of the most sacredly observed festivals in certain Mohammedan countries. Early in the eighth century the power of the Ommyads had extended to the borders of China, over North Africa, and all Spain. Before 720, the Abbaside movement had arisen, named from Abbas the paternal uncle of Mahomet. His descendants enjoyed the greatest consideration among the Moslems, and on Ali's son's death remained nearest of kin to the Prophet. The Ommyad Caliphs, however, insulted them so shamefully that they conceived the idea of supplanting the ruling dynasty, and allied to themselves Ali's party, by giving out that one of his descendants had appointed an Abbaside, Mohammed, his heir. The advance of the Moslems into Europe was now first checked by Charles Martel in 732, who defeated Abdel-Rahman near Poitiers, and afterwards drove the invaders back into Spain.

Various provinces of the Arab Empire broke away and set up for themselves. The Ommyad dynasty fell in 750, and Abu 'l-Abbas became Caliph at Cufa on the Euphrates. The establishment of the dynasty cost, it is said, 600,000 lives. The next caliph, Mansur, transferred his capital to Bagdad, which was long the most famous Moslem city. Meanwhile Africa and Spain revolted from the power of the Abbasides, but they made great progress in Asia Minor. The most celebrated Eastern caliph, Harun-al-Raschid (786-809), was devoted in his religious duties, especially in pilgrimage, and attempted to secure the succession to the Caliphate to his three sons in order, by a deed which he hung up in the Kaaba, which, however, his eldest son destroyed, and in consequence lost his crown and his life five years after his accession. The second son of Harun, Maimun, after a stormy beginning, led a life of literary ease, encouraged authors, and set himself to overthrow the widespread doctrine that the Koran was the uncreated word of God; and his successor continued the same policy. From their time the power of the Eastern Caliphate declined. Razi (934-940) was the last Caliph who led prayers and preached to the people. In 910 the Fatimite dynasty was founded in Egypt, by Obaid Allah, surnamed the Mahdi, "the directed one," hence fit to guide others, and assuming to be a descendant of Fatimah, and consequently entering into the rights of Ali. The empire of the Fatimites lasted in Egypt and North Africa till 1171. The Ommyad Caliphs of Cordova, in Spain, maintained their rule from 755 to 1236, and the Moorish Caliphs, or Sultans, of Granada, held sway from 1238 to 1492.

Meanwhile the Crusades had contributed greatly to the decline of the Eastern Caliphate. At first the Arab conquerors of Palestine, in the seventh century, allowed Christian pilgrims to Jerusalem to build a church and a hospital. Under the Fatimite Caliphs

The Crusades.

MOSQUE OF AHMED KHIAGA, AND MARKET PLACE, BAGDAD.

who conquered Palestine and Syria in the tenth century, the position of Christians was less favourable. In 1065 the Seljuk Turks from the Caucasus, new converts to

Islam, overrunning Palestine, committed great atrocities on Christians. This resulted in the first Crusade, which was successful in wresting Syria, Palestine, and much of Asia Minor from the Mahometans (1099). But this dominion was practically won back by Saladin, *Saladin.* a Kurdish chieftain who had made himself Sultan of Egypt, and the Christians remained free to make pilgrimages to Jerusalem exempt from taxation. A still more formidable enemy to the Caliphs, however, approached from the north and east, in the person of Jenghiz Khan and the Mongols. Finally *Fall of Bagdad.* Hulaga, the Mongol sovereign, took Bagdad in 1258, and destroyed the Eastern Caliphate. Before this, however, governor after governor of dependent provinces had become practically independent; *Various sultanates.* and hence we find one power at Kairwan, in Tripoli, another in Fez (Morocco), another in Khorasan, and others in various parts of India. The Ottoman Turks set up their dynasty in Constantinople in 1299, and it still continues.

In giving an account of modern Islam we must first direct attention to the two predominant and hostile divisions into which it is divided, and which date *Sunnites and Shiites.* back to the early times of the Caliphate. The Sunnites, followers of the Tradition or path (Sunnah), acknowledge the first four caliphs as rightful successors of Mahomet, and accept the six "authentic" books of tradition, in addition to the Koran, as the guide of faith and conduct. This does not imply that the Shiites, the other great division, reject the Traditions, but the Sunnites have appropriated the name; while the Shiites, or "followers" of Ali, reject the right of the first four caliphs as true successors of the Prophet, and reckon Ali, Mahomet's cousin, as the first true imam or caliph. They call themselves the true believers, and are also known as the imamiyahs, believing that Islam consists in knowledge of the rightful imam. They have traditions of the nomination of Ali to succeed him by Mahomet, and believe that special revelations were made to Fatima, Ali's wife, which were inherited by the last imam, the Mahdi. They recognise in all twelve imams, including Ali, his sons Hasan and Hosain, Ali, son of Hosain, and seven of his descendants, the last, Mohammed, the so-called Mahdi, or Director, being supposed to be still alive, though withdrawn from sight, to reappear in the last days, according to the Prophet's prediction.

The Sunnites are the majority in Arabia, Turkey, North Africa, India, Turkestan, Afghanistan, and Eastern Asia, and in all they number something like 150 millions; while the Shiites are most numerous in Persia and in India, though scattered here and there throughout Islam. They are variously estimated at between ten and twenty millions. Besides these, there are the Abadiyeh of Oman and Zanzibar, and the Zirdites of Yemen, estimated by Mr. Blunt at four and two millions respectively, and the Wahhabis in Nejd and some other regions, said to number eight millions. Consequently the followers of Mahomet at the present day cannot be reckoned fewer than 175 millions. *Distribution and numbers.*

Besides the existent sects, we may mention among those of the past, the followers of Hasan of Basra, in the first century of Islam, who set himself to settle dogmatic difficulties which the Koran left unsolved. One of his disciples, Wasil, founded the sect of the Motazilites (dissentient), or Kadarites, recognising man's power (kadar) over his own actions, in contradistinction to the orthodox view of predestination. Wasil denied the eternity of the attributes of God, reasoning that if they were eternal, they constituted so many independent deities. Wasil objected to predestination, that it was incompatible with the belief in future rewards and punishments; he also admitted a purgatory. Another sect, the Jabarites, agreed with the Motazilites as to the attributes of God, but maintained the most uncompromising view of predestination, denying to man the slightest share in shaping his own conduct. Somewhat like the Calvinists, they believed that every man was predestined to heaven or hell, and, more consistent than the Calvinists, they denied human responsibility. A third sect, the Sifatites, *Various sects. Motazilites. Jabarites.*

ENTRY OF OMAR INTO JERUSALEM.

partisans of the attributes, interpreted the Koranic accounts of God literally, and were gross anthropomorphists.

Another form of dissent from the Koran and its orthodox upholders arose in the middle of the seventh century, among the partisans of Ali. It refused to acknowledge the exclusive right of the Koreish to furnish a Caliph and Imam to Islam, and maintained that the origin of the leader of the faithful was a matter of indifference, if he did his duty well. This sect, known as the Kharijites, were truer followers of Mahomet than the orthodox; they held that a man was responsible for his actions, in spite of predestination, and that a great sinner could not be a good Moslem. They were ultimately suppressed in Asia, but long continued to have much influence in northern Africa. These sects, together with the Shiites, subsequently described, were the "protestants" to whom, by antagonism, much of the character of Mohammedan orthodoxy is due. The Sunnis are divided into four principal sects, the Malikites, Hanifites, Shafiites, and Hanbalites; named after their founders, Malik, Abu Hanifa, Shafii, and Ibn Hanbal. These were all established under the Abbaside Caliphs, and really differ comparatively little from one another. The first great collection of the traditions of Mahomet was made by Malik, at Medina, in the eighth century. These he regarded as superseding human judgment. Abu Hanifa, his contemporary, who died at Bagdad in 770, eclipsed him in fame, being the main pillar of the deductive method, which undertook to create precedents in Moslem law by analogy, in agreement with the spirit of the Koran, the Tradition, and the decisions of the first four caliphs. His system, known as the Hanifite law, is the most followed of any. Shafii (born 770), a descendant of the Prophet's grandfather, a pupil of Malik, founded an intermediate system between the deductive and the traditional. One of his pupils, Ibn Hanbal, founded the fourth orthodox sect, which was a kind of puritanism, aiming at restoring the primitive purity of religious observances. His followers are now comparatively few, though it

*Kharijites.*

*Malikites.*

*Hanifites.*

*Shafiites.*

*Hanbalites.*

is alleged that the Wahhabis represent the spirit of his teaching.

INTERIOR OF A MOSQUE, CAIRO,
(Showing the Pulpit and the Kiblah).

Moslem orthodoxy has become fixed within narrow limits, and does not vary much from century to century

or from place to place. Its discussions and learning are confined to a narrow kind of scholasticism, analogous to that of the Middle Age schoolmen.  *The ulema.*
Even more than in the Roman Catholic Church, the believers are in the hands of a clergy, the *ulema*, or knowers (singular *alim*), who, without being endued with any temporal power, and without having any ordination or apostolical succession, constitute a spiritual hierarchy of despotic power and enormous influence. In fact, they are much more powerful, socially and politically, than the temporal rulers of Moslem countries. As a specimen of their strong self-assertion, we may quote the declaration of the ulema in Spain, when the Sultan Mansur threatened them for opposing him: "All the evil you say of us applies to yourself; you seek unjust gains, and support your injustice by threats; you take bribes and practise ungodliness in the world. But we are guides on the path of righteousness, lights in the darkness, and bulwarks of Islam. We decide what is just or unjust, and declare the right. Through us the precepts of religion are maintained. We know that the Sultan will soon think better of the matter; but if he persists, every act of his government will be null, for every treaty of peace and war, every act of sale and purchase, is valid only through our testimony." Leaving the vizier's presence, they were followed by the Sultan's apology before they had passed out of the palace gate.

The mode in which the numbers of the ulema are kept up is by a sort of university education, which is now chiefly obtainable at the famous mosque of El Azhar, at Cairo, but formerly from the famous universities of Damascus, Bagdad, Kairwan, Seville, Cordova, etc., where there were thousands of students. They almost all come from the lower classes, in whom fanaticism is most abundant, and not unfrequently obtain permission to sleep in the mosque, and receive daily rations from the funds of the mosque. They enter their names according to their respective sects, and attend the lectures of their professors, which are given around the pillars of the great court. The subjects are Arabic, Mohammedan dogma, the Koran, tradition, and the law. The Hanafite decisions are most effective in law courts; but nevertheless the Shafiite and Malikite students are much more numerous, and there are very few Hanbalites. The work of a professor is not mentally onerous, for, strange to say, they merely give explanations from commentaries, being forbidden to add anything of their own. There are various standard compendiums and treatises of great length, consisting chiefly of arguments like those of the medieval school-men, which the students have to master. A few other subjects, such as rhetoric and logic, may be taken up; but the general course is very narrow, and confirms the natural narrowness of the pupils. All that does not directly appertain to theology is regarded as superfluous or injurious. Theology, being considered to be already perfect, can supply no opportunity of progress beyond a certain narrow limit. "All originality is crushed out, and a blind and ludicrous dependence on written tradition—even in things profane —takes its place." The students, after three or four years thus spent, having obtained certificates from the professors, gain a government appointment in a law court, or become teachers, prayer-leaders, cadis, or muftis in the smaller towns, or occupy themselves in the various offices for which a theologian is required. There are many sources from which an income may be derived, gifts being not the least abundant of these; and the higher ulema back up their brethren in all ways, so that they form in effect a powerful corporation. There is no charge for the instruction given in El-Azhar, and there is no endowment for the professors. In Bokhara there is still a considerable attempt at theological education, and there are eighty colleges or schools attached to mosques; but they are for the most part centres of mere fanatic ignorance. In India every considerable mosque has its college of divinity students, and their heads are generally termed mollahs (or maulawis); some of them are good Arabic scholars, but are otherwise very ignorant.

Considering their unofficial position, it is surprising how great a power the ulema wield. This is in consequence of their representing the spiritual influence of the Prophet;

ENTRANCE TO THE MEDRESSÉ (COLLEGE) OF ABDUL AZIZ KHAN, BOKHARA.

while even the Sultan of Turkey, though he calls himself "the successor of the Prophet," cannot exercise the powers of a pope. He however nominates the Sheikh-ul-Islam (senior or president of Islam), or mufti of Constantinople, who represents him among the ulema, and whose judgments on points of faith and law cannot be appealed against. But the choice of this personage is limited to the mollahs, or chiefs of religious bodies; and as no one can become one of the ulema but by examination and certification by older ulema, the priesthood is thus animated by a powerful *esprit de corps*.

The imams, or leaders in prayer, are the most important essential officials of the mosques. The true imam, or caliph of all the Moslems, is the deputy or representative of the Prophet, and should perform almost every function which Mahomet performed; but the term has become applied to the leader of any system or school of theology or law, and to leaders in prayer at all mosques. There is no ceremony of ordination, nor is any ministerial act performed by the imam, except that of standing in front and repeating the prayers and reciting the Koran. In fact, wherever there are three worshippers, one of them must act as imam and the other two follow him. Tradition says that the Prophet spoke thus: "Let him act as imam to a congregation who knows the Koran thoroughly; and if all present should be equal in that respect, then let him perform who is best informed in the rules of prayer; and if they are equal in this respect also, let him act as imam who has fled for the sake of Islam; and if equal in this respect likewise, let that person act who is oldest; but the governed must not act as imam to the governor."

Imams.

Passing now to the teachings and beliefs of these "clergy" and of intelligent Moslems,—although they rely so much on the Koran, they have imperceptibly developed and codified much teaching that is not formally contained therein. For instance, as to the personality and nature of God, their detailed statements are to a large extent worthy of Christian doctors and full of philosophic acumen. Of course,

Extra-Koranic beliefs.

believing so absolutely in predestination and control by the Almighty, they hold doctrines which large sections of Christendom would reject, and which come very near to complete Pantheism. Thus the words "There is no God but God," to the Moslem, to quote Mr. Palgrave's language, "imply that this one supreme Being is also the only Agent, the only Force, the only act existing throughout the universe, and leave to all beings else nothing but pure unconditional passiveness, alike in movement or in quiescence, in action or in capacity." Thus even all evil, so-called, is His creation. Yet "He has with respect to His creatures one main feeling and source of action, namely, jealousy of them, lest they should perchance attribute to themselves something of what is His alone. Hence He is ever more prone to punish than to reward, to inflict pain than to bestow pleasure." (*Central and Eastern Arabia.*) It is a consequence of this position, that no pre-eminence can rightfully be claimed before God by any man; all are equally His servants.

There is one exalted name of God, supposed only to be known to the prophets and great saints; and it is said that Mahomet declared that whoever calls upon God by that name will obtain all his desires. Consequently the Moslem fakirs and mystics spend much of their time in trying to find it out; those who assert that they know it gain great influence over the superstitious. The attributes of God are classified under the heads of "Life, Knowledge, Power, Will, Hearing, Seeing, and Speech."

As a specimen of the best kind of Moslem theological statement, we may quote from the famous scholastic divine Al-Ghazzali in the eleventh century (1058–1111). He writes thus of the essence of God: "He is one, and hath no partner; singular, without anything like Him; uniform, having no contrary; separate, having no equal. He is ancient, having no first; eternal, having no beginning; remaining for ever, having no end; continuing to eternity, without any termination. He persists without ceasing to be; remains without failing and never did cease, nor ever shall cease to be described by glorious attributes, nor is subject to any decree so as to be determined by any precise limits or set times, but is the First and the Last, and is within and without. . . . He is too holy to be subject to change, or any local motion; neither do any accidents dwell in Him, nor any contingencies befall Him,—but He abides through all generations with His glorious attributes, free from all danger of dissolution. As to the attribute of perfection, He wants no addition to His perfection." And so on through a long exposition. This is quoted, not as proving

MOSLEM POSTURES OF PRAYER.

any originality in the Moslem beliefs, but as showing the high level attained in some directions, and as a proof that, so far as regards the Divine attributes, Christians have much in common with Moslems—a fact which should moderate denunciations or censure, and give rise to an attitude of tolerance.

With such beliefs as to the absoluteness of Divine control, it is surprising that Mahometans should admit the possibility of sin; but they do this, although there have been long discussions on predestination, and strong endeavours to reconcile it with man's responsibility. Learned Mohammedans divide sins into two classes: the kabirah, or great, which condemn the sinner to a purgatorial hell; and saghirah or little sins, inherent in man's nature. The great sins are generally stated as seventeen in number: infidelity, despairing of God's mercy, considering oneself safe from His wrath, bearing false witness, constantly committing little sins, falsely charging a Moslem with adultery, taking a false oath, drinking wine, practising magic, defrauding orphans of their property, usury, committing adultery, unnatural crimes, stealing, murder, cowardice in battle with infidels, disobedience to parents. Sins.

Mahometans are considerably given to oaths, and, it may be imagined, at times run great risks of condemnation for perjury. The Koran itself contains many extreme oaths, and it is not surprising that Mahomet's followers imitate him in this. There are many fine distinctions drawn, after the Talmudic manner, as to the various kinds and qualities of oaths, and the guilt of breaking them. The most effective oaths are, saying three times "By the great God," taking hold of the Koran and saying "By what this contains of the Word of God," placing a sword on the Koran and saying "I impose on myself divorcement." Notwithstanding this, lying is pretty frequent among "the faithful." Mahometan oaths.

As to abstinence from wine and intoxicating liquors, this is one of the most characteristic Moslem virtues; but in many cases the rule of abstinence is broken through. It is to the credit of Moslem consistency, that opium and tobacco have been recognised as included under the same ban as wine; but the supposed prohibition is less regarded than in the case of intoxicants. Abstinence.

One of the special prohibitions generally observed, is that which forbids eating pork; and there is reason in this in hot climates. Moreover various animals' flesh is forbidden as food, the list being very like that of the Mosaic code. The Koran says (ii. 167) Restrictions on eating.

"O ye who believe, eat of the good things with which we have supplied you, and give God thanks if ye are His worshippers. Only that which dieth of itself, and blood, and swine's flesh, and that over which any other name than that of God hath been invoked, hath God forbidden you." But no flesh may be lawfully eaten unless the animal has been killed in orthodox Mahometan fashion, *i.e.* by cutting the windpipe and gullet through, repeating at the same time, "In the name of God, God is great."

MOSLEM POSTURES OF PRAYER.

According to the traditions, beasts and birds of prey may not be eaten. Moslems have no religious objection to eating with Jews and Christians, provided the meat or drink be lawful for them, and in fact eat with them in various countries, but not in India, where hatred of a conquering race has established the custom of exclusiveness.

The extreme attention of most Mahometans to ablution of the hands, mouth, and nose before eating, is well known. It is a religious ceremony, depending on the traditional precepts of the prophet. His followers are to eat in God's name, to return thanks, to eat with their right hand, and with their shoes off. The devil, it is said, has power over that food which is eaten without remembering God. Before beginning, it is necessary to say "Bismillah!" (in the name of God), and after finishing, "Glory to God!" Ablution is also essential before worship. The Koran (v. 8) says, "O Believers, when ye prepare yourselves for prayer, wash your faces and hands up to the elbows, and wipe your hands and your feet to the ankles." The detail of this ablution is elaborate, but with practice it is performed in three minutes, the worshipper reciting prayers or pious ejaculations meanwhile. The full ablution is not insisted on before each prayer time, if nothing unclean has been touched and no impurity contracted. When water cannot be had, ablution may be performed with dust or sand. In special cases washing of the whole body is prescribed, and among these occasions are the admission of a convert, Friday prayers, the great festivals, and the washing of the dead. The Tradition says, that he who performs ablution thoroughly will extract all sin from his body, even though it may be lurking under his finger nails. *Ablution.*

The Moslem rule is, that public prayer shall be entirely in Arabic, and the place of prayer must be free from impurity. Before it commences the muezzin or crier gives the call to prayer from the minaret or outside the mosque, adding in the early morning "Prayer is better than sleep." The first recitation is given by the imam's "follower," or by the crier, and is the same as the call to prayers, with the addition, "Verily, prayers are now ready." The regular prayers then begin, all standing, with the following: "I have purposed to offer up to God only, with a sincere heart this morning (or afternoon, or evening), with my face towards the kiblah, two (or more) rakeh prayers." The word *rakeh* signifies a form of prayer; *farz* are prayers enjoined by God; *sunnah*, those founded on the Tradition of Mahomet; *nafl*, the voluntary performance of two *rakehs*. The num- *Public prayer.*

ber of *rakehs* to be said varies for the different hours of prayer; at night seven are said after all the usual series have been gone through. A devout Moslem will go through the same form of prayer seventy-five times in the day. Any travelling of the eyes or mind, a cough, etc., vitiates the prayer, and the worshipper must recite all again. Yet a late-comer, after reciting the preliminary, and the "God is great," may join the congregation at the stage which they have reached.

The *subhan* follows, ascribing holiness and praise to God and praising His name, followed by the declaration, "I seek refuge from God from cursed Satan." Then follows the first chapter of the Koran, after which the worshipper may repeat as many chapters of the Koran as he desires, but at least should say one long or two short verses. Very frequently the 122nd, a short chapter, is chosen: "Say: He is God alone: God the Eternal. He begetteth not and is not begotten; and there is none like unto Him." "God is great," and "I extol the holiness of my Lord, the great," are repeated frequently in various attitudes of devotion. After every two rakehs the following prayer is offered: "O God, have mercy on Mahomet and on his descendants, as Thou didst have mercy on Abraham and his descendants. Thou art to be praised, and Thou art great"; and also, "O God our Lord, give us the blessings of this life, and also the blessings of life everlasting. Save us from the torments of fire." At the end of prayers follows the salaam: "The peace and mercy of God be with you!" repeated once with the head turned to the right and once to the left, followed by the supplication, a series of prayers from the Koran or the Tradition, and not infrequently said in the vernacular.

There are also special prayers for Friday, for a traveller, at funerals during the fast, during eclipses, etc.; but the specialty consists rather in the number of extra *rakehs* than in the substance of the prayers. There are many directions for prayers in the Traditions, and promises or assertions of blessing for special acts of prayer. One curious regulation is as follows: "When any one of you says his prayers, he must have something in front of him, but if he cannot find anything he must put his walking-stick into the ground, or if it be hard, place it lengthways before him; but if he has no staff, he must draw a line on the ground, after which there will be no detriment to his prayers from any one passing in front of him." Sincere as the Moslem may be, one cannot but see how mechanical and superstitious his devotions tend to become when governed by such multitudinous formalities and repeated so often; and, in fact, the lip-service of a large proportion of Mohammedans is notoriously combined with deceit and evil.

The Friday sermon is given at the time of noonday prayer, and on the two great festivals at the prayer after sunrise. There is usually a special preacher who delivers this, after the first four sets of prayers. It is in Arabic, and includes prayers for Mahomet, his companions, and the sovereign. Its nature is a matter of choice with the preacher, but it consists very largely of assertions of the various Moslem doctrines. An eloquent New Year's Day sermon given in Lane's "Modern Egyptians" contains the following passages: "O servants of God, your lives have been gradually curtailed, and year after year hath passed away and ye are sleeping on the bed of indolence, and on the pillow of iniquity. Ye pass by the tombs of your predecessors, and fear not the assault of destiny and destruction, as if others departed from the world and ye must of necessity remain in it. Ye rejoice at the arrival of new years, as if they brought an increase to the term of life, and swim in the seas of desires and enlarge your hopes, and in every way exceed other people in presumption; and ye are sluggish in doing good. Oh, how great a calamity is this! God teacheth by an allegory. Know ye not that in the curtailment of time by indolence and sleep there is very great trouble? Know ye not that the night and day divide the lives of numerous souls? Ye are now between two years. . . . Is any of you determining upon diligence in doing good in the year to come? or repenting of his failings in the things that are passed?" etc. In the latter half of the sermon: "O God, assist the forces of the Moslems, and the armies of the Unitarians [*i.e.* believers in the one God]! O God, frustrate the infidels and the polytheists, Thine enemies, the enemies of the religion! O God, invert

EGYPTIAN FUNERAL PROCESSION.

their banners and ruin their habitations, and give them and their wealth as booty to the Moslems!" etc. "O Lord, we have acted unjustly towards our own souls, and if Thou do not forgive us and be merciful to us we shall surely be of those who perish."

**Circumcision.** Circumcision, usually performed on boys between the ages of five and twelve, is not a sacred rite, though ordained by the Tradition. There is nothing about it in the Koran, and no record of Mahomet's circumcision. Marriage also is celebrated with very little religious ceremony; at the making and signing of the marriage contract the opening chapter of the Koran is recited, together with an address or exhortation and some Koranic prayers and recitations. **Marriage.** The actual marriage may be performed with much or little religious ceremony, according to the discretion of the cadi or other person performing it; and the ceremony does not take place in a mosque. The bridegroom usually repeats after the cadi, "I desire forgiveness of God;" four short chapters of the Koran, the creed, and a profession of belief in God, the angels, the Koran, the Prophet, the Resurrection, etc. The bridegroom then formally consents to the marriage, and the cadi prays that mutual love may reign between the couple, as between Adam and Eve, Abraham and Sarah, Joseph and Zuleika, Moses and Sarah, Mohammed and Ayesha, Ali and Fatima." The legal regulations about marriage are more properly political than religious; four lawful wives are permitted. Divorce is easy, needing only that the husband should say to his wife, "Thou art divorced," after which three months' waiting is enjoined, when the divorce is permanent. A husband may divorce his wife after **Divorce.** any misbehaviour, or without assigning cause. In some few cases a wife may obtain a divorce. Concubinage with any woman held as a slave is **Concubinage.** lawful; and among the Shiahs, temporary marriages, for a few hours, afford the most degrading form of concubinage. In other respects slaves are usually well treated, and often attached to their masters and mistresses. The Tradition praises and blesses the **Slaves.** emancipation of slaves, and they are not infrequently emancipated, especially at the death of the owner. But the absolute power which a Moslem master has over the life and person of his slave is most deleterious to the character of both; and this, together with the looseness of matrimonial relations, constitutes perhaps the most evil feature of Islam.

The Koran teaches that the hour of death is fixed for every one; and in the Tradition Mahomet teaches that it is sinful to wish for death. "Wish not for death, not even if thou art a doer of good works, for peradventure thou mayst increase them with an increase of life. Nor even if thou art a sinner, for with increase of life thou mayest obtain God's pardon." He is also reported to have said, "Whosoever loves to meet God, God will love to meet him, and whoever dislikes to meet God, God will dislike to meet him. When death comes near a believer, God gives him a spirit of resignation, so that there is nothing a believer likes so much as death."

*Death.*

When a Moslem is about to die, some skilled reader of the Koran is sent for, that he may read the 36th chapter to tranquillise the soul. The creed is also said aloud by all present. Early burial is the rule in Islam, as the sooner the dead are buried the sooner they are believed to reach heaven; while the bad man must be buried quickly that his lot may not fall upon his family. The burial service is believed to be based on the practice of Mahomet. It may properly be recited by the nearest relative, but is usually led by the family imam or the cadi. It is said in a mosque or in some open space, and includes many of the ordinary prayers, with prayer for the soul of the deceased, after which the people say: "It is the decree of God," to which the chief mourner replies, "I am pleased with the will of God," and then says to the people, "There is permission to depart." After this the body is placed on its back in the grave, with the head to the north and the face turned towards Mecca, the words of burial being, "We commit thee to earth in the name of God, and in the religion of the Prophet." On the third day after burial it is usual for the relatives to visit the grave and recite selections from the Koran, the whole of it being sometimes recited by mollahs paid for the purpose.

*Burial.*

Funeral processions on foot are the rule with Moslems, and it is a meritorious act to carry the bier. This is done at a quick pace, that the righteous may arrive soon at happiness. The elaborate funeral processions of Egypt are well described by Lane ("Modern Egyptians," *Minerva Library*,) and we must refer readers to this book for many excellent accounts of Islam in Egypt.

*Funeral processions.*

We have already given an account of the Moslem doctrine of Paradise, but we may here give a summary of what Mahomet is alleged to have said about the immediate fate of the faithful dead. At death, white-faced angels descend to meet them, and at first sit apart, while the Angel of Death comes and calls the pure soul to come forth to God's pardon and pleasure. When the soul comes out, the Angel of Death takes it, but the other angels take it from him immediately, and carry it upwards to heaven, where it is received by God, his name is inscribed in the register of good Moslems, and then the soul is returned again to the body to wait for the resurrection with joy. Similarly an infidel is attended by black-faced angels, after which the Angel of Death comes and bids the impure one come forth to the wrath of God. The angels take the soul up to the highest heaven, when God says, "Write his history in Sijjin," that is, the lowest earth; and the soul is thrown down with violence. It is again replaced in the body, and endures misery, and begs that the resurrection may be delayed. There can be no doubt that the Moslem believes seriously in a future life and state of rewards and punishments; but his idea of paradise is usually very material, and it can largely be secured by ceremonial and formal merits.

*The immediate fate of the soul.*

Mohammedan mosques are much less varied and complex in their structure than Christian churches. They are usually square buildings of stone or brick, with an open central court-yard, and cloisters and cells around for students. In the centre of the wall turned towards Mecca and farthest removed from the entrance, is a niche, the kiblah, which indicates the direction of the Kaaba; and the pulpit is placed to the right of

*Mosques.*

this. A large tank is in the court-yard, at which ceremonial ablutions can be performed. Frequently in Egypt, Turkey, and Syria, however, the mosques are completely covered buildings. The side turned towards Mecca is the only extensive covered area in most mosques. In front of the pulpit there may be a raised platform from which exhortations are chanted, and lecterns for the reading of the Koran. There are also minarets, or peculiar turrets not diminishing regularly in size, but only at successive stages marked by external galleries, from the uppermost of which the muezzin or crier sounds the calls to prayer day and night. Blind men are often employed in this office, since they cannot see into the privacy of houses from their elevated station.

The mosques are often most costly buildings, decked with elaborate carving in marble or other stone, inlaid with mosaics, agates, etc. The kiblah and the pulpit are elaborate works of art, and many forms of gorgeous ornament are lavished upon various other parts of the mosque. Windows of rich tracery pierced in marble or stucco, filled with richly coloured glass in small pieces, often occur. Many mosques have rich treasures of valuable Arabic manuscripts.

Most mosques have considerable endowments, managed by an officer who often appoints the imams, of whom one recites the Koran and leads the daily prayers, while the other, known in Arabia and Egypt as the khatib, preaches the Friday sermon. The imams usually have some other occupation, such as school-teaching or trade. The mosques are used as places of general resort; and between prayer-times people are to be seen discussing secular topics, and even eating and sleeping in them, contrary to the precepts of the Prophet. They are also very generally used as places of rest and abode for travellers.

*Endowment and Government.*

The Sacred Mosque at Mecca and the Prophet's Mosque at Medina must be more particularly described. The former, which contains the Kaaba, (Cube-House) or House of the Sacred Black Stone, is 250 paces long by 200 broad, enclosed on all sides

*The Sacred Mosque at Mecca.*

by a colonnade with quadruple rows of pillars more than twenty feet high on the east side, and triple rows on the remaining sides. Above every four pillars, supported on

EGYPTIAN MOHAMMEDAN TOMB WITH THE ENTRANCE UNCOVERED.

pointed arches, rises a small dome, externally whitened. These domes are said to be 152 in number. Lamps hang from every arch, some being lighted every night, and all during Ramadan. A great outer wall encloses the colonnade: parts of this are ancient, having escaped the various destructions and repairs which have occurred. Some of the walls are gaudily painted in stripes of red, yellow, and blue, as also are the minarets. The style of the columns is in general coarse Saracenic.

Seven paved causeways converge towards the Kaaba, an oblong building which might almost be called a low tower, eighteen paces long, fourteen broad, and thirty-five to forty feet high; the roof is flat. It is roughly built of grey stone, the present building dating from 1627. There is only one door into it, on the north side, about seven feet from the ground, and it is only opened two or three times a year. The famous "Black Stone" is let into the wall at the north-east corner of the building, about four or five feet from the ground. Burckhardt described it as an irregular oval about seven inches in diameter, with an undulated surface, composed of about a dozen smaller stones of different sizes and shapes, joined by a little cement and surrounded by a silver setting. It appears to be a meteoric stone; but its present surface does not show its nature, for it is greatly worn by the millions of touches and kisses it has received. Its colour is a deep reddish brown, approaching black. On the north side of the Kaaba near the door is a little hollow in the ground lined with marble, in which it is thought meritorious to pray, as it is the spot where Abraham and Ishmael, the fabulous builders of the Kaaba, are said to have kneaded their chalk and mud for mortar.

In continuation of a pre-Moslem custom, a covering (the kisweh or veil) of black silk stuff conceals the exterior of the walls of the Kaaba (the roof being bare), openings being left to show the black stone and another stone at the south-east corner. A new veil is put on every year, in the first month, after the Kaaba has been left bare for about a fortnight. At first it is tucked up high by cords, afterwards it is gradually let down, but is not fastened tightly, so that any wind moves it slowly. These movements are treated by the worshippers as signs of the presence of its guardian angels.

Opposite the four sides of the Kaaba are four small erections, used respectively by the imams of the four orthodox sects to lead the devotions of their followers. One of these for the Shafiites is over the well Zamzam, which yields an everflowing supply of water for drinking and ablution to the Meccans, and is believed by the Moslems to be the well found in the wilderness by Hagar. This building is beautifully ornamented with coloured marbles. At one time the shereef of Mecca exacted a high price for this water; but one of the first acts of the Wahhabis was to abolish this payment, and the water is now distributed gratis, except that a small charge is made when it is drawn up and presented by the regular water carriers. It is regarded as a certain cure for all diseases, and a great improver of health, rendering even prayers to God more acceptable. Enormous quantities of it are drunk by some persons; many strip themselves and have bucketsful thrown over them; and few pilgrims leave Mecca without taking some of this water to drink in illness or for their ablution after death.

A movable wooden staircase on wheels is used for entering the Kaaba, being ordinarily kept at some distance. Not very far from this is the pulpit, of white marble, highly ornamented, the preacher's station being surmounted by a gilt polygonal steeple. Here several of the elder ulemas in Mecca preach in rotation, girt in a white cloak covering head and body, and with a stick in the hand as if prepared against a sudden surprise, as in the early ages of Islam. Round the base of the pulpit the congregation deposit their shoes. Besides one or two other less important buildings, the enclosure of the sacred mosque contains a small one which is said to contain the sacred stone upon which Abraham stood to build the original Kaaba, and believed to show an impression of his foot; but this stone is always kept entirely covered. At this building worshippers regularly pray for the good offices of Abraham.

The larger part of the enclosure consists of gravelled spaces which, together with part of the marble pavement surrounding the Kaaba, is covered at evening prayer with carpets from sixty to eighty feet long and four feet wide, which are rolled up after prayers. Other parts are covered with pilgrims' own carpets, or with mats which they bring with them. During the pilgrimage this vast space is sometimes nearly half filled, although the Meccans believe that the mosque could contain all the faithful at once. Burckhardt could never count more than ten thousand persons in it at one time. The mosque has no fewer than nineteen gates, one of these, the Bab-es-Salam, being that by which every pilgrim must enter it. None are ever closed; indeed, they have no doors. Burckhardt entered at all hours of the night and always found people there, either at prayers or walking about. There are seven minarets on the exterior of the mosque. A number of houses which formerly supported the wall of the mosque are now private property, mostly let out to the richest pilgrims, and with windows looking into the mosque, giving the privilege of performing Friday's devotions in their own houses.

This sacred mosque is the one true temple of the Mohammedans, and inasmuch as it contains the Kaaba towards which every Moslem turns in prayer, it is the only place of prayer where believers can turn in any direction they please and yet fulfil the law. It will be very evident from the description of other mosques, how different they are in plan from this. It is a striking commentary on the aim of Mahomet to uphold the unity and spiritual worship of God, that an Arab idol of long standing should be the object most venerated by his followers. Sura ii. 144, 145 says, "From whatever place thou comest forth, then turn thy face towards the Sacred Mosque; for this is a duty enjoined by thy Lord."

Here is the most convenient place for describing the Sacred Hajj, or pilgrimage to Mecca. Just as the old **The Sacred** Arab idol, or fetish, is the central object of **Hajj, or** Moslem reverence, so the pilgrimage to Mecca, **pilgrimage.** which had existed long before Islam, has become the greatest function of the religion. Every Moslem is properly bound to make a pilgrimage to Mecca once in his life, and it should be completed in the twelfth month of the Moslem year, although an ordinary pilgrimage may

## MOSQUE OF ST. SOPHIA, CONSTANTINOPLE. 143

MOSQUE OF ST. SOPHIA, CONSTANTINOPLE.

be made at any season. Most essential features are the visits to sacred spots in the neighbourhood of Mecca, and the pilgrimage ends with a visit to the Kaaba. We cannot detail the numerous features of interest attending the setting out for Mecca from distant countries, the troubles and inconveniences of the journey or voyage, the sacrifices which good Moslems will make to accomplish this great life-object. We will simply note that the number who reached Mecca in 1880 was computed by Mr. Blunt as somewhat over 93,000, of whom 33,000 were Arab pilgrims, 15,000 British subjects from India, 12,000 Malays chiefly from Java and other Dutch possessions, 9,500 subjects of the Ottoman sultan, 8,500 Persians, 6,000 Egyptians, 6,000 North Africans, 2,000 Soudanese negroes, and 1,000 Zanzibaris, etc. Thus in fifty years about five millions of pilgrims may visit Mecca. Probably only 3 or 4 per cent. of Moslems ever see Mecca; but multitudes of others long for the opportunity.

There are three points essential to the lawful completeness of the pilgrimage: the wearing of no garment but the *ihram*, consisting of two seamless wrappers, one girding the waist and the other loosely thrown over the shoulders; to stand in Arafat, the Mount of Recognition, twelve miles from Mecca, where Eve is related to have been found by Adam; and to make the circuit round the Kaaba. There are five other observances which are obligatory, but their omission does not constitute absolute infidelity, although it is a sin. These are, to stay in Al Muzdalifa, halfway between Mina and Arafat; to run between the hills of Safa and Marwah; to perform the ceremony of casting the pebbles at Mina; to make an extra circuit of the Kaaba, if not Meccans; and to shave the head at the end of the pilgrimage.

When the pilgrim arrives at the last stage, near Mecca, the ceremonies begin by his bathing, saying two rakeh prayers, then putting on the pilgrim's garb, after which he neither anoints his head, pares his nails, nor shaves until the whole of the ceremonies are over. Facing Mecca, he says aloud what is termed the intention: "O God, I purpose to make the hajj; make this service easy to me and accept it from me." He then goes to the city, reciting or singing the pilgrims' song (p. 91), enters the sacred mosque, kisses the black stone, and makes the circuit of the Kaaba seven times, three times at a run, four times slowly, each time kissing the black stone and touching the other sacred stone. He then says two prayers at the station of Abraham, returns and once more kisses the black stone. He next goes to the so-called hill of Safa, 76 paces from the mosque, and three times recites the Moslem creed, adding, "He hath performed His promise, and hath aided His servant, and hath put to flight the hosts of infidels by Himself alone." He then runs from this hill to that of Marwah seven times and back, repeating the same sentences each time on each hill. This is usually done on the sixth day, and on the seventh the khutbah or sermon at the mosque is listened to. On the eighth day the journey is made to Mina; on the ninth the pilgrim goes to Mount Arafat, and after saying prayers and hearing a sermon, stands on the hill and shouts Labbeik, and recites prayers and texts till sunset. Early on the next day a second stand is made by torchlight for a short time round the mosque of Muzdalifa between Mina and Arafat; but the chief ceremony on this day is at Mina. This is the day of sacrifice, on which the pilgrim throws seven stones at each of three pillars in Mina, saying, "In the name of God the Almighty, I do this, and in hatred of the devil and his shame." Then a victim has to be slain at Mina, from a sheep to a camel, according to the pilgrim's means, part of the flesh being given to the poor; and finally, Mecca must be visited again and the black stone kissed. At this time a great fair takes place at Mina, and the sacrifice may be made on any day of the fair. The pilgrim then gets shaved, takes off his pilgrim's garb, and the pilgrimage is over.

Shiites allow performance of the pilgrimage by deputy, and it is considered very meritorious to pay the expenses of one who cannot afford it. But any Moslem who has not made the pilgrimage may leave money to some one else to make the pilgrimage, and is thus considered to have fulfilled his duty. The pilgrim becomes known as a hadji, and retains that title ever afterwards before his proper name. Notwithstanding ablutions, the Meccan

MOSQUE OF THE PALACE, KHIVA.

assemblages are dangerous centres of infectious diseases; and Mecca is reported to be a hotbed of vice.[1] The

[1] For interesting speculations as to the origin of all the ceremonies at Mecca, see W. Robertson Smith, art. "Mecca," *Encyclopædia Britannica*.

whole Meccan pilgrimage strikes an outside observer as a strangely meaningless superstition, one that does not elevate the character of the worshippers, and only produces an inordinate self-satisfaction on its completion. Its great utility to Mohammedanism is evident, in giving it a centre and a uniting impulse.

A visit is very generally made to Medina after the pilgrimage is over, except by Wahhabis, who regard such a visit as idolatry. The Prophet's mosque is a very extensive building, much larger than the original one; it is between 400 and 500 feet long by about 300 in breadth, with an elaborate principal gate leading into a deep portico with ten rows of pillars, along the southern wall. Near the farther end of this is a walled enclosure without doors, believed to contain the graves of Mahomet, Abubekr and Omar, and close to this is a similar building which encloses the tomb of Fatima. Both are enclosed within an iron railing covered with brass wire-work. Through some small apertures pilgrims address prayers for intercession to the prophet and the other saints. The idea of Mahomet's coffin being suspended in the air by magnets is an European fable. There is a great dome above the prophet's tomb, and there are striking minarets; but otherwise the mosque is not very remarkable in construction, and is not more than 400 years old. *The Prophet's mosque at Medina.*

The Mosque of the Caliph Omar, at Jerusalem, built soon after his entry into the city in 637, was supposed to be built upon the site of Solomon's Temple, and to be the place to which Mahomet was carried from Mecca on his celebrated "night-journey." The original small building still exists, though it is uncertain whether it is a chamber east of the next mentioned, or that to the west, known as the Mosque of the Mogrebins. Abd el Malik, Caliph of Damascus, built another mosque here in 691. It is a square covered building with seven aisles, as large as many of our cathedrals, and it lacks the square court usually found in mosques. Its north porch was added in the fourteenth century; the rest of the building is very barn-like. *The Mosque of Omar.*

The building called by Europeans "the Mosque of Omar," is certainly not Omar's, and it is rightly termed **The Dome of** "the Dome of the Rock," according to Moslem **the Rock.** nomenclature. It is a beautiful octagonal build-

MOSQUE OF OMAR, "DOME OF THE ROCK," JERUSALEM.

ing of 160 feet diameter, with a high circular dome, and it is according to Fergusson a nearly unaltered Christian building of the 4th century, erected by the Emperor

Constantine. Its pillars are of the most precious marble, either from Herod's or Hadrian's temple; and exquisite mosaics and magnificent painted glass windows combine to make it one of the most beautiful buildings in the world.

The great mosque at Damascus, successively a heathen temple and a Christian church, was, in the first century of Islam, used jointly by Christians and Moslems. The present splendid building was then erected by the Caliph Walid. It is 508 feet by 320, enclosing a very large court. The covered side has three aisles, and is 126 feet wide. *Great mosque at Damascus.*

One of the finest mosques of the typical form was that at Cordova, in Spain, built in 786–796, now transformed into the cathedral. The original main covered part has no fewer than twenty rows of marble columns, and they are so arranged as to appear to stretch without end in every direction, like the Hall of pillars at Karnak. Moreover, formerly rows of orange trees formed aisles in the open court continuing the lines of the columns. Among the notable mosques of this normal type are those of Amr, Old Cairo, that of El-Azhar at Cairo, the great mosque of Old Delhi, and those of Fez and Kairwan. *The Mosque of Cordova.*

The mosques of most complex structure are those of Cairo, the reason being that subsidiary buildings, such as schools, colleges, courts of justice, hospitals, etc., have been aggregated around them. The mosque of the Sultan Hasan (14th century) is cruciform in plan, the central court open, the eastern arm forming the place of prayer and preaching, and the domed tomb of the sultan being east of this. There is a splendid entrance on the north-west, with a very high arch. Many pages might be devoted to these splendid mosques; but we must only notice the tomb-mosques of the Egyptian sultans, outside the walls of Cairo. They have beautiful domes and minarets; and they owe much to Byzantine, Persian, and even Christian gothic architecture, Islam itself having produced few great original architects. There are over four hundred mosques in Cairo. Northern Africa has many fine mosques. Persia has but *Mosques and tombs at Cairo.*

ENCAMPMENT OF PILGRIMS IN THE VALLEY OF MINA.

a few fine early mosques remaining. At Ispahan there is the splendid Masjid Shah, built by Shah Abbas I. (1585-1629), with a very large pyriform dome, 165 feet high.

When the Turks took Constantinople, in 1453, they at once appropriated seven or eight of the chief Christian churches as mosques, and at the head of them St. Sophia, which they sincerely admired and set to work to imitate; 100 different mosques at Constantinople testify to the influence of this type. We may briefly describe it here as an actual Mohammedan mosque, though constructed as a Christian church by the Emperor Justinian, in 532-537, the architect being Anthemius. It is almost a square of 250 feet added to a nave of more than 200 feet long. Externally it has little beauty, and its great beauty is internal, the great dome being continued by two half domes east and west. The arches on which the great dome rests are about 100 feet across and 120 feet high. The pillars are of the most precious marbles or porphyry, the capitals admirably carved; all the flat surfaces are covered with exquisite mosaics. Fergusson calls it the most perfect and beautiful Christian church. The mosque of Suleiman the Magnificent adopts the combined dome form, has a great forecourt, and on the opposite side a large garden containing the tombs of the founder and members of his family.  *St. Sophia at Constantinople.*

Indian mosques and tombs are among the most splendid and varied buildings of that country, rich in splendid buildings as it is. The Moslems, carrying the dome and minaret ideas with them, elaborated and adapted them to the native architecture, and produced a succession of styles, as numerous as all European styles, and all worthy of notice. We can only mention a few remarkable features. The mosques and tombs of Ahmedabad, of Bejapore, the tomb of Mahmoud, with its extraordinary dome larger than that of the Pantheon at Rome, externally 198 feet high, and the mosques of Agra and Delhi compare even with the exquisite Hindu temples. The great mosque (Jummoo Musjid) at Delhi, with its grand porch with pointed arch, its lofty minarets  *Indian mosques and tombs.*

and three great pyriform domes, its courtyard with open colonnades, was, like the Pearl Mosque at Agra, built by Shah Jehan. The latter is entirely of white marble from base to summit, without any ornament. The Taj Mehal at Agra is the most perfect mausoleum perhaps in the world, also erected by Shah Jehan to contain the remains of his favourite wife, Minutaz Mehal, who died in 1631. He meant to build a more splendid one for himself, but died before accomplishing his intention, and he now rests beside her in the Taj Mehal. The whole is enclosed in exquisite gardens; within is a very large court with splendid gateway, leading to a platform 18 feet high and 313 feet square, upon which are two beautiful detached minarets, and the mausoleum 186 feet square, with the corners cut off. The dome is 58 feet in diameter and 80 feet high, covering the show-tombs, a vault beneath containing the true tombs. Light is admitted through marble trellis-work of exquisite design. Indeed, the whole building is of white marble, and visitors say that no words can express its beauty. All the important parts are inlaid with precious stones in exquisite designs.

# CHAPTER VII.
## Modern Islam. Part II.

The Bairam festival—Ramadan—The breaking of the fast—The Kisweh and the Mahmal—Other fasts and festivals—The Moharram fast—The holy war.—The dervishes or fakirs—Various orders—Rifayeh—Dancing dervishes—Performance in Tashkend—Various rites—The Dóseh—Saints—Worship of deceased saints—Sufism—Relation to pantheism—The Shiites—Their chief distinctions—Their mollahs and colleges—Persian dervishes—Passion plays—Babism—Ali the Bab—Abadites and Zeidites—The Wahhabis—Their founder—His teaching—His champion—The Wahhabi kingdom—Mecca and Medina taken—Defeats by Mehemet Ali and Ibrahim—Extension in India—Special doctrines and defects—The Druses—Origin—Hakim—Durazi—Hamza—Recent history—Tenets—Seven great duties—The Akals — Meetings — Turkey— Kerbela — Meshed — India—China—North Africa—Central and Eastern Africa—Contrast between Pagan and Moslem Negro—The Koran unifies and elevates the Negro.

THE year of twelve lunar months is still observed by Moslems, and is eleven days short of the solar year; thus it brings round all the festivals in turn to different seasons. For ordinary purposes of life, however, the solar year is used. The festivals and fasts of the Mohammedan year are of great importance. They have already been incidentally referred to, and we need only here describe certain special points. The Feast of Sacrifice, in Turkey and Egypt known as the Bairam festival, is the great festival of the year. As part of the Meccan pilgrimage we have already described it, but it is observed all over Islam on the same day, the tenth of the last month of the Mohammedan year, as a time of great rejoicing. A special place outside the city is chosen for the special festival prayers, which are led by the imam, and afterwards a sermon is delivered, emphasising the significance of the day, and commending the offering of sacrifices as capable of carrying the believer across the narrow bridge or road to Paradise. On returning home, the head of each family takes an animal—a sheep, cow, goat, or camel, according to his means or the number of his family—turns its head towards Mecca, and says, "In the name of the great God: verily my prayers, my sacrifice, my life, my death, belong to God, the Lord of the worlds. He has no partner: that is what I am bidden; for I am first of those who are Moslems:" after which he kills the animal. One-third of the flesh is kept for the family, one-third is given to relations, and one-third to the poor.

The fast of Ramadan, the ninth month of the Moslem year, has been already explained. Its observance in the letter is rigorously necessary for all good Moslems, except the sick, the infirm, nursing and pregnant women, young children, and travellers. When the month falls in the hot season, the day-long fast is extremely trying, for not a drop of water may be drunk during the day; also twenty additional rakehs or forms of prayer must be gone through after the night prayer. It is customary for good Moslems to stay for considerable periods in the mosques during this month, reading the Koran, and refraining from conversation on worldly affairs. It is imagined by many that the Mohammedan fast of thirty days was derived from the Christian Lent.

<small>Ramadan.</small>

The Feast of Alms, or minor festival, is kept on the day after Ramadan is over, and is called the Festival of Breaking the Fast. After the general distribution of alms, there are special prayers outside the city, followed by a sermon, special petitions for remission of sins, recovery of the sick, rain and abundance of corn, safety from misfortune, and freedom from debt. After the service the people salute and congratulate one another, and then spend the day in feasting and rejoicing. In Egypt it is a custom to visit the tombs of relatives on this or the following days, the visitors often carrying palm-branches to lay on the tombs, reciting the creed,

<small>The breaking of the fast.</small>

A DERVISH.

PILGRIM TO MECCA.

and more or less of the Koran. This is not the custom in India, where tombs are visited in the Mohurram festival.

There is a considerable festival in Cairo a few days after this, when the Kisweh, or covering of the Kaaba, is con-
**The Kisweh and the Mahmal.** veyed from the citadel to the mosque of the Hasanein, to be sewn together and lined before the pilgrimage. An elaborate procession which escorts it is well described by Lane. The Mahmal, or canopy, is carried at the same time, but has also a grand procession of its own two or three weeks later, before the departure of the great caravan of pilgrims. The Mahmal is a covered litter or canopy borne on a camel, as an emblem of royalty originally sent to represent a sultana of Egypt in her absence.

A festival largely observed in India, is the fifteenth day of Shaban, the eighth month, when it is said that God
**Other fasts and festivals.** registers all the actions of mankind, and all births and deaths for the coming year. Originally intended to be observed as a fast, it has become a festival, and is a great occasion for letting off fireworks. New Year's Day is a great festival of the Persians. The last Wednesday of Safar, the second month, is observed in some parts of Islam as a feast, commemorating a mitigation of Mahomet's last illness and his last bath. The birthday of Mahomet on the twelfth of the third month, is kept in Turkey, Egypt, and some parts of India, alms being distributed and additional religious exercises being performed.

The first ten days of the first month, Moharram, are kept in memory of the martyrdom of Hasan and Hosein,
**The Moharram fast.** as days of lamentation, by Shiites only; but the tenth day is kept as a fast by Sunnites generally, as being the day on which heaven and hell, life and death, Adam and Eve, were created.

There can be no doubt that the propagation of Islam by the Jihad, or holy war, has been one of the most
**The holy war.** potent means of securing its success. It is enjoined in the Koran as a religious duty. But there is nothing which forbids the spread of Islam by

peaceful persuasion and example, and at the present day this is largely the method by which the Moslem faith is being diffused in Africa. It is enjoined, however, that when an infidel country is conquered, the people shall be offered the option of becoming Moslems, of paying a poll-tax for protection (except in the case of Arabian idolaters and apostates), or death by the sword. It is held by the Hanifites that the injunction is sufficiently obeyed when any one tribe of Moslems is engaged in spreading the religion by the sword. It is not held right to attack any infidels without previously calling upon them to accept the faith. There are many detailed regulations for the conduct of a sacred war in the books of Mohammedan law.

The fakirs or dervishes are very prominent characters in Islam, answering in some ways to the Christian monks in the middle ages. The word dervish—more accurately *darweesh*—is a Persian word, signifying those who beg from door to door; the Arabic *fakir* means "poor" before God, not necessarily poor in a worldly sense. Both terms are in general use for those who lead a religious life, with special practices or exercises. There are many fakirs or dervishes who, while professing to be Mahometans, do not follow the Koran; those who obey the Mohammedan law are of very varied types or orders, all having special rules, many of which it is impossible to ascertain, being known only to the votaries themselves, and kept strictly secret. It is claimed, but without foundation, that they deduce their origin from the brotherhood which was formed in the first year of the flight between the emigrants from Mecca and the citizens of Medina, establishing a community of property and common religious rites of penitence and of mortification. These men took the name of Sufis (the meaning of which word is uncertain), and it now designates any Moslem devoted to religious contemplation, exercises, and painful rites. They practically include the fakirs. A long history might be given of the various orders of dervishes, their founders and their history; and their existence is a standing contradiction of Mahomet's com-

*[margin: The dervishes or fakirs.]*

mand, "Let there be no monasticism in Islam." Tradition says that Mahomet declared, "The retirement which becomes my people is to sit in a corner of a mosque and wait for the time of prayer." We can only give a few details out of many.

One order, the Baktashiyeh, which was founded by a native of Bokhara, and which gave rise to the Janissaries, **Various orders.** is marked by the mystic girdle, which the members put off and on seven times: saying at the successive times, "I tie up greediness, and unbind generosity;" "I tie up anger, and unbind meekness;" "I tie up avarice, and unbind piety;" "I tie up ignorance, and unbind the fear of God;" "I tie up passion, and unbind the love of God;" "I tie up hunger, and unbind (spiritual) contentment;" "I tie up Satanism, and unbind Divineness."

The Rifayeh dervishes, very numerous in Egypt, include a sect who pretend to thrust iron spikes into their **Rifayeh.** eyes and bodies without injuring themselves, to pass swords through their bodies and thick needles through their cheeks without wound or pain. Another of their sects handle serpents with impunity (but have first extracted their fangs); it is this sect whose head or sheikh performs the ceremony of the dóseh (see p. 160).

The Dancing or Whirling Dervishes are the most popular order in the Turkish empire. Their usual services **Dancing dervishes.** take place every Wednesday and Sunday at two o'clock. Their special exercise consists in spinning round, dancing, and turning with extraordinary speed, their bell-shaped petticoats thus acquiring a whirling umbrella shape.

Mr. Eugene Schuyler, in his book on Turkestan, has graphically described the exercises which he saw in the **Performance in Tashkend.** mosque at Tashkend. A considerable number of men were on their knees in front of the kiblah, reciting prayers with loud cries and violent movements of the body, the prayers being as follows: "My defence is in Allah! May Allah be magnified! My light, Mohammed—God bless him! There is no God but God!" These words were chanted hundreds of times over in a low voice, the devotees' heads being violently thrown to the left over the shoulder, then back, then

THE MAHMAL (p. 156).

over the right shoulder, then down. The movements, at first slow, continually increased in speed, till the performers were exhausted. " When their voices became entirely hoarse with one cry, another was begun, and finally the cry was struck up of 'Hai, Hai! Allah Hai!' (Live, Allah, the immortal), at first slowly, with an inclination of the body to the ground; then the rhythm grew faster and in cadence, the body became more and more vertical, until at once they all stood up; the measure still increased in rapidity, and each one placing his hand on the shoulder of his neighbour, and thus forming several concentric rings, they moved in a mass from side to side of the mosque, leaping about, and always crying, "Hai, Allah Hai!'" and this was only a small part of one performance.

Some of the rites of the dervishes are observed only by particular orders, some by many orders. Some observe a forty days' fast occasionally (that is, from daybreak to sunset each day), others confine themselves in a cell in a sepulchre-mosque north of Cairo, remaining there three days and nights, scarcely eating during that period, on the occasion of the festival of the saint of the mosque. During this time they continually repeat certain special forms of prayer, coming out of their cells into the mosque to join in the five daily prayers, and making no answer to any one who speaks to them but "There is no God but God."

*Various rites.*

Almost all the dervishes in Egypt, says Lane, are tradesmen, artisans, or agriculturists, and only occasionally join in the ceremonies of their orders. Some do nothing but perform their special religious exercises at the festivals of saints and at private entertainments, and chant in funeral processions. Some are water-carriers, a few wander about and subsist on alms, wearing fantastic or characteristic dresses. Many Turkish and Persian wandering dervishes in Egypt are among the most importunate for alms.

A volume might be filled with accounts of the dervishes, but we can only give in any detail a notice of the ceremony of the *Dóseh*, or "treading" on prostrate dervishes by the horse of the sheikh or chief of the Saadiyeh dervishes, preacher of the mosque of the Hasanein. After noon prayers on a certain Friday, when

*The dóseh.*

the Prophet's miraculous ascent to heaven is celebrated, the sheikh, seated on a horse of moderate size, goes to visit the sheikh El Bikree, who is the head of all the dervishes of Egypt. Before he reaches his destination, a considerable number of dervishes lie down upon the ground, side by side, as close as possible, with backs upward, legs extended, and arms placed together beneath their foreheads, and constantly murmuring "Allah!" Twelve or more dervishes then run along over their backs, some beating little drums and exclaiming "Allah!" Then the sheikh approaches on his horse, and with some little difficulty the animal is urged over the prostrate bodies, being led by two men who themselves also run over the bodies. Apparently no one is hurt, and all jump up and follow the sheikh immediately. Each receives two treads from the horse, and their escaping injury is considered to be a miracle granted specially to the sheikh of this order. Another remarkable performance of a dervish order is the chewing of a mouthful of redhot charcoal without showing any sign of pain. Epileptic fits often occur during some dervish performances.

Nearly akin to the regard paid to dervishes is the worship of reputed saints, both living and dead. Many of the reputed saints of Egypt and other Mahometan countries are harmless lunatics or idiots whose mind is imagined to be in heaven. Some even go about naked, others in the strangest or most absurd garbs. The term *wali*, properly applicable only to a very eminent saint, has consequently become degraded to mean also "fool" or simpleton. Any privilege and reverence is readily accorded to such; and it is believed that there exists a certain most holy wali, who is not known as such, and who may perhaps be seen anywhere. He is reported to be almost constantly seated at Mecca on the roof of the Kaaba, and at the gate of Cairo called Bab Zuweyleh. Many persons when they pass this gate recite the Moslem prayer, and give alms to a beggar seated there. Persons having headaches drive a nail into the door to charm away the pain; sufferers from toothache extract a tooth and insert it in a crevice of the door. The holiest wali is believed to be able to transport himself in an instant from Mecca to Cairo, and also to wander at will through the world, distributing, through other walis, blessings and evils. Many walis, who often live in desert places, are regularly supplied with food by the faithful. In numerous cases they are believed to have the power of working miracles.

Deceased saints are venerated and even worshipped more than living ones. Large mosques are erected over the tombs of the more celebrated; and even minor saints in Egypt are honoured with small square white-washed buildings crowned with a cupola. Over the saint's vault is an oblong monument, usually covered by silk or linen, with some words from the Koran worked upon it. The most notable memorial of a saint in Egypt is the great mosque of the Hasanen, in which the head of Hosain, the son of Ali and grandson of Mahomet, is said to be buried. The people regard the deceased saints as interceding for them with God, and consequently make offerings and pay visits of veneration to them, reciting the Moslem prayer before the door of the monument and on each of its four sides, also saying, " O God, I have transferred the merit of what I have recited from the excellent Koran to the person to whom this place is dedicated," and prayers are said in which the saint's help as intercessor is besought. Almost every village in Egypt has some patron saint, whose tomb is visited by the people on a particular day of the week, making various offerings or vows; and all the chief saints have anniversary festivals or molids, when varied special observances are gone through, when many persons visit the tombs to obtain special blessings, and dervishes perform their exercises or portions of the Koran.

*Worship of deceased saints.*

Sufism as a form of mysticism is far from being exhausted by an account of the dervishes or of reverence for saints. They all agree in giving a mystic spiritual meaning to the Koran, and consider that their system has existed since the foundation of the world. In fact, it is a Moslem adaptation of the Vedanta Hindu philosophy, and the allied philosophy of Buddhism, together with some influence from the early Christian

*Sufism.*

anchorites. They all profess implicit obedience to a spiritual guide, and that they are either inspired by God Himself, or are in union with God. The leading doctrines of Sufism may be thus expressed: God alone exists, and is in all things, and all things are in Him. All beings are an emanation from Him, and are not really distinct from Him. There is no real difference between good and evil, all being from and in God, who fixes man's actions. The soul existed before the body, in which it is constrained, and longs to be set free by death to return to the Divinity. The main occupation of the Sufi is to meditate on the unity of God, to perform the exercises of his special order, and to progress rightly in the journey of life. This journey is described in different stages, the lowest of which is the observance of the law. Later, in answer to his prayers, he reaches the true love of God, followed by the desire for seclusion, which by contemplation leads to knowledge. Often this produces ecstasy, during which direct revelation of truth from God may be received, through which union with God may be reached even in the present life. It is this union which the eccentric exercises of the dervishes are designed to promote. There is a considerable literature describing Sufi thought, for which subject Hughes's "Dictionary of Islam," and Palmer's "Oriental Mysticism," may be consulted.

Poetry is a very prominent feature in Sufism; and indeed the poetry of Saadi and the odes of Hafiz are as a sort of Scripture to the Persian Sufis. The author of the "Masnawi" (A.D. 1302) thus expresses some Sufi doctrines:—

> "Are we fools? We are God's captivity.
> Are we wise? We are His promenade.
> Are we sleeping? We are drunk with God.
> Are we waking? Then we are His heralds.
> Are we weeping? Then His clouds of wrath.
> Are we laughing? Flashes of His love."

Mahmoud writes:—

> "All sects but multiply the I and thou;
> This I and thou belong to partial being.
> When I and thou and several being vanish,
> Then mosque and church shall find thee nevermore."

A poem of another author has the following lines:—

> "Joy! joy!" I triumph now; no more I know
> Myself as simply me. I burn with love.
> The centre is within me, and its wonder
> Lies as a circle everywhere about me."

Thus we see that Sufism is really a form of pantheism, and, strangely like the Buddhist, the votary seeks to lose **Relation to pantheism.** his own identity. Sufism is not true Mohammedanism, but rather an erection starting from it, of a mystic creed in which the inner light or some spiritual teacher becomes paramount, and which can dispense with moral law. Consequently one Sufi sect openly neglects morality, and professes community of property and women. Such people regard any sin they are inclined to as imposed by fate; and do not consider themselves guilty whatever they may do.

We pass by a natural transition to the Shiites, who abound in Persia, the stronghold of mysticism. The word **The Shiites.** Shiah literally means "followers," that is of Ali, the husband of Fatima. They maintain, as we have already said, that Ali was the first true imam or caliph, and that true religion consists in the knowledge of the rightful imams. Of these the leading sect, or Twelveans, recognise twelve; the last, Mohammed Abu l'Kasim, being supposed to be still alive, and to be about to appear as a precursor of the Day of Judgment. This is why pretenders to this title appear at various times, and, if favoured by circumstances, gain such a large following. But the apparently simple faith of the Shiites has admitted of much controversy and schism, and there are nearly as many sects of them as of Sunnites.

The principal differences between Shiites and Sunnites, says Prof. A. Müller in the *Encyclopædia Britannica*, **Their chief distinctions.** depend on their legitimistic opinions (*i.e.* their opinion as to the rightful imams or caliphs), or are accommodations of the rites of Islam to the Persian nationality, or else are petty matters affecting ceremonial. Thus they reject all the "Traditions" of the Sunnites as being compiled under illegitimate caliphs, and they have their own body of tradition, alleged to be compiled under Ali, but not genuine. They add to the ordinary Moslem

THE DOSEH.

creed, "and Ali is the Wali (vicegerent or confidant) of God." Some of their sects regard Ali as Divine, and many of them recognise him as partaking of the Divine nature. Those who have deeply studied Persian Mohammedanism, like Sir Lewis Pelly, have discovered that the Shiite schism is really an expression of the race antagonism between the Iranian Aryans of Persia and the Semites.

The Shiites reject the conclusions of the four great schools of Sunnite law founded on the Traditions, and *Their mollahs and colleges.* derive all their law from the Koran; but they depend upon their mollahs or religious teachers to declare its correct interpretation. The mollahs are trained in madrasas, or colleges attached to the mosques; but their training is inferior to that of Cairo and Bokhara. The most noted Shiite madrasa is at Kerbela, 50 miles south-west of Bagdad, in the Turkish dominions, said to be the scene of the martyrdom of Hosain the son of Ali. The students, when passed out of the colleges, become local mollahs, and later may join the college in a larger town, each of which has a chief mollah known as the Sheikh ul Islam. Certain presidents of the chief mosques are known as *mujtahids* or "enlightened doctors," and their opinion is taken as final in all matters of Moslem law and doctrine. In Persia the cadi is an inferior judge who acts instead of the Sheikh ul Islam in special cases; a mufti, or solicitor for the court, prepares cases to come before the cadi. There was for long a sort of war between the Government of Persia and the Mohammedan doctors; and the Government has good ground of offence in the corruption of the courts, while the rights of spiritual asylum and protection by the clergy are most valuable to the common people.

The Persian dervishes belonging to the Shiites are, it is said, more immoral and unworthy of respect than any *Persian dervishes.* others. "At the great feasts especially they quarter themselves impudently in wealthy houses, and deafen the indwellers with their unceasing cry of *Yá hakk* ('O truth!' the mystical equivalent of 'O God!'). The wise and modest dervish who in Saadi's poems tells the greatest Sultan the truth as to the hollowness of his royal state has degenerated into the half-mad and insolent hanger-on who thrusts himself into audience-chambers and claims the seat of honour beside the grandees. The multitude of these motley vagabonds, some harmless, others dangerous, is explained by the love of idleness, buffoonery, and story-telling, which is even more marked in Persia than in other parts of the East." (M.)

Undoubtedly Islam as practised in Persia is a very degenerate cult. The great majority of those who profess it belie it by their lives. They attach much more importance to their distinctions from Sunnites and Jews than to the teaching of the Koran. The Persian "natural turn for lying and hypocrisy" comes out very evidently in their religion. Private drunkenness and mere temporary "marriages" are very common among them, and the mollahs even countenance them.

The Persians set great store by religious festivals and shows. While they celebrate the great sacrificial feast or Bairam festival, they attach the greatest importance to the Moharram (see p. 567), which <small>Passion plays.</small> is celebrated by passion-plays, consisting of several parts, one of which is enacted on each successive day of the mourning. In these are most pathetically and vividly set forth the events of the life of Hosain and the tragedy of his death; and the spectators become fanatically excited as they witness the successive scenes. "I have seen some of the most violent of them," says Morier, "as they vociferated, 'O Hosain!' walk about the streets almost naked, with only their loins covered, and their bodies streaming with blood, by the voluntary cuts which they have given to themselves, either as acts of love, anguish, or mortification." The Shiites, who are very numerous in Oude and in other parts of India, also celebrate the martyrdom of Hasan and Hosain at the Moharram festival by miracle plays, which are fully described by Sir Lewis Pelly in his "Miracle Play." We illustrate the Moharram festival at Bombay by a representation of a procession.

Yet there is some vitality remaining in Persian Mohammedanism, as evidenced by the growth of sects which aim at purifying or improving the popular religion. Some hold Ali to be a divine incar- <small>Babism.</small>

nation, others explain away the resurrection. The most remarkable of the modern sects, however, is that founded by Ali, a young man of Shiraz, in 1843. He taught a sort of communism and pantheism, the unity of God, and the re-absorption of all things in Him; that God reveals His will by a series of messengers who are divine as well as human, each being the revealer of some new truth. Of these Moses, Jesus, Mahomet, and himself were the chief, while he looked for a greater to come after him, the great Revealer. A fanciful theory of numbers, especially connected with the number 19, was one of his specialities. He chose 18 chief disciples, who with himself made up 19. The great work of revelation was to contain 19 chapters, of which he wrote eleven, leaving the rest to be written by his successor, etc. His person was most attractive, his life pious and regular, and his doctrine gained such sway that the State became alarmed. He took the title of "the Bâb," that is "the Door," the only one through which men can reach God. He discountenanced polygamy, forbade divorce, and abolished the veiling of women. He also sternly exposed the vices of the mollahs: and consequently they were his bitter enemies. This fact secured him toleration by the Government for some time, and his converts spread his cult widely in Persia. One of his chief followers, Hosain, formed a camp of Babis, as the new religionists were called, at Castle Tebersy, which in 1848 was stormed and Hosain killed. In various provinces the Government attacked the Babis, imprisoned and martyred men, women, and children, and killed the Bâb himself under circumstances of great cruelty and contumely on 18th July, 1849. A new Bâb, indicated by supposed divine signs, was chosen by his followers, named Yahya. A further massacre of the Babis took place in 1852, since which time the sect has not dared to show itself openly, though zealously propagated in secret. It is unknown whether the new Bâb is still living, and how many Babis there are is doubtful. A recent traveller puts them at 100,000 (see *Contemporary Review*, Dec., 1885). They write many books, which are secretly circulated, and their teachings are said to have taken the greatest hold of the most intelligent classes in Persia.

We must briefly mention two heretical sects, possibly descended from the Khawarij, who revolted from Ali after the battle of Siffin, being offended because he submitted his right to the Caliphate to human decision, when according to them it ought to be left to Divine arbitrament. They also believed that any man might be made Caliph, of whatever tribe or nation, provided he were a just person, and also that a Caliph who was a wrong-doer might be put to death or deposed. The Abadiyeh of Oman and Zanzibar hold this doctrine at the present day, and are said to number four millions. They reject a vast quantity of Sunnite traditions, and have no communion with Sunnites. The Zeidites of Yemen are probably akin to them in belief, rejecting the traditional Caliphate, but passing themselves off as Sunnites when on pilgrimage. They do not number more than two millions. *Abadites and Zeidites.*

The Wahhabi movement, now nearly two centuries old, has been one of the most potent that has ever arisen in Islam, and is by no means extinct, though shorn of much of its former influence. It arose by the preaching of Mohammed Abd el Wahhab, the son of Wahhab, whose name has been given to the movement, since his own proper name would have confused it with that of the Prophet. He was born in the centre of Nejd, the great desert tract in Arabia, in 1691, was educated as a Hanbalite, visited and studied at Mecca, Basra (Bassorah), Bagdad, and Medina, and returning home started his mission as a religious teacher. Fired with zeal for primitive Islam and hatred for the extravagances, excrescences, and evils he had noted in various Moslem countries, he taught the pure unity of God, rejected all the traditions except those derived from the Companions of the Prophet, and claimed the right of private judgment as to the Koran and the Traditions. He abolished the invocation and worship of saints and the dead, and forbade the use of intoxicants and tobacco, the wearing of silver *The Wahhabis. Their founder. His teaching.*

and gold, and every practice forbidden by the Koran. Thus his movement partook both of Puritanism and Protestantism.

The new teacher began to preach at about forty years old, and soon drew down upon himself great opposition.

*His champion.* He had to take refuge at Deraieh, with Mohammed ibn Saood, who espoused his cause eagerly, and sought to establish his own conquests on the basis or pretext of the new doctrines. He began a career of conquest which extended the Wahhabi principles and the rule of his own dynasty over the greater part of Arabia. On Ibn Saood's death, in 1765, Nejd was a strong kingdom, and his son's successor, Abd-ul-Aziz, assumed the titles of imam and sultan. The founder of *The Wahhabi kingdom.* the Wahhabis lived on till 1787. Abd-ul-Aziz continued his conquests till 1803, when he was murdered by a Persian fanatic. His son Saood took Kerbela, containing the tombs of the Shiite caliphs, and destroyed everything that savoured of idolatry, from the golden dome of Hosain's tomb to the smallest tobacco *Mecca and Medina taken.* pipe. In 1803 he took Mecca and performed similar destruction, though without any personal outrage on the people. Medina was taken in 1804, and the dome over the Prophet's tomb was destroyed. The usual pilgrimages were now suspended, none but those who conformed to Wahhabi views being allowed to approach the holy places.

The Sultan of Turkey was at last roused to vigorous action, and in a succession of campaigns under Mehemet *Defeat by Mehemet Ali and Ibrahim.* Ali and Ibrahim Pasha, lasting from 1811 to 1818, the Wahhabi dominion was practically crushed, and Deraieh, its capital, destroyed. In a short time, however, the Wahhabis showed signs of revival, and Riad in Nejd became its stronghold, and the capital of a kingdom which gradually extended over the greater part of the central desert land of Arabia, although it never regained its supremacy in Oman, Bahrein, and Yemen.

When it appeared destined to extinction, the Wahhabi faith was still taught by some teachers at Mecca; and

# SCENE IN THE MOHARRAM FESTIVAL, BOMBAY.

SCENE IN THE MOHARRAM FESTIVAL, BOMBAY.
A Taboot (model of Hosain's tomb) carried in procession.

Seyyid Ahmed, a freebooter of Bareilly, but a descendant of the Prophet, learning the truth from them, returned from Mecca in 1822, resolved to reclaim Northern India to the true belief of Islam. He was hailed as the true caliph or mahdi, propagated the Wahhabi doctrines widely, started a religious war in 1826 against the Sikhs, but failed after some years' time. But in more recent years Wahhabism has been still more widely spread in India by books, and is now exercising a powerful influence there.

<small>Extension in India.</small>

Some of the doctrines of the Wahhabis, beyond those already mentioned, are: that at the last day Mahomet will obtain permission of God to intercede for His people; that no prostration or perambulation of saints is lawful, not even of Mahomet's at Medina; that women should not visit graves, because of their excessive weeping; that only four festivals should be observed —those of the Sacrifice, of the Breaking of the Fast (after Ramadan), the 10th Moharram, and the Night of Power.

<small>Special doctrines.</small>

No doubt Wahhabism has some strong features; but it is too completely reactionary and puritanical. Its end, if it were successful, would be to spread a Moslem propagandism over the world; and it would refuse to recognise anything not known during the early years of Islam. What injured it more than anything, was its capture and exclusive possession of Mecca and Medina, and the destruction of venerated objects and relics there.

<small>Its defects.</small>

The Druses may be most conveniently mentioned here. They inhabit the mountains of Lebanon and Anti-Lebanon, and the Hauran to the east of the Sea of Galilee, and extend as far north as Beyrout, and east to Damascus. Altogether they number about 70,000, having over 100 towns and villages of their own, and occupy more than twice as many in common with Christians. They appear to have originated from mixed Arab, Kurd, and other—even Indian—tribes, who aggregated there in a spirit of lawlessness and self-defence, beginning as far back as pre-Moslem times.

<small>The Druses.</small>

<small>Origin.</small>

The sixth Fatimite caliph in Egypt, Hakim Biamrillah, who began to reign at Cairo in A.D. 1019, a tyrannical and half-insane ruler, believed that he had direct communication with the Deity, and indeed was an incarnation of the Divine. In 1029 these claims were publicly asserted in Cairo, and supported by his confessor Darazi. The latter had to fly, owing to the popular indignation. He took refuge in Western Hermon, and propagated his belief considerably. A little later, however, Hakim's vizier, Hamza, a Persian mystic, was more successful in elaborating the new doctrine with various additions of his own, and succeeded in getting it widely accepted. Hakim was at last assassinated, in 1032; but it was given out by Hamza that he was only gone for a time, and that his followers were to expect his coming again with confidence. Darazi was termed a heretic by Hamza, and is still hated by the Druses, who probably derive their name from him, while Hamza is revered as the founder of their faith. We cannot detail their subsequent history, which is told in Churchill's "Druses and Maronites," 1862. They have nearly always been at war among themselves, with the Christians, or with the Turks. In modern times they became bitterly hostile to their neighbours the (Christian) Maronites, and the most cruel warfare was carried on for many years between them (1841–1861). It was at last composed on the appointment of a Christian governor independent of the district (1864), since which time disturbances have practically ceased.

*Hakim.*

*Darazi.*

*Hamza.*

*Recent history.*

The Druses are extremely conservative, and do not seek to make converts. Their doctrines include, together with much of the Koran and Sufism, a considerable infusion from the Pentateuch and the Gospels. They believe in one God, without seeking to define His nature or attributes, and call themselves Unitarians. God has, according to them, been at different epochs manifested to mankind in a human form, without weaknesses or imperfections, Ali and Hakim being among these. The latter was the last and final incarnation.

*Their tenets.*

Finally, when the troubles of the faithful have reached their fulness, Hakim will come again and overcome the world, so that the true religion may reign supreme. The first of God's creatures they name Universal Intelligence; he is always manifested together with the Divine Incarnation, and Hamza was the last of such manifestations. He alone has direct communication with God, and imparts his knowledge and gifts to all subordinate ministers. He will be the medium of Hakim's conquests, and will distribute rewards and punishments. The Universal Intelligence is also held to be the creator of every soul. At death souls pass into other bodies, and rise to a superior degree if truly attached to truth, or descend if they have neglected religious meditation.

The seven great duties of the Druses are: (1) Truth in speech (towards one another only), (2) mutual protection, (3) rejection of all other religions, (4) separation from all who are in error, (5) belief in the unity of God, (6) resignation to His will, (7) and obedience to His commands. Prayer is considered to be an impertinent attempt to interfere with God's designs; but the freewill of man is clearly held. The faithful are commanded to keep their doctrines secret from unbelievers, and to this end they are permitted to make outward profession of any religion which prevails around them.

*Seven great duties.*

There is a special class of Druses who alone are admitted into the deeper knowledge of the religion, known as the Akals. This class, constituting 15 per cent. of the whole people, is open to any one after a year's probation and proof that he will strictly keep the laws of the religion. All these abstain from tobacco and wine, and wear no gold or silver or gorgeous clothing. They are often ascetics, wear a distinctive white turban, and show great devotion and purity. Friday being their day of rest, as among the Mahometans, on Thursday evenings the Akals assemble in their plain meeting-houses in retired spots and read their religious books. These meeting-houses have revenues belonging to them, devoted to the poor and to showing hospitality. Their sacred books, which are numerous (in

*The Akals.*

*Meetings.*

# JUMMOO MUSJID, DELHI. 175

JUMMOO MUSJID, DELHI.

manuscript), are marked by a high tone of morality; and there is no proof of the allegations of nefarious practices which the Maronites have brought against them. For hospitality, charity, and fidelity to guests they stand high. Polygamy is forbidden; near relations often marry. Divorce is freely allowed. Those who die in righteousness are buried in their own houses. Numerous manuscripts of the Druses are to be found in European libraries.

A brief review of the distribution of Islam must suffice. The Sultan of Turkey is reputed the only true successor to the caliphs, and bears the title, "Successor of the Prophet." But he is very much under the control of the ulemas, headed by the sheikh-ul-Islam (or grand mufti), whom, however, he nominates as his deputy in the imamate. But he must choose him from among the mollahs or superior ulemas; and from his judgment on matters of law and religion there is no appeal. The conservative and dilatory spirit of the ulemas of Constantinople is one of the great obstacles to Turkish reform. The Turkish official and ruling classes are very largely hypocrites, unbelievers, or formalists; such reality as is found in Turkish Islam is chiefly to be met with in the lower classes. The ordinary Turk of Roumelia or Asia Minor to a large extent really believes and practises his religion. The very general profession of Islam in Arabia, Persia, and Syria will have been gathered from what has gone before. Kurdistan, Turkestan, and Tartary are mainly Mohammedan, as are Afghanistan and Beluchistan. Kerbela, not far from Bagdad, is the most holy place of the Shiites, having the tomb of Hosain, the son of Ali. They believe that whoever lives or dies there will have nothing to fear in the world to come; and many Shiites leave instructions in their wills that they shall be buried there. Besides the numerous caravans bringing dead bodies for burial, Kerbela is visited by many pilgrims.

*Turkey.*

*Kerbela.*

Next to Kerbela the Shiites revere Meshed, the capital of Khorasan, the burial place of the Imam Ali or Riza, the eighth imam. His shrine is annually visited by 100,000 pilgrims, and he is dealt with

*Meshed.*

as if actually living. Kum, between Teheran and Ispahan, is almost equally famous, as the shrine of Fatima, his sister.

The Mohammedans of India are largely found in

THE TAJ MEHAL, AGRA.

Bengal, the North-west Provinces, and the Punjab, and approach 50 millions in number. They have a vast influence, and are among the most zealous adherents of their faith. They have many magnificent mosques and mausoleums, as the Jummoo Musjid, at Delhi

(p. 175), the Taj Mehal at Agra (p. 177), etc., which we figure. Even in Benares, the great centre of Hinduism, there are 330 mosques.

Even in China Mohammedans exist in large numbers, though it is very difficult to estimate them exactly. In some parts of North China, however, they form a third of the population; but they are largely of foreign extraction, Turkish or Persian, and their settlement in China took place chiefly after A.D. 1000. They keep up the exclusiveness of their religion, sometimes marking their houses or signs with the words Hwei-hwei (Mahometan); but they are not unfrequently to be found in the Government service, and in office conform outwardly to the State religion. They read the Koran in Arabic, which is taught in the schools attached to the mosques; but the tenets of their religion are also learned from Chinese works. For their mosques they adopt the Chinese style, with some Western features; and they are ornamented with Arabic and Chinese inscriptions painted on monumental boards. The people are certainly not so attentive to daily prayer as in other countries, and they do not now make the pilgrimage to Mecca. Several million Malays are Mohammedans mostly under Dutch rule.

*China.*

In North Africa Islam shows some of its least inviting aspects, especially in Morocco. Here exclusiveness and antagonism to Christians are most markedly displayed. The Sherifs, or so-called descendants of the Prophet, hold sway and insult others with impunity; and the Marabuts or Saints claim and gain great reverence. In Tunis, the holy city of Kairwan is a noted almost exclusive domain of Islam, and has one of the finest mosques in Northern Africa.

*North Africa.*

In many countries Mohammedanism seems to be decaying, and to have lost all power to elevate the people; in Central Africa it is seen in most vigorous life, and it has succeeded where Christianity, as hitherto presented,—together with smallpox and the gin bottle,—has failed. No unprejudiced person who has compared the descriptions of the Moham-

*Central and Western Africa.*

medan countries of the Soudan and Western Africa with that of pagan negroes, can fail to admit that the former include the most active, intelligent, progressive of the Negro races. This may be partially due to admixture of Semitic, Abyssinian, or other non-negro blood; but this admixture is often slight, and many of the most zealous African Moslems are pure negroes. Who can deny that the fetishism of the Fantis and Ashantis is far lower than the belief in one God, the simple, regular Moslem prayers, the devoutness of mosque worship? or that the abstinence from intoxicants which Islam preaches is preferable in tropical climates to the indulgence of the European, to which he tempts his African brethren? The simplicity of the creed makes it easy of comprehension by the untutored African. In Islam "everything," as Mr. Joseph Thomson says (*Contemporary Review*, vol. 50, p. 883), " is within the range of the negro's comprehension—a very terrible One God, who sits in judgment, and a very real heaven and hell."

From the tenth century onwards Mahometanism has been advancing continuously in Africa, from Egypt and Abyssinia, spreading westward and southward, until now nearly all the large States stretching across the Soudan to the West Coast are under its sway. Many Christian observers testify to the contrast between a Mahometan and a heathen negro State. "The love of noisy terpsichorean performances, so noticeable in pagan communities," says Dr. Blyden, himself a negro Christian of high character and abilities, " disappears as the people come under the influence of Mohammedanism. It is not a fact that 'When the sun goes down, all Africa dances'; but it might be a fact, if it were not for the influence of Islam. Those who would once have sought pleasure in the excitement of the tomtom, now repair five times a day to the mosque, where they spend a quarter of an hour on each occasion in devotional exercises. After the labours of the day they assemble in groups near the mosque to hear the Koran recited, or the Traditions or some other book read." In every State schools have been established, in which the

*Contrast between pagan and Moslem negro.*

usual Moslem education is given; and few villages are now without several men who can read or write Arabic. In some cases they even go for further education to Cairo. The polygamy which Islam sanctions is not attended with the seclusion or veiling of women imposed in other countries, and there are several other respects in which Islam in the Soudan is more tolerant than elsewhere. Still there have been many religious wars in the Soudan; and in Bornu the position of non-converts has been aggravated by their being always liable to be carried away into slavery. Even in Lagos Mahometan schools are to be found, as well as followers of the Prophet who have made the pilgrimage to Mecca.

The influence of the Koran as an educator has been very marked in Africa, especially in unifying, supplying common ground for study and worship, and inspiring a common antagonism to paganism. "Even where the ideas are not fully understood," says Dr. Blyden, "the words seem to possess for them a nameless beauty and music, a subtle and indefinable charm, incomprehensible to those acquainted only with European languages." No translations could replace it, and thus Arabic is now spreading far and wide. Moreover, just as Islam in former times produced many a hero-prophet, so in modern times has it been in Moslem Africa, although Europe has known nothing of it. Among those in the middle of this century may be mentioned the Sheikh Omaru Al-Hajj, a native of Futah Toro, between Timbuctoo and the West Coast. He was a great proselytiser and religious leader, banished paganism from Sego, and elevated and purified the Mahometanism of several Fulah nations. He wrote many Arabic works in prose and poetry; and his poems are recited and sung in many Moslem towns and villages from Sierra Leone as far inland as Kano. And the feeling he had is shared in a degree by all negro Moslems. To propagate Islam is the one object worthy of enthusiasm, whatever sufferings they or their opponents may have to endure. While Christian missions in Africa are an expensive exotic, only to a slight extent perma-

*The Koran unifies and elevates the negro.*

nently impressing the negro nature, the natives of the Soudan keep up mosques, services, schools, etc., and contribute to support the missionaries who come to them from Arabia or elsewhere; and this even in Sierra Leone. Good observers attribute this partly to the fact that Mohammedans do really place the negro convert on a moral level with themselves, give him a career that inspires him with ambition, and practically make him respect himself. Moreover, Islam has done in Africa what it has scarcely done anywhere else, except in China—it has adapted many of its customs to suit the negro. The Arab type has been grafted on the negro, and has not wrecked it. Since the influence of Timbuctoo, which was a replica of Morocco, has given way to that of Kuka and Kano, the negro amalgamation has gone on rapidly, and much stability, as well as power of spreading, has been imparted to African Islam. Perhaps, above all, the Arab constitution has suited the climate of Africa; the Arab has found his way everywhere. His skin has not repelled the negro, nor contrasted too greatly with his. The two races have understood one another far better than the higher European.

Thus, on the whole, we may anticipate a great future for Islam in Africa and in India. Even in other regions, where religion seems sunk in evil, we may yet witness an uprising of moral and spiritual reform which may revivify the popular religion. Christians may and should acknowledge freely the important elements of truth which they hold in common with Mohammedans; yet they cannot shut their eyes to the evils of slavery and fatalism, of polygamy and the subjection of women, which largely prevail throughout Islam, though not so extensively as many imagine.

[*Encyclopædia Britannica*: "Sunnites and Shiites," Prof. A. Müller (M.); Palmer, "Oriental Mysticism"; Lane's "Modern Egyptians;" W. S. Blunt, "The Future of Islam;" J. P. Brown, "The Dervishes;" Lady Anne Blunt, "A Pilgrimage to Nejd;" Eugène Schuyler's "Turkestan;" Edkin's "Religion in China," chap. xv.; Morier, "Second Journey through Persia"; "Christianity, Islam and the Negro Race," E. W. Blyden, LL.D.]

IDEAL ASSEMBLAGE OF THE GODS ON MOUNT OLYMPUS.

## CHAPTER VIII.

### The Ancient Greek Religion: The Gods.

Long study of classics—Nature- and ancestor- worship—Early simplicity—Local gods—Foreign influences—Succession of gods—Kronos—Personification of nature—Growth of myths—Early cosmogony—Local, tribal, or civic gods—Zeus—Hera—Pallas-Athēnē—Themis — Apollo —Delphi—Aphroditē—Dēmētēr—Hephaistos—Hestia—Arēs — Hermēs —Dionysos—Poseidon— Hadēs, or Pluto—Minor divinities—Characters of gods.

WHEN we come to the Aryan religions of Europe, we enter at first upon a domain which has been more thoroughly traversed and discussed than any we have previously described. For hundreds of years classical students have been engaged in making out the meaning of the Greek and Latin authors, and reconstructing and explaining their systems, histories, and philoso- Long study phies. It cannot be said that either Greece or of classics. Rome possessed Scriptures like the Vedas, though the Homeric hymns, the works of Hesiod, and various lost writings approached to this character; and there certainly is no special set of sacred books to which the Greeks and Romans appealed as of divine authority. Both on account of the literature being well known and accessible, and on account of its great bulk, we shall not here attempt anything like a full treatment of this subject, but shall rather seek to indicate the main ideas, and very briefly describe the personages of the Greek and Roman deities and the beliefs generally associated with them.

# THE ANCIENT GREEK RELIGION.

In Greek and Roman, as in Indian, religion we find a combination of nature-personification, nature-worship,

KRONOS.

**Nature- and ancestor-worship.** with that of deified heroes and ancestors. The original Pelasgians appear to have had no temples, and to have worshipped principally upon the tops of mountains. When they attained the conception of a supreme deity cannot be ascertained; but the earliest aspect of the Zeus, or supreme God, is that of the heaven, earth, or sky, just like Dyaus of the Veda. They also worshipped the same god under the title Father Zeus, Zeus pater (later developed into the Latin Diespiter and Jupiter). **Early simplicity.** This conception was retained, together with an open-air altar, long after the Greek cities were crowded with images and temples. St. Paul detected a relic of the old religion at Athens in the altar to "the unknown god," and it was no uncommon thing to see in Greece altars to the "pure," "great," and "merciful" gods unnamed, inspired by an old feeling which neither named nor represented the gods in word or by symbol.

As the primitive Pelasgians branched and migrated, they imagined new local gods or phases of divine beings, **Local gods.** possibly learning about them from people whom they conquered or enslaved. Later they mingled with the Phœnician voyagers, and saw their images of

HEPHAISTOS.

Astarte and Melcar, which latter they changed to Melicertes, and adapted to their own ideas. The Greeks who colonised the coasts of Asia Minor found plenty of material already there for the development of local or patron deities; some they adopted directly, to others they gave the attributes of their own national heroes.

*Foreign influences.*

HADES (PLUTO).

Whether it marks a series of changes of divinities or not, we find that the great god Zeus rests on a past history, traced by the poet Hesiod from Chaos, after whom arose Gaia, the earth, with Tartarus, the infernal region, below. Gaia was the parent of Ouranos, the Heaven; and from their intermarriage arose the twelve Titans, the Cyclopes and three hundred-handed beings. Ouranos was not at all satisfied to see his offspring, including Oceanus, Hyperion, Kronos (The Creator), Themis (Law), etc., multiplying, and concealed them in cavities of the earth. Finally, Kronos disabled and dethroned Ouranos, whose last offspring, Aphrodite, rose from the sea-foam opposite the island Kythera, and thence went to Cyprus; in both of which islands her worship was probably derived from that of the Phœnician Astarte. Each Titan was credited with a numerous offspring; very remarkable is the facility with which gods were multiplied by the Greeks. The children of Kronos,

*Succession of gods.*

APOLLO.

*Kronos.*

however, became most powerful, and included Hestia (Vesta), Dēmētēr, and Hērē (Juno), Hades uto, Poseidon, and Zeus, the latter destined to supplant his father. But Kronos, foreseeing destruction by one of his children, had swallowed the first five, and retained them still alive within himself. The birth of Zeus was concealed from him, a stone enveloped in swaddling clothes being substituted, and duly swallowed. Later, Zeus made his father eject the stone and the children; the stone being preserved and venerated near the temple of Delphi. And this is but a sample of an extraordinary number of myths which the Greeks related and believed about their gods.

What the sentiments properly termed religious had to do with the growth of Greek polytheism it is difficult to determine. The oldest names of the gods describe the elementary facts of nature. It probably can never be settled how far the old Greeks consciously personified the facts and forces of nature, and how far early modes of expression, not at all fictitious in intention, came to signify personal beings, which gradually became dissociated from the natural facts they represented. Early human beings, seeing the heavenly bodies, lightning, rain, trees, etc., probably imagined them to have life and consciousness like themselves, and saw in the rising, the course, and the setting of the sun facts in the history of the sun-being, which those who had fancy interpreted in their own fashion. Many myths undoubtedly sprang up in the attempt to explain part of the ritual. By the effect of natural selection, those beliefs which gave most pleasure, satisfied the instinct for the marvellous, or best appealed to feelings already in existence, persisted, and were firmly believed in, even after higher thoughts had been awakened. Some of these legends are very gross, and can only have persisted because religion is alway conservative. Then the imaginative minds set to work to give fuller and more artistic representations, to fill in details, to supply explanations of what seemed incongruous in the older myths; and often an old epithet of one being would give rise to a totally

*Personification of nature.*

new one, and to a secondary story or myth. And there can be little doubt that the sun supplied the source for many of these myths. As Sir G. W. Cox says: **Growth of myths.** "In the thought of these early ages the sun was the child of night or darkness; the dawn came before he was born, and died as he rose in the heavens. He strangled the serpents of the night; he went forth like a bridegroom out of his chamber, and like a giant to run his course. He had to do battle with clouds and storms. . . . Sometimes he was the lord of heaven and of light, irresistible in his divine strength; sometimes he toiled for others, not for himself, in a hard, unwilling servitude. His light and heat might give life, or destroy it. His chariot might scorch the regions over which it passed. . . . He would have many brides in many lands; and his offspring would assume aspects beautiful, strange, or horrible. His course might be brilliant and beneficent, or gloomy, sullen, and capricious." Thus we may see how it is to the creative and imaginative men among the early Greeks that we owe the growth of that marvellous mass of myth which is involved in their entire history. From the idea of the sun looking down on the earth, and producing a teeming harvest or countless progeny, the transition is easy to the sun-god marrying the earth-goddess, and becoming by her the parent of a vast family of beings; and by a further literalising of language, we have Zeus depicted as inspired by passions and lusts, having many wives, or assuming many forms to woo reluctant brides. And the deceased heroes of the race, no longer seen by their relatives, are imagined as becoming acquainted with the heavenly beings, being advanced by them to positions of honour, and finally, it may be, are identified with personalities, of whom it may be represented that they were mere temporary earthly embodiments.

We may pause here to refer to the cosmogony or history of the world as represented in the early Greek poems. The Hebrew belief that God formed man out of the dust of the earth is parallel with the **Early cosmogony.** Greek belief that man originated from the earth, untamed like the beasts, and was only gradually civilised by the gods and heroes who taught him useful arts, agriculture, house-building, etc. A tradition as old, or older, makes men the children of trees. Then came a period of degeneracy, and all the world was destroyed by a flood, from which only Deucalion and his wife Pyrrha were saved, in consequence of their piety, in an ark, in which they floated for nine days and nights, till it rested on the summits of Parnassus. From the bones (*i.e.*, stones) of their mother earth, cast over their shoulders, sprang men and women. It was by a displacement of this view that men came to be regarded as made by the gods, and as having passed through successive periods known as the Golden, the Silver, the Brazen, and the Iron Ages. The first age (when Kronos or Saturn was supreme) was one of unmixed bliss, all things growing freely; men were pure, happy, and long-lived, did no evil, and had no wars. In the Silver Age, when Zeus came into power, men were feebler and shorter-lived, fought with one another, and were not properly reverent to the gods. Consequently, they were banished to Hades, where they wandered restlessly, regretting their lost pleasures. The men of the Brazen Age were a new strong race, cruel and warlike, using brazen (or rather, bronze) tools and arms. The gods at length sent them also to Hades, and they were followed by the men of the Iron Age, who had to toil hard to gain food, and who also became sinful. These then were all drowned but Deuclion and Pyrrha, who became the father of Hellen, from whom the Hellenic people derived their origin. But this was by no means the only cosmogony of the Greeks, for which we must refer to separate works. In fact, every tribe or town may be said to have had a share in a cosmogony, at least, so far as concerned their own locality. As Mr. Grote says, "Every association of men traced back their union to some common progenitor, either their common

**Local, tribal, or civic gods.** god or some semi-divine person closely allied to him. A series of names of ancestors, with adventures ascribed to them, constituted for the Greeks their pre-historic past connected with the gods.

The names in this genealogy were largely their own names, or those of local objects, rivers, mountains, etc., embodied as persons, and introduced as acting or suffering. The personage from whom the community derived

HEAD OF ZEUS (FROM OTRICOLI).

their name was sometimes the son of the local god, or sometimes a man sprung from the earth, thought of as a goddess." We must now refer to the principal gods and their characteristics as accepted in the greatest period of Greece; but we have not space to describe even such a great hero-god as Herakles (Hercules), whose labours and significance as the patron god of the Dorians are well known, or Theseus, the patron god of Athens.

Zeus was the ruler of earth and heaven, the god producing storms, darkness, and rain; he controlled the phenomena of nature and the recurrence of seasons; kingly power was derived from him, and he upheld princes and rulers, and all the institutions of the State. As father of men, he watched over them, rewarding good deeds, such as charity, truth, and integrity; while he punished cruelty, false swearing, and want of hospitality. Zeus also, as father of the gods, saw that each of the gods performed his duty, settled their quarrels, and punished their defaults. His special home was on the cloud-capped top of Mount Olympus, in a palace of gold, silver, and ivory, built by Hephaistos (Vulcan), who had also built palaces for the other gods lower down.

*Zeus.*

In Greek art Zeus was represented as a man of noble appearance, serious and benign, with high forehead, thick hair, and flowing beard. An eagle, a bundle of thunderbolts, lightning, and a wreath of oak-leaves are his accompanying symbols. At one of the earliest places where he was worshipped,—Dodona, in Epirus,—he was chiefly adored as the sender of water or rain. There his voice was believed to be heard in the rustlings of an oak, interpreted by his priests. The worship at Dodona became inferior to that at Olympia, in Elis, where there was a magnificent statue of Zeus of ivory and gold, forty feet high, counted as one of the seven wonders. The appropriate sacrifices to Zeus were white bulls, cows, and goats.

Zeus appears as a polygamist, seven of his wives being immortals. His first wife, Metis (representing prudence and wisdom), was devoured by him in the belief that her offspring would depose him. After this he himself gave birth to Athēnē, his head being cloven for that purpose by Hephaistos. His remaining goddess wives were Themis (goddess of Justice), Eurynomē, Dēmētēr, Mnemosynē (goddess of Memory and mother of the nine Muses),

Leto, mother of Apollo and Artemis (Diana), and Hera (Juno) whose position became highest, so that she was regarded as queen of heaven.

THE FARNESE HERA.

Zeus was not only allied to numerous goddesses, but he visited mortal women under various disguises; Antiope, Leda, Europa, Kallisto, Alkmene, Semele, Io, and Danae are among these; and the children of Leda (Castor and

Pollux), Europa (Minos, Rhadamanthus), Alkmene (Herakles or Hercules), are world-famed types of heroes. No doubt the fables of Zeus becoming the father of earthly kings and heroes represent part of the process of their deification, so that much of the Greek mythology is resolvable into ancestor-worship.

**Hera.** Hera was generally regarded as the one truly married wife of Zeus (also his sister), and so became the protectress of married women. She was also figured as specially faithful to her husband, and thence was the representative of wifely virtue and the sanctity of the marriage bond. Jealous of any immor-

HERA AND IRIS.

ality, she was a strict censor of the misdoings of gods and men; and she is represented as vain of her beauty and jealous of any indignity. She became the mother of Ares (Mars), Hephaistos, and Hēbē, and was the special guardian of the Greek people. She is figured seated on a throne, with a sceptre in one hand and a pomegranate in the other, as a calm, beautiful, dignified matron, wearing a tunic and mantle. Her principal temples were at Argos and Samos; and on the first day of each month a ewe lamb and a sow were sacrificed to her.

## Pallas-Athene.

Pallas-Athēnē, whom we have already described as issuing from Zeus's head, was born fully armed, and she is the goddess of wisdom, protecting the State, law and order, the patroness of learning, science, art, and all arts and inventions. She is the type of chastity and purity. An ægis or shield was given to her by Zeus, which she whirled swiftly round her; in its centre was the awful Medusa's head, which changed all who looked at it into stone. Athēnē, among other arts, presided especially over spinning and weaving, in which she excelled. In statues, etc., she appears as a fully clad woman, serious, thoughtful, and earnest, with beautiful oval face and abundant hair, somewhat masculine on the whole.

PALLAS-ATHENE.

194 THE ANCIENT GREEK RELIGION.

As a war goddess in defence of the Greeks, of cities, and of innocent victims, she wears a helmet with a large plume, a golden staff, and her famous shield. While very

THE BELVEDERE APOLLO.

generally worshipped throughout Greece, she was specially the goddess of the Athenians, who built the great temple of the Parthenon to the virgin goddess, whose great statue by Phidias was enshrined there. The olive-tree was specially sacred to Athēnē, and rams, bulls, and cows were offered to her. The great Panathenaic festival was held in her honour.

Themis, the goddess of law and justice, presided over popular assemblies and guarded the rights of hospitality; even Zeus is represented as taking counsel with her. Her statues represent her with the scales of justice in her right hand, indicating her impartiality, which is further secured by her eyes being bandaged, so that no individual influence or prejudice should influence her. The sword in her right hand indicates the majesty and sovereignty of the law.  *Themis.*

Together with Zeus and Athēnē, Apollo may be named as constituting the greatest triad of the Greek gods; and in many ways Apollo, though described as a son of Zeus and deriving his power from him, is the god whose character and worship had the greatest influence upon the Greeks. There is no doubt that among the later Greek poets and philosophers Apollo was identified with Helios, the sun-god, although in Homer and for some centuries afterwards the two are quite distinct; but the epithet Phœbus, the shining one, is even in Homer applied to Apollo. It has been strongly held by some that Apollo was originally the sun-god, and that it was a process of development which made Helios a subordinate deity. We must not attempt to decide whence his worship was brought to Greece, whether from Egypt, the East, or the Hyperboreans; in fact, if sun-worship is a natural product, there is no necessity to regard it anywhere as imported. The settled tradition was, that he was born of Leto in the island of Delos, though several other places claimed his birth. Not long after his birth he suddenly appeared as a full-grown youth of divine strength and beauty, demanded a lyre and a bow, and announced that he would thenceforth make known to mortals the will of Zeus; whereupon he at once ascended to Olympus.  *Apollo.*

Apollo is described as the punisher and destroyer of

the wicked and insolent, as the god of medicine and warder-off of plagues and epidemics (father of Asclepios, the god of the healing art), as the god of prophecy, song, and music, as the protector of flocks and herds, and the founder of cities and leader of colonists, no colony being founded without consulting his oracle. Many of these characteristics are explicable in reference either to the sun as the great light of the earth, or to the heavenly illumination given to the spirit of man. We can see how, like the fierce sun of summer, he could be a bringer of pestilence and death, or like the genial orb he could give pasture to preserve the flocks. The rising sun awaking nature to life and rousing the birds to sing, gave foundation to Apollo's being the god of music, and hence of poetry. Prophecy was his, for nothing escaped his all-seeing eye. Not long after his ascent to Olympus, he again came back to earth and travelled through many countries, seeking a place in which to establish his oracle. It was fixed at Delphi, after he had destroyed the dragon Python (whence the epithet Pythian Apollo); but this was not his only oracle, though by far the most famous one. It actually became the national Greek oracle, which was even consulted by foreigners, Romans, Lydians, and others; and no Greek would undertake an important enterprise without consulting the oracle, whose priestess, as interpreted by the priests, gave utterances of world-famed dubiousness. No doubt the highest aspect of Apollo was that in which he appears as the pardoner of sin after repentance and the protector of those who expiated their crimes by long years of suffering. No evil deed escaped him, and hence expiatory offerings were often made to him.

The extraordinary abundance and often beautifully idyllic character of myths and stories about Apollo show how his nature had become part of the Greek mind and spirit. In sculpture and in the poets he is represented as gifted with eternal youth, joyous, and perfectly beautiful. His deep blue eyes, somewhat low but broad forehead, golden or bright chestnut hair falling in wavy locks, well suited this ideal. Laurel-crowned, wearing a purple robe, and carrying a silver bow, he looks the perfection of manly beauty. The celebrated Apollo in the Belvedere of the Vatican is a naked statue seven feet high, copied from one at Delphi. Among the appropriate surroundings or implements of Apollo are the bow and

ARTEMIS.

quiver, the lyre and plectrum, the raven, the shepherd's crook, the tripod, and the laurel. Wolves and hawks were sacrificed to him.

The Delphian temple was one of the most famous and magnificent of all Greek temples; its foundation dated

**Delphi.** before historic record, and it was for centuries the recipient of vast offerings from kings, States, and private persons who sought its counsel. The Pythian games were held at Delphi every fourth year, in honour of his victory over the Python; and two annual festivals celebrated the god's supposed departure at the beginning of winter to the Hyperborean region, and his return at the beginning of summer. Athens, Sparta, Delos, Thebes, etc., all had their distinctive festivals for Apollo.

In many ways the idea of Apollo represents an elevated aspect of Greek religion, having so much distinct moral teaching; for Apollo could only be rightly approached by those of pure heart who had duly examined themselves, and who practised self-control, though without any austerity. It is held that the Delphian oracle maintained a really high standard of moral and political conduct for several hundred years. Apollo is certainly one of the highest ideals of the Greek mind.

**Artemis.** Artemis is the twin and correlative of Apollo, the goddess of night and of the moon, of hunting and of chastity. In several of her functions she resembles Apollo, as in her relieving the sufferings of mortals, and her power of sending plagues and destruction. She devotes herself passionately to the chase, and always carries a bow and quiver and is attended by huntress-nymphs. Under this form she is especially termed the Arcadian Artemis, her temples being more numerous in Arcadia than in other parts of Greece. She especially protected the young, both children and animals. All her priests and priestesses were required to live chaste lives.

Artemis is represented as a head taller than her nymphs, slender and youthful, beautiful in feature but not gentle in expression, her figure graceful but somewhat masculine. Her hair is loosely knotted at the back of her head, and her short robe, not reaching to the knees, gives her abundant freedom for hunting. Of the many existing statues of Artemis, the most famous is in the Louvre, in which she is depicted rescuing a hunted deer from its pursuers. The bow, quiver, and spear belong to her equipment;

and the hind, dog, and wild boar are specially sacred to her. In Thrace dogs were sacrificed to Artemis.

Another form of Artemis was named the Tauric or Brauronian, from the statue of her at Brauron, in Attica, said to have been brought by Orestes from Taurica (the Crimea), where human sacrifices, especially of strangers, were offered to her. This is probably connected with bear-worship. The little Athenian girls imitated bears in her honour. These sacrifices, whatever their origin, were kept up both in Attica and Sparta till the days of Lycurgus. Afterwards at Sparta boys were cruelly scourged at her altar. Stags and goats were sacrificed to her.

The Ephesian Artemis was very distinct, being in fact identical with the old Chaldæan divinity Mitra (or Anaitis), the goddess at once of love and of the light of heaven. It was owing to this latter character that the Asiatic Greeks adapted this deity to the name of Artemis; but she retained her other character, also exercising sway in the land of Hades and permitting departed spirits to visit this world sometimes for counsel or for warning. Contrary to any Greek custom, her priests were eunuchs, and she was represented with many breasts. Her magnificent temple at Ephesus, often termed that of Diana (see Acts xix.), was one of the seven wonders of the world, being 425 feet long by 220 wide, having 127 columns, each 60 feet high, a great ebony statue of the goddess with a crown of turrets on the head, the body pillar-like and sculptured with rows of animals, and countless other rich treasures, statues, and paintings. It was destroyed by fire in 356 B.C. by Herostratus; but afterwards rebuilt, burnt by the Goths in 262 A.D., and utterly destroyed by the end of the fourth century.

The moon-goddess Sēlēnē became identified with Artemis. Hecate was a moon-goddess of the Thracians, at one time identified with Sēlēnē, at another with Persephone (see later).

There is abundant evidence that the worship of Aphroditē was originally derived from that of the Phœnician Astarte. But she became thoroughly Hellenised, and in

# THE ANCIENT GREEK RELIGION.

APHRODITE (MELOS).
(Commonly termed the Venus of Milo.)

**Aphroditē.** Homer takes a natural place as daughter of Zeus and Dionē, a sea-nymph; while we have already referred to Hesiod's account of her origin from Ouranos, her rising from the sea-foam, and her landing at Cyprus. In the popular creed of the Greeks, Aphroditē represented love, excited it in human beings, and by her special power ruled all creatures. In the Greek mind love and beauty were associated; and thus Aphroditē is perfectly beautiful and the goddess of beauty, which she could grant to her votaries. She was married to Hephaistos (Vulcan), but was unfaithful with Arēs (Mars) and others; these traditions representing the gradual decay of

## APHRODITE.

Greek morals, which at last made Aphroditē the patroness of courtesans. Her magic girdle was held capable of inspiring love for any one who wore it. Her principal festivals were held in spring, among flowers and sweet scents; some of them were undoubtedly of a licentious character. Eros (Cupid) is generally represented as her son and chief companion.

Aphroditē is variously represented in ancient art as clothed, half clothed, or nude, as bathing, or as armed (the latter at Cythera, Corinth, and Sparta). In every respect she is depicted as possessing the most perfect beauty of form and expression. The finest existing

BACCHUS.

DĒMĒTĒR.

statues of her are those of Melos (Milo), in the Louvre, of Capua, at Naples, and of the Medici, at Florence. The principal sacrifices made to Aphroditē were incense and garlands of flowers; but sometimes various animals were offered. The dove, swan, swallow, and sparrow were sacred to her.

Dēmētēr is another great goddess, intimately associated with the natural operations of agriculture, sowing and reaping. In this way she was associated with subterranean working; and many stories about her relate to the periodic death and quietude of nature

Dēmētēr.

and the recurring spring-time and harvest. She was the daughter of Kronos and Rhea, and became one of the wives of Zeus, to whom she bore Persephonē and Dionysos. The great myth about Dēmētēr and Persephonē relates to the carrying off of the latter to the subterranean regions by Pluto, to whom Zeus had promised her. Dēmētēr travelled far to seek her, but on finding out the truth abandoned Olympus and came to dwell among men, blessing those who received her kindly, and punishing those who repelled her. At last, however, unable to recover her daughter, she produced a famine on earth. Zeus, failing otherwise to reclaim her to Olympus, or restore fertility to the earth, sent Hermes to fetch back Persephonē, and arranged that she should spend only a part of the year (namely the winter) in the subterranean regions. Thus Dēmētēr was conciliated. We may see in this story a representation of the concealment or dormancy of the reproductive powers of the earth during the winter season. Some of the later Greek philosophers interpreted the disappearance and return of Persephonē as referring to the burial and resurrection of man. She was looked upon not only as a goddess of agricultural fertility, but also of marriage, and as a lawgiver and friend of peace. She was worshipped in Crete, Delos, Attica, and especially in Sicily. The worship was carried out by secret rites at the Eleusinian mysteries every five years, of which nothing certain is known, except that they were conducted by torchlight and with great solemnity.

Dēmētēr is depicted as of noble stature and bearing and matronly appearance; her hair was golden-yellow falling in curling locks. Sometimes she is represented sitting in a chariot drawn by winged horses; sometimes she is standing, with a sheaf or a bunch of poppies in one hand and a lighted torch in the other. She is always fully clad, and wears a garland of ears of corn or a simple riband round her hair. The appropriate offerings to her were figs, pine, fruits, etc. Her temples, known as Megara, were often in groves near towns.

Hephaistos (Vulcan), son of Zeus and Hera, was the

god of fire, as a natural phenomenon and as useful in the arts. He was fabled to possess a workshop with an anvil and twenty pairs of bellows in Olympus; there he made arms, utensils, etc., of marvellous workmanship; yet in the court of the gods he was the object of laughter, being lame, deformed, and slow. Various volcanic islands were also termed his workshops. He gave skill to human artists, and taught them to make their tools and other products. He was also reputed, like Athēnē, to have great healing powers. He was depicted as a man of powerful muscular frame, bearded, and wearing a small cap, his right arm raised to strike the anvil with a hammer, while with the left he is turning a thunderbolt which he is forging for Jove. In several temples he was jointly worshipped with Athēnē. He was specially worshipped at Lemnos.

*Hephaistos.*

Hestia (Vesta) was a goddess of fire, being a daughter of Kronos and Rhea, and especially the patroness of the domestic hearth and home life. Her worship became distinct from that of Zeus rather

*Hestia.*

HESTIA.

late; she is not mentioned in Homer. As represented at the house and temple altar fire, she shares in the

ARES (MARS).

sacrifices of all the gods. To her the first and last libations of the sacrificial meal were poured out. Her fire was always kept burning, or if extinguished it was again kindled by friction or from the sun's rays. As the goddess of the hearth, she also became the goddess of housebuilding; she was worshipped, not in special temples, but in the prytaneum or city hall, the city hearth, so to

HEAD OF THE BELVEDERE APOLLO.

speak; there the city entertained its benefactors, and thence colonists took a portion of the fire to their new abode.

Arēs, the god of war, son of Zeus and Hera, is represented as rejoicing in the actual business of war, its

tumult and carnage, wild and destructive and bloodthirsty.
**Ares.** His worship flourished in Thrace, and is reputed to have reached Greece from the north. He does not fight always on the same side, nor is he

HERMES.

uniformly victorious. He is represented as youthful, athletic, and muscular, carrying a great sword, with a shield. He had comparatively few temples; but it is related that human sacrifices were offered to him at Sparta.

Hermēs (Mercury), the messenger and herald of the gods, was the son of Zeus and Maia, one of the Pleiades; but there are traces of his being modified from an early Pelasgian nature divinity, the god of festivity, and bestower of flocks and herds. As messenger of the gods, he is the ideal skilful and eloquent speaker; and hence the tongues of sacrificed animals were offered to him. He was prudent and cunning, sagacious and shrewd, the promoter of social intercourse, and the reputed inventor of the alphabet, numbers, astronomy, weights and measures, etc. He was charioteer and cup-bearer to Zeus, the imparter of dreams to men, the giver of sleep, the conductor of the spirits of the dead to the lower world, the maker of treaties, the helper of commerce, the god of words, and protector of travellers. He watched over the rearing of children, and encouraged gymnastic exercises; as the giver of gain, he was regarded as the author of any stroke of good luck, and as presiding over the dice-box. He was said to have performed many acts of mischief and dexterity and even to be the god of thieves.

<small>Hermēs.</small>

Hermēs is represented in art as young and handsome, without beard, often in the attitude of running. He may wear a travelling hat with little wings, a herald's staff (caduceus) with entwined serpents, and wings at the top, and golden sandals. He was worshipped anciently in Arcadia, whence his worship spread to Athens and throughout Greece. Little images of him, known as Hermæ (being busts upon pillars of stone), were set up at cross roads and in streets, and apparently before the door of each house. Lambs and kids were among his special offerings, with incense, honey, and cakes. The palm-tree and the tortoise were sacred to him.

Dionysos, the god of wine, son of Zeus and Semele (called Bacchus in late Greek and Roman times), was related to have accidentally discovered the making of wine from the juice of the grape. The exhilaration produced by drinking it caused both Dionysos and his companions to burst into song, joyful exclamations, and dancing. The god extended the gift

<small>Dionysos, or Bacchus.</small>

to all mankind, that they might have more enjoyment, and forget care and sorrow. Consequently he journeyed through the world, planting the vine and instructing people how to make wine. Lycurgus, king of Thrace, disapproved of his wild revels, and banished him from his kingdom. Midas, king of Phrygia, was one of his most noted worshippers. The stories about Dionysos are extremely numerous, and many give accounts of the riotous exploits of his followers. But other accounts of him elevate his character. From being associated with the vine, he becomes the protector of trees in general; the wine-giver is an inspired being and a source of inspiration, and reveals the future by oracles; at the same time he heals diseases by revealing remedies in dreams. Thus he is accounted a promoter of peace and the well-being of States. His worship probably had a Phœnician origin. Later he was regarded as the patron of the drama.

Bacchus is represented in early times as a grave manly figure, bearded and robed like an oriental monarch; but later he appears as a beautiful but effeminate youth, his long curling hair adorned with vine or ivy leaves, his expression pleased and gentle. He carries in one hand a drinking-cup with two handles, in the other a thyrsus, or pole terminated with vine-leaves, a fir-cone, or other ornament. Humansacrifices are said to have been offered to him in early times; later, rams and goats were offered. Tigers, panthers, and dolphins were among his sacred animals. His attendant women are usually known as Bacchantes, and they are generally represented in violent enthusiasm or madness, with dishevelled hair.

Poseidon (Neptune), son of Kronos and Rhea, was the god of the sea, especially of the Mediterranean, and took the place of the older Oceanus. His most distinctive attribute was that of causing and quieting storms; and hence mariners poured out a libation to him before beginning a voyage, and made offerings on their safe return. He is represented as riding in a chariot drawn by sea-horses, at whose approach the waves became smooth. Hence he is greatly famed as the creator

**Poseidon.**

and tamer of horses, and the originator of horse races. He was the patron of fishermen, and had the power of sending great inundations and horrible sea-monsters on States which displeased him.

Poseidon is depicted in varying forms, a good deal resembling Zeus, without benignity, the hair usually disorderly, the figure massive, the eyes bright. His special symbol was the trident, a three-pointed fork with which he could stir up or allay storms and shake the earth. As signifying the contest between sea and land, he is fabled to have disputed the possession of several countries with other gods. He was accompanied by a crowd of minor divinities and attendants, including his wife Amphitritē, the Tritons, Nereids, dolphins, etc. He was specially worshipped in Peloponnesus and the coast towns of Greece. Black and white bulls were his appropriate sacrifices. We can only briefly refer to his wonderful palace beneath the waters, of which marvellous descriptions were given.

Hades, or Pluto, son of Kronos and Rhea, and monarch of the land of shades, is connected with a very important part of our study, the question of the future life: we shall therefore postpone details about his kingdom, merely noting that it was inhabited not only by the shades or spirits of deceased mortals, but also by dethroned deities. The name of this god was habitually left unmentioned; and those who invoked him struck the earth with their hands, and averted their faces when they sacrificed. According to Homer, he was the most detested of all the gods. He is depicted as very much like Zeus in feature, but stern and gloomy looking, his hair and beard being black. His wife Persephonē is seated beside him, and he holds a staff with which he drives the shades into the lower world. He was worshipped, though with fear, throughout Greece; and his sacrifices, consisting of black sheep, whose blood was allowed to run into a trench, were offered at night. Even his priests wore black robes. At a comparatively late period Pluto, as god of the lower world, was regarded as giver of all things dug out of the earth, and hence of the precious metals; so he became confounded with Plutus (wealth), originally quite a distinct divinity.

We have not space to describe a crowd of minor divinities, many of them important in the Greek way of looking at things, and connected with distinctive circumstances or events pertaining to human life. Such are the Fates, the Furies, the Gorgons, the Nereids, the Sirens, Nemesis, Thanatos (Death), Hebe, the Muses, the Graces, etc.

*Minor divinities.*

In the Greek religion, the gods are very generally represented with human characteristics, though usually heightened and ennobled; they required food and sleep, and married and had children. In passions they were like men, and frequently committed the same evil deeds as men. They are represented as punishing evil-doers, although in most cases the heaviest punishment is for neglecting to worship them. Their visits to and friendships for human beings are frequent; and the children of gods and mortals were heroes or demi-gods. If we invert this process, it will be seen that many gods have been imagined as a mode of accounting for the courage or prowess of real heroes. Of course, in addition to mortal powers, the Greek gods were gifted with all kinds of supernatural faculties, and many of these represent natural phenomena. In fact, while acknowledging that many attributes and achievements of deities are derived from those of heroes, and that some gods are deified heroes, we must admit that a great number of individual gods and of their attributes represent departments of nature and nature's workings, as idealised by the most imaginative and highly cultured people that ever lived.

*Characters of gods.*

[Sir G. W. Cox, "Mythology of the Aryan Nations"; Grote, Curtius, and Duncker's Histories of Greece; Berens, "Myths and Legends of Greece and Rome"; A. Lang, "Myth, Ritual, and Religion."]

## CHAPTER IX.

## Greek Sacrifices, Priests, Temples and Festivals, and Morals.

Sacrifice—Votive offerings—Kinds of sacrifices—Description—Slight consciousness of sin—The priests—State aspect of religion—Duties of priests—Their position—Private temples—A Greek festival—Wealth of temples—Early temples—The Greek styles—Sculpture—Altars—Oracles—The Delphian Oracle—Various beliefs—The great festivals—Religious origin and purpose—Rise of the drama—Marriage—Death and the future life—Funeral rites—Moral state of the Greeks.

IN presenting a picture of Greek religion, we are in the presence of difficulties of a kind more liable to mislead than in the case of any other people. Worship and ideas about the gods not only changed considerably from one age to another, but they varied largely from place to place, from State to State at the same time, no doubt in dependence upon the original ideas about local deities, but also in accordance with the great fertility of the Greek mind. Thus it would be impossible, without more space than we can give, to present a clear idea of the religious observances of any one State or city. Therefore what we say must be understood to be generalised to a considerable extent, and perhaps inapplicable to special localities.

**Sacrifice.** Inasmuch as sacrifice is the essential element of religious acts in such a religion as the Greek, we will begin the account of the practical side of it with this subject. The Greek, as far back as we know anything about him, offered gifts to his gods, in gratitude for their protection, to obtain their favour, either generally or in some particular instance, or to expiate some offence or appease the anger of the gods. The gratitude of individuals and of States led to the building of temples, the donation of statues, the offering of garlands, locks of hair, costly garments, vases, cups, candelabras, pictures, arms, etc. After successful wars a tenth part of the spoil **Votive offerings.** was often dedicated to the gods. On recovery from illness votive tablets and presents were given to temples of Asclepios. Persons who had escaped from shipwreck dedicated to Poseidon the dress which they had worn when in danger; and many other presents of gratitude for escape or for prosperity are recorded in Greek authors, showing that the Greek religion was real, and founded not merely on fear, but also on a sense of humble dependence on Divine protection and on the acknowledgment of gratitude for benefits received. Frequently the finest of flocks and herds or the firstfruits of agricultural produce were thus offered.

No doubt the early Greek gods, like dead human beings, were conceived as needing food, or capable of deriving **Kinds of sacrifices.** pleasure from it; and early sacrifices consisted largely of grains, either cooked or uncooked, and fruits; though with the increase of flocks these gained a predominant place among the offerings. The gods of the seas, rivers, etc., were fed by offerings thrown into the water, and the offerings to gods of the subterranean regions were buried. Ordinarily, when the deity is looked upon as benign, the meal offered is one which the god and his worshippers can share at the same time; and often ordinary meals were sanctified by invoking the gods to be present. Even in St. Paul's day most of the meat sold for ordinary food had been dedicated to the gods, small parts having been specially assigned to the god. It was an appropriate accompaniment of sacrifice to drink wine, part of which was poured on the altar or on the ground for the gods (compare the Soma and Haoma offerings of the Hindus and Parsis), to listen to music, or to dance. The entire sacrifice, by burning, of the animal offered was rare, though it is difficult to ascertain how extensively it once prevailed. We cannot here discuss the relation of special animal sacrifices to the totem system and totem worship by clans; but there can be little doubt that many special features of the early Greek sacrifices are due to it. The Greek religion, as accepted nationally, represents the combination of the beliefs of many diverse tribes, maritime, mountainous, pastoral, agricultural; and the discordant or strange features sometimes seen in the characters and sacrifices appropriate to the several gods are attributable to this combination.

In Homer we find that the legs were burnt, enclosed in fat, together with part of the intestines, and the worshippers consumed the rest. The smoke from the burning victims was believed to be peculiarly pleasing to the gods, and the greater the number of animals sacrificed the more meritorious was it. Hence States and wealthy individuals would frequently sacrifice "hecatombs" (not necessarily meaning a hundred victims); and such sacrifices were much in vogue at Athens. The head of a victim was usually sprinkled with roasted barley-meal mingled with salt, and adorned with garlands; a portion of hair from its head was thrown into the fire before it was killed. The head of the animal was drawn upwards when the offering was to one of the Olympian gods, and downwards if to the gods of the lower regions, or to deceased heroes. While the flesh was burning, wine and incense were cast upon it. At the time of sacrificing opportunity was taken to judge whether the god was propitious, for, if not, he would certainly give signs recognisable by the priests; these being derived from the movements of the still warm intestines, the phenomena of the altar fire, etc. The singing or chanting of hymns in praise of the gods, or recounting their actions, was a frequent accompaniment of the sacrifices; but few of those have come down to us. In general, the longer hymns are narratives of the principal stories current relating to the gods. Few of them can properly be compared with the "scriptures" we have already noticed. We may quote, however, the hymn to Athene, as translated by Chapman.

> " Pallas Athene only I begin
> To give my song, that makes war's terrible din;
> Is Patroness of cities, and with Mars
> Marshalled in all the care and cure of wars;
> And in everted cities fights and cries,
> But never doth herself set down or rise
> Before a city, but at both times she
> All injured people sets on foot and free.
>   Give, with thy war's force, fortune then to me;
>   And with thy wisdom's force, felicity."

The remainder of the hymns are just as much or as little "devotional" as this specimen; and taken by themselves they would indicate a race comparatively little conscious of "sin" as understood in modern times. To have displeased the gods was grievous, but the gods were not supposed to be governed by any inexorable standard of right and wrong; they could be appeased and persuaded, and even grievous faults could be, as it were, paid for or expiated by a proportionate animal sacrifice. The "Theogony" and the "Works and Days" of Hesiod are two of the most important poems which have come down to us, giving accounts of the gods and their doings, portions of which probably were chanted in their services.

<small>Slight consciousness of sin.</small>

That there were priests in ancient Greece, and that they exercised important functions and filled important positions in the Greek States, is evident from a very slight study of Greek literature; but it is difficult to realise their precise status without a knowledge of the entire social and political condition of the Greeks. The priests did not constitute a distinct and ordained order; there was no fixed or regular prin-

<small>The priests.</small>

ciple about the priesthood. Religion was above all an affair of the community, whose first business it was to fulfil the duties of the State towards the gods. Such duties must be performed for all by certain appointed persons, or by the head of the State, whether king or general. In early Greece we find that the king frequently sacrificed on behalf of the people; and when kings ceased to reign, the priestly functions were given to elected leaders or magistrates, such as the *archon basileus* at Athens. Where this course fell into abeyance, we find the priest as the elected or hereditary minister of a temple, charged to fulfil all the due rites of the worship there celebrated, and paid from the temple revenues or by the gifts of worshippers. Subordinate bodies, such as the *phratriæ*, had common religious duties which were discharged by chosen members. The State kept watch over any infraction of duty towards the gods by private persons, and each family discharged its private religious duties through its head. The priesthood of certain gods became hereditary in particular families on account, sometimes, of the supposed hereditary transmission of prophetical power, or of the knowledge of certain traditional rites. Some priests were merely appointed for a term of years; in some cases the succession was to brothers, and to the sons of the eldest brother; sometimes the priesthood was purchased, or was granted for special services.

In Greece we have the spectacle of a people, with strong religious feelings, in whom the public or State aspect of religion permanently predominated over the ecclesiastical. The priesthood did not become the ruling power; art, literature, and politics used religion as part of their inheritance, without placing their consciences in commission to an order of priests. Although the priests claimed and gained the benefit of protection from the gods they served, they were by no means exempt from criticism, and they were not in general allowed to control the funds of the temples. The tenure of the priesthood by unworthy persons was jealously guarded against, and persons of high birth were preferred.

*State aspect of religion.*

**Duties of priests.** The priest of a temple had specially to superintend the ritual of his temple, to protect it from improper intruders, and to see that the sacrifices were properly performed. He was also charged with all, or nearly all, the interpretation of the will of the gods, and, especially in regard to the sacrifices, he had to note all signs indicating the approval or disapproval of the gods. In this he had the aid of skilled soothsayers, who noted the manner in which the victim approached the altar, and whether he made sounds or not; the colour and smoothness of the intestines, the appearances of the flame and smoke of the altar, etc. It was specially important, too, that no irreverent or frivolous words should be uttered by the bystanders. The flight of birds and the phenomena of the heavens were also observed for the purposes of drawing omens. The diviners who interpreted dreams and told fortunes, though they enjoyed considerable favour in Greece, had no regular connection with the temples or the priests. Within their temples the priests had great authority, being able to excommunicate those who broke their regulations, and invoking curses on them before which the stoutest-hearted Greek quailed. Such offences were stigmatised as impiety, and often heavily punished by fines or boycotting.

**Position of priests.** Notwithstanding the limitations we have mentioned, a Greek priest had no mean position, especially in virtue of his office as interpreter and representative of the god. The priests could solve the State's difficulties when disaster or pestilence occurred, and in the case of the greater oracles which were consulted by all Greece, they occupied a position which no great man in a single State could attain. At public festivals they occupied special seats of honour, and sometimes appeared decked with the costume and attributes of the god they served. Consequently the position was sought after by the wealthy, who in their turn could gratify the people by splendid ceremonies and costly festivals. Naturally such persons tended to gather about them assistants to perform the more laborious or irksome portions of their duty, such as revealers of the mysteries to the uniniti-

# THE PARTHENON, ATHENS.

THE PARTHENON, ATHENS.

ated, torch-bearers, proclaimers of rites, bearers of sacred water, etc.; and not a few slaves were attached to the temples to perform menial offices. Each temple had its appropriate series of services, according to the character of the god and the State.

But public, national, or State temples were not the only ones in which the services of priests were required.

**Private temples.** They were not infrequently founded by private persons or societies, and endowed with estates to keep up a succession of priests and services. They might be founded in honour of success in an enterprise, in honour of a deceased friend or relative, in obedience to dreams or oracles. Xenophon, for instance, devoted a tenth of certain spoil of war to buy an estate in Lakonia, on which he built a temple to the Ephesian Artemis, surrounded by a forest full of wild animals, let to a tenant who had to give one-tenth of the produce to a festival in honour of Artemis, and also to keep the temple in repair. In other cases rites for the dead were associated with a temple, and periodical gatherings of a family were enjoined, which remind us of Chinese ancestral worship. There were also numerous religious corporations or associations devoted to the worship of some particular divinity, holding assemblies, building temples, choosing priests, making regulations enforced by fines. Really these assemblies formed limited churches, governed by the church assembly. Many of these were founded in large cities for the worship of gods not worshipped by that particular city.

The most complete account of the ritual of a Greek festival is given in an inscription from Andania, in

**A Greek festival.** Messenia. The twin gods known as Kabiri were there celebrated, together with Demeter, Apollo, Hermes, and a local nymph, by a body of priests and priestesses chosen by lot out of the tribes of the city, who had to swear to conduct the ritual in accordance with prescribed form. They had the custody of the sacred books and the chest in which they were kept. Strict regulations are laid down as to the dress of the priests and priestesses, limiting the cost, prescribing the absence of paint and of gold ornaments. The procession included a leader, the priest of the deities, the president of the games, the sacrificers and flute-players; then sacred virgins, priestesses, and priests. The victims were

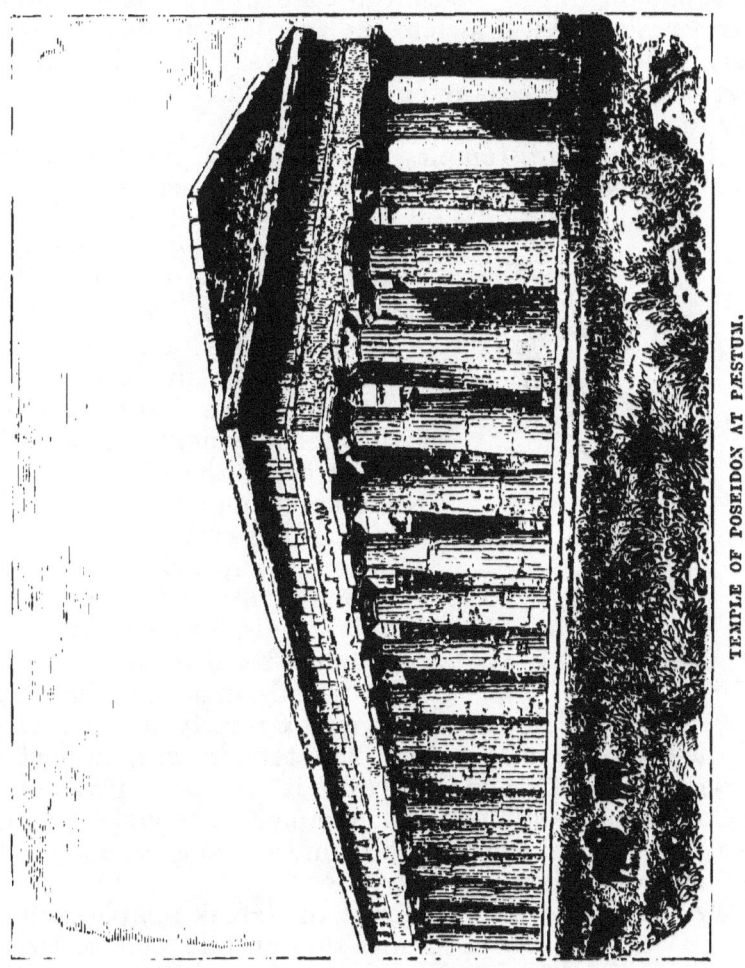

TEMPLE OF POSEIDON AT PÆSTUM.

also led in procession; they included a large number of lambs, a sow for Demeter, a two-year-old pig to the Kabiri, a ram to Hermes, etc., and all victims were to be without blemish. After the sacrifices, the portions not given to the gods were eaten by the priests, priestesses, and virgins, the musicians and other assistants. Complete provision was made for a market to supply the crowds gathered to the festival, and for the judgment of offenders during its continuance, as well as for public warm baths. All brawlers and sacrilegious persons were sternly denounced; and there is every sign that in the best period of Greece public opinion was strongly against any unseemly conduct at the festivals.

The wealth of temples became very great from the accumulated offerings of devout worshippers and States. As a temple grew in fame, it attracted wealthy foreigners and even foreign kings to its worship. The place being sacred, money was often deposited there, and invested either in loans or in property. The State undertook the management of all the property of the civic temples, issuing commissions from time to time, or regularly appointing officers to supervise the temple accounts. Apart from property which could be dealt with, the temples became very rich in votive offerings, and as these varied extremely with the taste of the giver or of his time, the temple was, in fact, a museum of art; and wherever it has been possible to explore the site of an ancient temple, it has yielded many treasures and much valuable information, especially in the form of dedicatory inscriptions.

HERMES.

*Wealth of temples.*

We must now briefly refer to the Greek temples, which succeeded the early open-air altars on hills and in sacred enclosures. We see a strange likeness to the fetish enclosures of the African negro in the placing of the images of gods and heroes in hollow trees as a habitation in early times. Then, as architecture developed, the sacred image was covered and protected

*Early temples.*

in dark buildings only lighted from the door, or by lamps. This period of the history of Greek temples is almost entirely prehistoric, for the Greeks in early times had so far progressed as to build fine temples of the well-known oblong form, almost always adorned with a row or rows of columns in various styles or arrangements. Certain types, associated with or invented by a particular state or tribe, became peculiar to certain gods, probably from having been early used for their temples. Thus the Doric style was used in the temples of Zeus and Ares; the Ionic, in those of Apollo, Artemis and Dionysos; the Corinthian, of Hestia. Most of the **The Greek styles.**
chief temples, besides the porch with columns, had a vestibule, a large cella or habitation of the god or gods, in which the statues of the gods were placed, facing the entrance, and a chamber in the rear, often used as a treasury. When the temple was a famous oracle, the cella was kept closed to all but priests and the initi-

THESEUS.

ated, and its violation by others brought the severest punishments. The temples afforded the Greeks the utmost scope for their sculpture, in the capitals, friezes, pediments, etc.; and while no light was admitted into the cella from the sides, it was frequently partly open above. The entire series of legends about the gods was represented in sculpture, and the highest skill and costliest materials were lavished on the statues of the gods, which are in reality only to be distinguished from the "idols" of other religions in the greater beauty and imaginative power they displayed. This is not degrading the beautiful images of the gods; **Sculpture.**

for few so-called idols have ever been imagined to be anything in themselves, apart from the spirit of a god believed to reside in, or to visit them; yet the rudest image made by a savage may represent as true an act of devotion and submission of himself to the unseen powers as the most magnificent Greek statue. Who can assign relative merits in this the most difficult of all fields? But as we have shown the savage as not destitute of genuine religion, so do we demonstrate the same fact for the Greek, whom St. Paul recognised as "very attentive to religion." Among the most notable Greek temples were those of Zeus at Olympia, of Athene Parthenos (known as the Parthenon), and Theseus at Athens, of Zeus at Ægina, Artemis at Ephesus, Athene at Syracuse, the Erechtheum and Propyleum at Athens. The Spartans were conspicuous for their lack of grand temples. We must not omit to note that the porch of every temple had a font containing holy water, consecrated by dipping into it a burning torch from the altar. With this water, all those who entered to take part in the sacrifices were sprinkled.

ASCLEPIOS (ÆSCULAPIUS).

Altar.

The altar was an indispensable part of the temple, and indeed existed before there were temples. The early Greek word for altar signifies any elevation, and then came to mean any elevation used for worship. Originally it was always in the open air; but when temples were built, the altar for burnt sacrifices continued in the open in front of the temple, while a smaller altar was placed in front of the statues of the gods in the cella. They might be made of earth, turf, or stones, and might be built anywhere on occasion, especially during war; but in the temples they were built of regular masonry, raised several feet, either of a round or of an oblong shape. They were decked with flowers and ornamented with appropriate sculpture, and either bore the name of the god or gods to whom they were devoted, or some representation of them. The inner altars were used for kneeling in prayer, and for the offering of incense and other non-living sacrifices. Altars were universally held to be places of refuge for criminals or unfortunate persons; the altars had horns, of which refugees took hold. Solemn oaths were also taken at altars. Some altars, as that of Zeus at Olympia, on which offerings of hundreds of animals were made, were of great size. The gods of the lower world, however, had no altars, the blood of the sacrifices made to them being received in ditches or trenches.

No part of the Greek religion was more devoutly believed in than the oracular utterances delivered at many shrines. The gods were believed to make communications to mankind through some medium, an inspired priestess or priest, or by dreams or signs. There were comparatively few oracles of Zeus, who was supposed to be too far from men's affairs to enter into close relations with them. Thus his will was revealed through Apollo and other gods, and even through heroes. Oracles of Zeus were given at Olympia from the inspection of victims, and at Dodona from sounds produced by the wind in a grove of trees. *Oracles.*

The oracle of Apollo at Delphi so far outgrew all others in fame that it has become the typical example. Here, in the innermost sanctuary, in front of the statue of Apollo, was an altar fire always burning, and in the centre was a small opening in the ground, from which at times an intoxicating or sulphureous smoke arose. Over this was placed a tripod, upon which the prophetess, known as Pythia, took her seat. The smoke ascending produced a kind of delirium in the prophetess, who, while it lasted, uttered various sounds which were believed to contain revelations from Apollo. These being taken down by the priests were interpreted by them to the people, being often given in hexameters, and conveyed in language that admitted of more than one interpretation. Many oracles, however, were quite direct and *The Delphian Oracle.*

plain, so that the modern meaning attached to "oracular utterances" is not quite just to the originals. The oracle was believed to give answers to every one of pure heart, but no answer could be obtained by a criminal until he had atoned for his crime. At first oracles were only given once a year; later, certain days were set apart every month, when the oracle could be consulted on payment of a fee, and sacrifice of a goat, an ox, or a sheep. The Pythia prepared for her function by fasting for three days, bathing, and sacrificing laurel leaves and barley flour to Apollo. The priests of this oracle belonged to certain noble families of Delphi, and were appointed for life. No doubt the credit of the oracle was principally due to them; they were of high birth, and had the most advantageous opportunities for gaining education and worldly wisdom, especially as Delphi was visited by embassies from every Greek city, as well as others; and there are grounds for believing that for a long period they were actuated by lofty ideas and constituted a means of elevation and of religious conservation. "In the earliest time we can trace the influence of the oracles discouraging the relentless blood-feud, distinguishing classes of murder, and allowing purification and expiation in certain cases. They make the sanctity of oaths between man and man a special duty; Apollo regards even hesitation to keep a pledge as already a sin. They are the centre of unions or amphictyonies which bind their members to observe certain duties, and show mercy to their fellow-members; and Delphi, as the oracle of an amphictyony including great part of Greece, had an important share in promoting the ideal unity of the whole country" (*Ency. Brit.*, "Oracle"). During the great struggle for supremacy between Athens and Sparta the Delphic oracle showed an increasing partiality towards Sparta, and gradually the Athenians and their allies lost their respect for it; but it continued to be consulted down to the time of the emperor Julian.

At an early time the spirits of the dead were believed to appear and give counsel; later the inquirer went to sleep over the grave of a hero, who appeared to him in a

OLYMPIA RESTORED.

dream. At the oracle of Amphiaraus near Oropus, where the hero had risen from the earth to become a god, the inquirer slept in the temple on the skin of a ram which he had sacrificed, after abstaining from food for twenty-four hours. Oracles were also at one time believed to be given by Mother Earth, being the abode of the dead, who could still give counsel to their descendants. The conception that Themis and Apollo gave oracles at Delphi appears to have been later than this.

<small>Various beliefs.</small>

In addition to regular or occasional religious worship at the temples, the Greeks had a religious bond and influence of a yet more powerful nature, in the public festivals kept by every State of any importance, or by numerous States in common. So far as their origin can be discerned, they are shared between celebrations of ancestral heroes and of the seasons or their successive phenomena, usually associated with a god or gods whose worship was specially appropriate to the season. There is evidence, however, that their number and splendour increased during the early historic period, and at last we find the Greeks of Tarentum keeping more festivals than working days. At Athens in the height of its prosperity fifty or sixty days were kept free from all business by magisterial order. The chief of these were the greater and the lesser Dionysiac, the Eleusinian, the Panathenaic, and the Thesmophorian. Thebes celebrated the Daphnephoria every ninth year. But the most influential of all the great meetings of the Greeks were the four panhellenic festivals, known as the Olympic, the Pythian, Nemean, and Isthmian games. Whatever the origin of the Olympian festival might be, it was lost in obscurity, and at a very early date the games had assumed such importance that during their celebration all warfare was stayed for a month, and the territory of Elis was regarded as sacred for the time being. One great part of the festival consisted of sacrifices to the gods by the Eleans, by the conquerors in the games, by representatives of other States, and by private persons. We cannot here

<small>The great festivals.</small>

<small>Religious origin and purpose.</small>

refer to the contests of strength and artistic skill which formed so celebrated a part of the festival, but note that they expressed the strong Greek feeling that men honoured Zeus best by the harmonious discipline of both body and mind; and consequently it is not surprising that the Olympic festival continued long after the Greeks had succumbed to Rome, the last being held in A.D. 393. The German excavations at Olympia in 1875-81 have made known the elaborate nature of the buildings and appliances, of the sculptures and works of art which existed in connection with these great games. The honours given to victors on their return home show how deeply these contests affected the national sentiment; some extolled their lot as divine. It is even recorded that altars were built and sacrifices offered to some victors.

The Pythian games and numerous other festivals were of special interest from their including poetic recitations, often original, and from their connection with the rise of the drama. As Dr. Donaldson says, in his "Greek Theatre": "The susceptible Athenian, whose land was the dwelling-place of gods and ancestral heroes, to whom the clear blue sky, the swift-winged breezes, the river fountains, the Ægean gay with its countless smiles, and the teeming earth from which he believed his ancestors were immediately created, were alike instinct with an awe-pervading spirit of divinity; the Athenian, who loved the beautiful, but loved it because it was divine, who looked upon all that genius could invent, or art execute, as but the less unworthy offering to his pantheism; and considered all his festivals and all his amusements as only a means of withdrawing the soul from the world's business, and turning it to the love and worship of God,—how could he keep back from the object of his adoration the fairest and best of his works?" The dramatic features in the stories of the gods and heroes suggested most natural subjects for dramatic representation, and these were most conspicuous in the festivals of Apollo at Delphi, of Demeter and Persephone at Eleusis, and of Dionysos at Eleusis and Delphi. The Eleusinian mysteries were the most famous

*Rise of the drama.*

and popular of all, and were specially marked by magnificence and by the secrecy of some rites, to which is owing our ignorance about them. Their importance does not seem to have depended upon any dogmatic instruction, but they were believed to educate the people in reverence for the deity. Silence, excitement, and rapt devotion were typical of the spectators, and the fasting, long ceremonies, and night wanderings which preceded the actual mysteries, heightened their effect. The touching and kissing of holy things, the hearing and repeating of traditional songs, the dramatic representation of incidents in the lives of the gods, appear to have formed important parts of the ceremonial. The worship of

THE MUSES—CALLIOPE, CLIO, ERATO, EUTERPE, MELPOMENE.

Dionysos had similar variations to that of the sun-god. His sufferings and misfortunes were dramatically bewailed, and his gifts of light and wine, etc., were celebrated with rites which, at first licentious, remained so, because of the conservatism of ritual. We cannot further follow this most interesting topic, and simply remark that we find in Greece, as in India, that everything, especially every invention, every art, every faculty, was under the patronage of, and intimately connected with, the popular religion. We must acknowledge that the Greeks, in their best periods, were true to their religious beliefs, and carried them out most thoroughly.

We cannot trace the stages by which marriage came

to be placed under religious sanctions: but we may believe that this process was almost simultaneous with the growth of belief in the relation of the gods to human conduct, and the necessity of pleasing them if good fortune were to attend a man. Cecrops was fabled to have instituted marriage in Athens, as well as the worship of the gods. Marriages between very near kin took place in early Greece, and dislike to such marriages was the growth of a later age, though it never proceeded so far as among Jews and Christians. Celibacy was decidedly frowned upon, and sometimes punished by Greek law; and one reason for marriage

*Marriage.*

THE MUSES—POLYHYMNIA, TERPSICHORE, THALIA, AND URANIA.

was that a succession of descendants might be kept up by every man, as worshippers or ministers of the godhead and of the family gods; indeed, they practically worshipped their ancestors. In connection with marriages (which did not take place till an adult age was reached), sacrifices or offerings were made to the gods presiding over marriage (Hera, Artemis, the Fates, and sometimes others), by the father of the bride; and after the marriage the husband offered a sacrifice. There was no religious ceremony which constituted the marriage; and wives occupied a comparatively low place in Greek estimation.

Death and the events succeeding it occupied a prominent place in the Greek mind. From Homer we gather that at death the spirit, occupying a shadowy outline of the body, was driven by Hades into his dominions in the lower world (Erebus); and we read that the shades occupied themselves in regretting lost pleasures, or past changes of fortune, but were only half conscious, except when roused by drinking the blood of sacrifices offered to them by living friends. The heroes enjoyed a more happy state, but longed for their former life. It was not till Egyptian ideas had influenced the Greeks that a doctrine of future rewards and punishments according to actions was taught. Hermes became recognised as the guide of mortals to the lower regions, where Hades received them hospitably; so that his kingdom ceased to be regarded as one of gloom. Three rivers had to be crossed by all, namely, Acheron (sorrow), Cocytus (lamentation), and Styx (intense darkness), the latter flowing nine times round Erebus. It was necessary to be ferried over the Styx by a grim boatman named Charon, who would take none but those who had received funeral rites, and brought with them a coin as toll; otherwise they must wander restlessly for a hundred years on the banks of the river. On the other side of the Styx was

*Death and the future life.*

THE GRACES—AGLAIA, THALIA, EUPHROSYNE.

THE FURIES—TISIPHONE, MEGÆRA, ALECTO.

the seat of Minos, who received confessions from and judged all shades, and announced their sentences, whether of happiness or misery. Cerberus, the three-headed dog, guarded his tribunal, and allowed no shade to emerge when once within the portals. The happy passed first into the palace of Hades and Persephone and received their greeting, and then set out for the Elysian fields, full of all delights, where they occupied themselves with their favourite pursuits, the hunter resuming his bow and arrows, the musician his lyre, the soldier his arms. According to the doctrine associated with the name of Pythagoras, after the shades had remained in Elysium for a thousand years, they returned to earth to occupy fresh bodies.

THE FATES—CLOTHO, LACHESIS, ATROPOS.

Those who had been condemned as guilty were conducted from Minos to the great judgment hall of Rhadamanthus, who announced in detail the punishments which each would receive in Tartarus, a gloomy region far below Hades. The Furies then seized the culprits, scourged them with whips, and hurled them down into Tartarus.

Naturally we find these ideas influencing the funeral rites of the Greeks. The greatest horror was felt at the idea of not receiving burial, and any passer who found a corpse felt it his duty at least to throw some earth upon it. Indeed, the deceased were regarded as having both a legal and moral right to burial. Burning was also in vogue among the Greeks, but probably not so much as burial in historic times. The body was anointed and decked with flowers and dressed in white: an obolus was put in its mouth for Charon, and a honey-cake by its side for Cerberus. When the body was laid out, painted vases were placed by the side of the bed, and afterwards buried with it. In early times, sacrifices (and sometimes captives) were offered previous to the burial; but these had ceased in Plato's time. The coffins for burial were usually of earthenware or baked clay. There were no specially consecrated grounds for burial, convenience and sometimes beauty of situation being the chief considerations. Those who had taken part in the funeral required purification before they could enter the temples. Sacrifices were offered on the third, ninth, and thirtieth days after the funeral, the latter ending the mourning. On certain days the tombs, which were often very handsome, were decked with flowers, and offerings of flowers and sometimes of food were made to the deceased.

We may now briefly endeavour to comprehend the moral state produced by, or co-existent with, the Greek religion. In the Homeric poems the cardinal virtue of truth does not appear to be in great esteem. "To deceive an enemy is meritorious, to deceive a stranger innocent, to deceive even a friend perfectly unobjectionable, if any object is to be gained." (M.) Most of the leading characters in the Iliad and Odyssey do not hesitate to lie, and the same is the case with the gods. "Zeus deceives both gods and men; the other gods deceive Zeus." The one check on deceit is the presence of the gods, who, if adjured by an oath, will certainly punish falsehood. Apollo and Menelaus are truthful characters, but even they have their defects. Might was practically right, and while Homer describes persons guilty of manslaughter or murder as going into exile or paying pecuniary compensation, it is not till after the Homeric period that a guilty person requires purification by special religious ceremonies. It would be easy to show that courage was really defective in the Homeric times, and could not readily be produced even by appeals to the gods. The sad condition of orphans, widows, and old people is graphically depicted in Homer, and the possession of women by the stronger and the

## THE TEMPLE OF ARTEMIS, EPHESUS. 233

conqueror is an acknowledged fact. The Homeric world, far from representing an early age of pure morality, is one of still rudimentary moral and religious ideas. The

TEMPLE OF ARTEMIS (DIANA), EPHESUS.

gods are but larger copies of men, and the best, if high in comparison with some conceptions of gods, are low when compared with the highest. The best character among the gods, Pallas-Athene, is, as Mr. Hayman, in his "Odyssey," says, without tenderness or tie of any sort, never owns obligation, is pitiless, unscrupulous in partisanship, and full of dissimulation; she whispers base motives of the good, beats down the strong, and mocks the weak, while true to a comrade or friend. Practically, the power of the chiefs, or of the aristocratic caste, was supreme in the Homeric and Hesiodic times, and their morals were on the whole selfish, and the common people followed their example. So there was every chance for the religious pretenders or believers who attributed troubles to the displeasure of the gods, and brought forward their prescriptions for appeasing or persuading them. Thus religion not based on morals grew in strength, and in time, and by the aid of importations from Egypt, the East, and Thrace, became full of excitements and orgies, sensuality and immorality. At the same time, and even down to the time of Herodotus, there lingered in parts of Greece horrible customs of human sacrifice.

The age of the tyrants was to some extent favourable to morals, for the tyrants put down excesses of immorality and prepared the way for wide-spread improvements such as those introduced by Solon and Pisistratus. In some minds a higher morality arose; poets and philosophers began to doubt the old mythologies, and to rest in a general belief in the Deity, in divine virtue and justice, confessing themselves unable to reconcile this belief with the facts of life. Theognis says that no man works with a sure knowledge whether the result will be good or evil; and the general view of the moralists of the time was that although Providence rewarded virtue, the reward was often withheld, and it was therefore best to follow the stream, and to gratify the passions of love and revenge. The lower orders thus had no elevating influence to raise them. It was held to be a shame to remain sober among men who were drunk. Romantic friendships were however not uncommon, and women were perhaps better esteemed and treated than in the Homeric days. Avarice and selfishness were common, and pleasure was universally sought. In most places old age was little honoured, though Lycurgus's ordinance to honour the old stands out in marked contrast. Honesty was largely honoured in the breach, and from the times of Herodotus to that of Cicero we hear of Greek untruthfulness and want of fidelity to their word. At the same time there was much kindly care of and affection for the young, and honourable justice.

The great period of Athens was warlike, and led to a greater ferocity, cruelty, and unscrupulousness of feeling. Oaths and promises were less kept than ever; party and state were everything. The ideal of womanhood was lowered; but there was a greater kindliness towards slaves. Many of the richer Athenians, however, set all morality at defiance, and their example was sufficient to start and maintain a degradation of morality which led to the ruin of Greece. When the old mythology was undermined there was not enough that was solid in the Greek religion to keep morals pure. While the oracles were respected and managed by impartial priests who represented the best ideas current, the moral standard was much better than at a later period when they had become partial and subservient to state factions, and when the best minds of Greece were engaged in politics, art, poetry and philosophy. The philosophers were raising their heads, it is true, and seeking for the true good, and many of them gave systematic instruction in conduct; but meanwhile the people were going to ruin, and the philosophers had little as yet to communicate.

[Mahaffy, "Social Life in Greece," "Greek Life and Thought." (M.) C. T. Newton, "Greek Religion illustrated by Inscriptions," *Nineteenth Century*, vols. iii. and iv. Articles, "Mysteries," "Priest," "Sacrifices," "Temple," "Encyclopædia Britannica," Grote's, Curtius's, and Duncker's "Histories of Greece."]

## CHAPTER X.
## Socrates, Plato, and other Greek Philosophers.

Socrates—His mode of life—His discharge of religious duties—His sign or dæmon—Socrates not really a sceptic—Socrates and the Deity—His views of Providence—Socrates a teacher of morals—His ardour for knowledge—His personal appearance—Socrates before his judges—His condemnation—The death penalty—Socrates on the future life—His death—Plato—His view of the body as evil—Virtue the highest good—Morals and the State—Views of the Deity—Aristotle—The Megarians—The Cynics—The Cyrenaics—Epicurus—The Stoics—Morals—Greeks in other lands—Polybius.

BEFORE Socrates, Greek philosophers like Thales, Pythagoras, Heraclitus, Democritus, and Protagoras had vainly tried to get at the secret of the universe and the true basis of conduct, and Protagoras had arrived at the conclusion that the human consciousness is the only standard of what is and what is not. It was reserved for Socrates the Athenian (*circ.* 470-399 B.C.) to start a new era by exhaustively showing how little men really knew, especially about divine government. He rejected all the popular mythology, which represented the gods as having committed actions which would be disgraceful in the worst of men. But he was no despiser of the gods; in fact, his friends claimed that he was "so pious that he did nothing without taking counsel of the gods; so just that he never did an injury to any man, whilst he was the benefactor of his associates; so temperate that he never preferred pleasure to right; so wise that in judging of good and evil he was never at fault. His self-control was absolute; his powers of endurance were unfailing; he had so schooled himself to moderation that his scanty means satisfied all his wants. To want nothing, he said, is divine; to want as little as possible is the nearest possible approach to the divine life;" and he practised what he taught, yet knew how to enjoy himself heartily. Like almost all the greatest teachers and reformers we have written of, his teaching was mainly conversational, and he left no books; but like them, also, his memory impressed itself upon his pupils and friends, so that we have more than one striking record and picture of the greatest soul among the Greeks.

Highly educated in Greek learning and a sculptor in early life, Socrates soon gave up statuary for his public mission, believing that he had a divine com- **His mode** mission to convict other men of their ignorance, **of life.** and so help them to improve. His wife, Xanthippe, led him an unhappy life with her shrewish temper, and his sons appear to have been unworthy of him. He showed bravery as a soldier at Potidæa and elsewhere, and on several important occasions he manifested great public spirit and courage in withstanding popular and aristocratic sentiment or commands. But most of his life was spent in his sacred duty, that of showing men their ignorance and helping them to choose right paths in practical morality. As Xenophon represents him, he caused many to turn from evil ways by inducing them to seek after virtue. In every way he could discover to be beneficial, he disciplined both his mind and his body, and he refused all payments for his instruction. We shall perhaps best elucidate his character, so far as it relates to morals and religion, by referring to the accusation brought against him in B.C. 399, that he was guilty, first, of denying the gods recognised by the State and introducing new divinities, and secondly of cor- **His discharge** rupting the young. In answer to this, Xeno- **of religious** phon alleges that he was frequently seen sacri- **duties.** ficing both at his own house and on the public altars;

and it appears that he accepted the established beliefs so far as they did not plainly conflict with his conscience, especially where they dealt with matters of which the gods seemed to have reserved all real knowledge to themselves. It was on human conduct and knowledge that he concentrated his attention. Yet he incurred opposition as being an innovator, for he sought to expunge from popular belief the fictions of the poets; and he avowed that he derived guidance from an inward "divinity," or "divine sign," often spoken of as the "dæmon" of Socrates, and sometimes as an intelligent spiritual companion or guardian spirit. But it is not correct to say that he regarded himself as possessed by a divinity or a guardian spirit. "According to Xenophon," says Dr. Henry Jackson (*Encyclopædia Britannica*, 9th ed.), "the sign was a warning, either to do or not to do, which it would be folly to neglect, not superseding ordinary prudence, but dealing with those uncertainties in respect of which other men found guidance in oracles and tokens; Socrates believed in it profoundly, and never disobeyed it. According to Plato, the sign was a 'voice' which warned Socrates to refrain from some act which he contemplated; he heard it frequently and on the most trifling occasions; the phenomenon dated from his early years, and was, so far as he knew, peculiar to himself." It has been suggested, with considerable plausibility, by Mr. Jackson, that the rational suggestions of his own brain, exceptionally valuable in consequence of his accuracy and intelligence, appeared to be

SOCRATES.

His sign, or dæmon.

heard by him as a voice speaking to him; others see in the "divine sign" the voice of conscience and instinct combined; while some may regard it as a direct Divine voice. This difficulty we cannot solve; but Xenophon uses this phenomenon to show that Socrates had a personal sign which was parallel to the divination of the other Greeks by birds and voices and sacrifices. But Socrates declared those bereft of their senses who had recourse to divination with a view to solving questions upon which the gods had given men power to decide themselves.

Socrates, seeming to his contemporaries to be a sceptic, was the most genuine believer of his time, so far as he thought he had grounds for belief. When the Delphian oracle pronounced him the wisest of men, he sought to discover some one wiser than himself, and succeeded only in finding people who thought they knew, whereas they were self-deluded. Still Socrates felt that he did not possess the wisdom with which he was credited, for, said he, God only is wise, and the oracle only meant to say, "He is the wisest who, like Socrates, knows that his wisdom is in truth worth nothing." About the Deity Socrates would put forward little that was dogmatic. He believed in a Supreme Being who was an intelligent and beneficent Creator of all things, and he prayed to the gods to grant him good gifts, believing that they best knew what was good. He gave as proofs of the existence of "the divine," the providential order of nature, the universality of the belief in it, and the revelations and warnings given to men by signs and oracles. He appealed very strongly to the argument from design, proclaiming that the evident purpose of vast numbers of things showed that they were produced by intelligence. The arguments of Socrates on these subjects have been made familiar to generations of schoolboys in Xenophon's "Memorabilia." We will quote part of one of his central arguments from Mr. Levien's translation.

*Socrates not really a sceptic.*

*Socrates and the Deity.*

"It did not, however, satisfy the Deity to take an interest in man's body only, but, what is the most important point of all, He also implanted in him that most excellent essence—his soul. But in the first place, of what other animal does the mind comprehend the fact of the existence of the gods as the organisers of so stupendous and excellent a system? and what other race except that of men offers service to the gods? or what intelligence exists more adapted than that of man to make provision against cold and heat, or hunger and thirst, or to alleviate disease, or to practise feats of strength, or to labour for instruction, or more capable of remembering what it may have heard or seen or learned? For is it not clearly manifest to you that men pass their lives like gods as compared with other creatures, and excel them in the nature both of their minds and bodies? For neither could a creature endowed with the body of an ox and the feelings of a man accomplish its wishes; nor do such animals as possess hands, but are devoid of intelligence, obtain any benefit thereby. But do you, who enjoy both these stupendous advantages, think that the gods have no regard for you?" Again, "You must not imagine that while your vision is capable of ranging over a distance of many furlongs, the eye of the Deity is unable to survey the universe at a glance. Nor should you suppose that while your mind can contemplate things that are taking place at home and in Egypt and Sicily, the Divine Intelligence is insufficient to regard all things simultaneously. . . . So with regard to the gods, you should make the experiment whether, if you cultivate them, they will not vouchsafe to you their guidance in matters which are unrevealed to mankind in general; and you may thus recognise the fact that the nature of the Deity is so stupendously constituted as to be able to see all things at once, and to hear all things, and to be present everywhere, and to take cognisance of everything at the same time."

*His views of Providence.*

It will at once be evident that we here have a style and matter of teaching never reached by any of the religions we have previously spoken of, and perhaps only approached by that of Zoroaster. To speak of Socrates simply as the greatest of the heathens does him injustice, unless it is clearly understood that the term heathen simply means a non-Christian. We cannot but rank him as one of the greatest of men, pre-eminent as an original thinker and independent character, and as a teacher of divine things.

He was equally eminent as a moral teacher. Far from being a corrupter of youth, we have abundant testimony that he was a corrector of young men's morals, and always tried to raise them, to inspire in them a sense of duty, of responsibility for the use of their intellect and conscience, and to lead them to spend their lives usefully and nobly. His moral teachings, if followed out, would have saved many a king or state or parliament, in presumably more enlightened times, from disaster. He did not believe in appointing men who succumbed to gluttony, crime, sensuality, and other vices to posts of difficulty and danger; in committing the education of children or the care of property to intemperate men. He regarded temperance (in the broad sense) as the foundation of virtue, and any one who accepted money readily from others as setting up masters over himself and binding himself to a most degrading slavery; rather he preferred to live more humbly than a slave. He rejoiced especially in having estimable friends; and if he knew of any good thing, he thought it a great joy to impart it to them. To him justice and every kind of virtue was wisdom, and he had a belief, too sanguine, that those who recognised this would never prefer to do any but just and virtuous actions. For a man not to know himself, and to imagine he knew things of which he was ignorant, he considered to be a very near approach to insanity. And therefore he did his utmost to cure that kind of insanity, and to lead men not merely to like abstract goodness or intelligence or knowledge, but to be good inwardly and to gain acquirements which were of practical value. But this man who, chief among his fellows, sought to raise and benefit youth, was charged with being a corrupting influence.

*Socrates a teacher of morals.*

"In Socrates," says Professor Sidgwick, "for the first

time, we find the combination of a genuine ardour for knowledge, and a paramount interest in conduct." By his dialectic art he brought home their ignorance to those who talked with him, and then hammered home his conviction that their ignorance of the good and evil in human life was the source of all practical error. He was above all practical, for "he knew no good that was not good for something in particular;" he taught that good is self-consistent, that the beautiful is also profitable and useful, and the virtuous also agreeable, in every instance. He demanded that every man should know what he was doing and why, should act on consistent principles, and should carry them out firmly and vigorously. This most trying of all demands, persistently enforced by criticism of those who acted contrariwise, was at last sufficient to bring about his ruin.

*His ardour for knowledge.*

The great teacher was not of gainly or prepossessing appearance. Short, thick-necked, with prominent eyes, broad, upturned nostrils, large mouth and thick lips, he in fact embodied the opposite of beauty of form. He lived meanly that he might carry out his mission, and took a sort of delight in making himself out to be the dullest person, or the most ignoble, or the most vile, and thus blunted the force of any shafts that might be levelled against him. He was willing to be of no account, to be despised, to be misjudged, in order that he might win those who could rise by his teaching. And he was willing to die rather than give up truth and conscience or curry favour with his judges.

*Socrates' personal appearance.*

When brought before a dikastery (consisting of between 500 and 600 citizens), to answer a charge of which the penalty sought was death, Socrates delivered in his defence the noble speech of which we have the substance in the "Apology" of Plato. The accusers, he said, had hardly uttered a word of truth, and had been most shameless. He condescended so far as to expound his course of life and the reasons for it, as we have already partially detailed them. He would use

*Socrates before his judges.*

no arts to secure an acquittal, but relied on truth alone. "For if, O men of Athens, by force of persuasion and entreaty, I could overpower your oaths, then I should be teaching you to believe that there are no gods, and convict myself, in my own defence, of not believing in them. But that is not the case; for I do believe that there are gods, and in a far higher sense than that in which any of my accusers believe in them. And to you and to God I commit my cause, to be determined by you as is best for you and me." He had refrained from preparing a set defence, believing that his just and blameless life were the best defence, and also because his divine sign had forbidden him. If he were condemned, he would be condemned unjustly, which would disgrace his judges, but not him; rather it would gain him sympathy and praise. He even seems to have thought that the fit end of his life, as divinely determined, had come. In any case he would not beseech his inferiors to let him live.

The die was cast, and by a majority of five Socrates was adjudged guilty. He disdained now to suggest any less penalty than the extreme one, a penalty which the majority would gladly have mitigated. *His condemnation.* Rather, he loftily expressed his belief that, inasmuch as he had been engaged for many years in conferring the greatest benefits on Athens and its people, he deserved a public maintenance in the Prytaneum at the cost of the State. At last, in compliance with his friends' entreaties, he proposed that he should be fined the small sum of thirty minæ.

The conclusion of the "Apology," after his condemnation to death had been pronounced, is one of the most affecting and sublime of all speeches. "The difficulty, my friends," he says, "is not in avoiding death, but in avoiding unrighteousness; for that runs faster than death." *His accusers were condemned by the truth to suffer the penalty of villainy and wrong.* He supposed that these things were fated; and he thought that they were well. There was great reason to hope that death is a good; it was either a state of nothingness or a migration of the soul from this world to another. Even considered as a perfect, peaceful sleep, he said, "to die is gain, for eternity is then only a single night. But if death is the journey to another place, and there, as men say, all the dead are, what good, O my friends and judges, can be greater than this? . . . Above all, I shall then be able to continue my search into true and false knowledge; and I shall find out who is wise, and who pretends to be wise and is not. . . . In another world they do not put a man to death for asking questions, assuredly not. For besides being happier in that world than in this, they will be immortal, if what is said is true. Wherefore, O judges, be of good cheer about death, and know of a certainty that no evil can happen to a good man, either in life or after death. He and his are not neglected by the gods; nor has my own approaching end happened by mere chance. But I see clearly that to die and be released was better for me. . . . I am not angry with my condemners, or with my accusers; they have done me no harm, although they did not mean to do me any good; and for this I may gently blame them. . . . The hour of departure has arrived, and we go our ways—I to die and you to live. Which is better, God only knows."

**Socrates on the future life.** Having refused to take advantage of an opportunity which his friends had provided for his escape, especially because he will not break the laws of the State under which he has lived peaceably so long, on the last day of his life Socrates is represented, in Plato's dialogue entitled "Phædo," as having delivered his opinions on the future life. He disapproves of suicide; "a man should wait, and not take his own life until God summons him." Yet he acknowledges that he ought to be grieved at death, if he were not persuaded that he was going to gods who are wise and good, and to men departed who are better than those he would leave behind. By death the foolishness of the body would be cleared away, and those who loved wisdom and purity in this life would be pure and hold converse with other pure souls, and know the light of truth. The impure souls at death have to pay the penalty of their evil life, and he supposes that they wander among tombs and sepulchres, till finally they are born again in another body, probably of a fierce or evil animal. He believes indeed that the soul exists before the body, as proved he thinks by the apparent reminiscences of previous states. Hence that which pre-existed cannot be destroyed by the mere death of the body. The lesson is drawn that the greatest care should be taken of the soul, and that the danger of neglect is truly awful. There is no release or salvation from evil except the attainment of the highest virtue or wisdom. He accepts the essence of the current doctrine of Hades and Tartarus, and of the sentences of reward and punishment there awarded. Those who have duly purified themselves with philosophy "live henceforth altogether without the body in mansions fairer than these, which may not be described, and of which the time would fail me to tell." He does not venture to say that his description is exactly true, but he thinks something of the kind is true, and the pure man who has arrayed the soul in her own proper jewels — temperance, justice, courage, nobility, and truth—is ready to journey to the other world. He would not have his friends sorrow at his hard lot, or say at his burial, "Thus we lay out Socrates," or "Thus we follow him to the grave or bury him;" they must say to themselves that they are burying his body only.

But their sorrow was not taken away by his words; they felt as if they were being bereaved of a father, and that they should spend the rest of their lives as orphans. The jailer coming in to tell him that the appointed time for drinking the cup of hemlock had come, called him the noblest and gentlest and best of all who ever came there, and burst into tears. "Then," said Socrates, "I may and must ask the gods to prosper my journey from this to that other world—even so— and so be it according to my prayer." Then he drank the poison quite cheerfully and **His death.** readily. As the poison was taking effect, he said, "Crito, I owe a cock to Asclepios; will you remember to pay the debt?" "The debt shall be paid," answered Crito. Possibly the philosopher meant that he was now restored by death to health, and would make the usual offering to the god of health.

Thus died the man whom Plato terms the wisest, greatest, and best man he had ever known. Truly he, being dead, yet speaketh. The life and death of Socrates did not indeed produce a new religion in Greece, but as represented by Plato and Xenophon, he became the true founder of most of the greatest philosophies of life and mind, and the influence of his life and death can never die. Of no man can it more truly be said that he lived up to the light he had, gained all the light he could, conquered human evil and the fear of death, and fearlessly trusted the Divine.

Having thus given in outline an account of Socrates and his teaching, we can give much less space to Plato, whose significance as a religious teacher is far less than his importance as a philosopher. As the pupil and friend of Socrates, he is of the utmost value as a recorder, more or less literal, of his teachings. His life (427–347 B.C.) is of less special note because he lived very quietly and unobtrusively, teaching in the grove named after Academus, whence his school is known as the Academy, and in his own garden. In dealing with those portions of his extensive writings which belong most clearly to our subject, we must begin with the moral teachings, for with him religion and morals are one. Plato, seeing that earthly life can never be free from evil, says that we must flee away as quickly as possible to God, by making ourselves like Him through virtue and wisdom. The body is an evil, the grave of the higher life; unrighteousness, arising in the soul, allies itself to the lower elements of the body, and develops all kinds of evil. Every man must seek the highest good, which is virtue. The virtuous man alone is free. Only he who takes hold on the Eternal can be truly satisfied. True philosophy is one with perfect morality. Virtue is its own reward, as vice is its own punishment. Virtue is rewarded in the life to come, and vice punished. The just man must do only good, even to his enemies; but the State, Plato held, might use untruth as a means of government. He also held views about marriage which were by no means lofty; he considered the question merely as a means of providing healthy youths to build up the State. Still he sought the elevation of women, both physically, mentally, and morally, and especially by making them share the training and pursuits of men to a considerable extent. In regard to another evil of the Greek social condition, he was little in advance of his time, for he upheld slavery, though he tried to improve the treatment of slaves. He had a low opinion of trade and agriculture as occupations for intelligent men. His political scheme ("*Republic*," "*Politicus*," "*Laws*") contained many elements related to morals, but they are too numerous to be detailed, and are seldom made to depend on his religious belief.

PLATO.

The State, as an ideal, was the main object of his "Republic," and to obtain and maintain good citizens, he described conditions of communism in property, wives and children, and of exposure of sickly new-born infants, which we may doubt whether he would have soberly put into practice. Modern anthropology has taught us that numerous races have approached Plato's ideal in some of these respects, without securing the advantages he desired to gain; and we must remember that Plato's theoretical discussion justifies no one in doing for private ends what he imagined a State to ordain solely for the common good. It is unnecessary to occupy space in condemning what no civilised race is at all likely to enforce or sanction.

Plato recognises one Eternal and Invisible God, perfectly true and good, the highest ideal, the Maker and Father of all. He is unchangeable and perfect, and will never show Himself to man other than as He is. Thus he is absolutely against all mythological stories of the gods which fall below this ideal. God being pure and good can produce or originate no evil; He does anything that can be done; He has wisely adapted means to ends; He knows everything, cares and provides for all in the best way, rewards virtue and punishes vice. He recognises also certain created gods, who represent or are the universe and the heavenly bodies. He uses the name Zeus for the soul of the universe, and frequently when he speaks of gods, he is evidently describing the Supreme Deity. He again and again combats the popular beliefs. The gods are above pleasure and pain, and cannot be bribed and persuaded by prayers and offerings. Divine Providence looks after small as well as great things and persons, and all things conduce to the true welfare of those whom the gods love. According to Plato the worship of God consists especially in a desire to be good, and the strenuous endeavour to attain the ideal. God is good, and man must strive to be like Him. He would maintain the old forms of religious worship, made pure and moral; and he would not only reverence guardian spirits (dæmons), but would have distinguished men reverenced as such after their death. He would punish atheism and other offences against religion, but would allow the young to be taught by myths and stories which he did not himself believe, regarding such as necessary stages towards the truth.

*Views of the Deity.*

Aristotle (384-322 B.C.) is often regarded as the great practical and scientific philosopher as opposed to Plato the idealist; but it is necessary to remember that he was a pupil of Plato, and that much of their teaching is in agreement. We shall only refer to the teaching of Aristotle upon morals and religion, which forms but a small part of his works. He makes man's

*Aristotle.*

highest good to consist in the exercise of his reason, which he places above the exercise of the moral virtues. He describes the brave man consciously encountering death for a worthy object, because he feels that it is beautiful to do so; and this illustrates his somewhat artistic conception of the excellence of virtue. He maintains that slavery is based on nature, and that certain races are intended to be subject. Women are distinctly inferior to men, and he objects to Plato's scheme for their education and elevation.

As to the cause of all things, Aristotle is not very clear. He speaks of a personal mover of all things, enjoying bliss for ever, wrapt in lofty contemplation upon Himself. Man is too inferior to God for Him to concern Himself about his affairs; and thus Aristotle can give us no light upon a future life, immortality, Providence, and prayer.

The chief schools beside the Platonic, which owed their origin to the pupils of Socrates, were the Megarian, the Cynic, and the Cyrenaic. The former, of which Euclid (not the geometer) was the founder, held that what is not good has no real existence, and that God sums up all intelligence, reason, and goodness. The Cynics, of whom Antisthenes and Diogenes were the greatest, deprecated theory and glorified action and self-control. Virtuous conduct based on wisdom and prudence was the only thing to make men happy; pleasure was the greatest evil. Their virtue being sufficient for them, they became self-sufficient boasters. They lived as beggars, with no property at all, and were more arrogant than the rich and powerful; and in contempt for convention they despised much of ordinary morality. The Cyrenaics, represented first by Aristippus, made pleasure the chief good, but kept a mastery over the desires. To Aristippus no possession was more valuable than contentment, no disease worse than avarice; he valued freedom above everything. He cared nothing for the popular notions about the gods. Epicureanism was the natural successor of the Cyrenaic philosophy, as Stoicism was of the Cynic.

Epicurus has too often been referred to as the type of the sensualist, but he was far from being so. While he regarded pleasure as the need and end of every one, he lived a sparing and quiet life, preferring pleasures of the mind to those of the body, and making virtue his aim because it conferred the most permanent and truest pleasure. He however places the family at a discount. "The sage," he says, "will not marry and beget children, nor will he take part in State affairs. He will not form hard and fast judgments; he will not believe all sinners to be equally depraved, nor all sages equally wise." He gathered around him a society of intimates, who lived in simple community, eating barley bread and drinking chiefly water. A remarkable degree of attachment subsisted between him and his pupils, who were exceedingly numerous. After his death statues were erected in his honour at Athens, where he lived for thirty-six years. Epicurus does not figure as a religious teacher. He does not deny the existence of the gods, but believes that human affairs are beneath their ken, and that they do not interfere even in the grand phenomena of nature. His philosophy found a remarkable exponent in the Roman Lucretius, and had great influence at Rome for centuries.

EPICURUS.

The Stoics, with Zeno at their head, took up the Cynic views of self-control as the means of regenerating the soul of man, and urged the discovery of the laws governing the world as indicating man's best path to perfect happiness. The whole world was under a Divine order or Providence, of which all the gods were but temporary or local manifestations. Passion was necessarily wrong, giving an erroneous judgment of what is desirable or to be shunned. Pain was not to disquiet a man, and all the causes that disturb man's spirit were not to ruffle the sage. Yet conformity to nature was their motto; and if desire, passion, and pain are not part of nature, what is? So the Stoics were as little consistent as many other schools; but they had a multitude of adherents. And well it might be so, for their views gave consolation to many an unfortunate or downtrodden man, by giving him a kingdom within himself, where no tyrant could control his thoughts or hinder him from having serene delights. Pyrrho, the Sceptic, is perhaps most interesting to us, since he taught what is practically a philosophy of feeling, the cultivation of good feelings, thus approaching somewhat to Christianity; at the same time he denied that any safe criterion of intellectual judgment had ever been found, though he did not go so far as to say there was none.

Up to and beyond the Christian era, the philosophic schools of Greece held sway, and attracted most of the best intellect of Greece and Rome. There arose a sharper distinction than ever between the learned and the common people whom they contemned; and we have little to show that the latter were in any way elevated by the teachings or influence of the former. The morals of the people continued to degenerate, or at least ceased to improve, with the decay of real faith in the gods; while the philosophic schools became more and more recognised and honoured by the great and powerful. At the same time the traditional beliefs were kept up. Public oaths were made in the names of many gods, and the comedians were styled priests of Dionysos. *Morals.*

In the wider Greece developed after the death of Alexander are many interesting phenomena relating to Greek religion. Thus Zeus Hades was imported from Sinope to Alexandria, and identified with the Egyptian god Serapis. The Museum and the Library founded there by the same great Ptolemy (Soter) were alike precursors of the wide diffusion of Greek learning which was one day to have so great an influence on and through Christianity. We find hymns written to order for the Greek monarchs of Egypt, celebrating Greek feasts and lauding the kings as almost on a level *Greeks in other lands.*

with the gods, and expressing a commonplace view of the old Greek religion. Later, the Ptolemies learnt to build temples to the old Egyptian gods; but Greek did not by any means fuse with Egyptian religion.

We may conclude this chapter by an account of the views of Polybius, who lived through the greater part of the second century B.C., and the irretrievable subjugation of Greece by Rome. He may be taken as a type of the best Greeks of the time. He was devoted to truth, and believed in the moral government of the world, and in retributive providence. He hated meanness and lack of self-respect. But he had no great inspiration to regenerate his people; and his teaching of the lessons of history, while of much interest, roused no enthusiasm. Whether from a decay that was inevitable or not, in Greece religion and national life were dead.

[Xenophon's "Memorabilia"; Plato's works (Jowett's translation); Grote's "History of Greece," vols. iv. and vii.; Zeller's "Socrates and the Socratic Schools" and "Plato and the Older Academy."]

MONUMENTS ON THE APPIAN WAY NEAR ROME.

## CHAPTER XI.
## The Roman Religion.

Early Roman religion—Origin—The Latins—Etruscan religion—Jupiter—Festivals—Juno—Mars—Janus—Minerva—Vesta—Flora—Vertumnus—Pales—Terminus—Comus and Libitina—Other gods—Prophetic nymphs—The Greek gods Romanised—The Penates or household gods—The Lares—The Manes—The Lemures—The Genii—Roman temples—Priests—The Vestal virgins—The Flamens—The Pontiffs—Divination—The Augurs—Relation to the magistrates—Funeral ceremonies—The calendar of festivals—Abstract deities—Essence of the religion—Keepers of the Sibylline books—Moral character of early Romans—Hellenism—Cybele—Bacchus—Degradation of morals—The later republic—Decay of religion—Julius Cæsar—The Empire—Imperial apotheosis—New beliefs—Seneca—Moral state of the empire.

ALTHOUGH the Romans were akin in stock to the Greeks, and were originally, to some extent, similar in religion, the divergences in political history and in **Early Roman religion.** personal and civic temperament were so great as to develop concurrently a decidedly distinct type of religion. The disunion of Greece was contrasted with the gradual achievement of unity in Italy; the variety of Greek gods was represented in Rome by a compendious worship, tribal gods being retained by the combined people of early Rome, and later the Greek gods being either adopted *de novo*, or identified with some of the old Italian divinities. Many of the deities most familiar to us by Roman names were scarcely known, and certainly were not worshipped at Rome during the period when the little city was, by slow and stern discipline, rendering certain its future conquest of the world.

Yet, to begin with, the Roman and the Greek religious notions were the same. Nature worship, personification **Origin.** of natural forces, hero and ancestor worship, were combined in various degrees. Spirits were imagined in every natural phenomenon, and concerned in the perpetual reproduction of creation and creatures; but from an early time the Romans viewed their religion more seriously than the Greeks, were less gay and confident, more gloomy and prudent. Their worship was much more marked by fear and awe, and they dared not handle the persons and names of their gods so freely. Consequently their mythology is very deficient in imagination, and there is almost an entire lack of those marvellous stories in which Greece was so prolific. Yet Rome in its way was prolific in regard to religion, for a special spirit was designated in relation to every action, every place, every object; each man, each family, each clan had its own guardian spirit; and for every State or city separate gods were recognised, who, however, might be admitted into the Roman worship by resolution of the people. One feature may be taken as common to the Roman religious ideas, that of naming them according to their qualities, and by abstract terms. The Roman gods do not marry and have children, and do not walk about unseen among mortals. Yet they unquestionably gained a powerful hold on the minds of the people who reverenced them, and we owe to them the most significant word Religion.

That Alba was a more primitive religious and national centre than Rome was borne witness to even during the time of Rome's greatness by the continuation of the Latin festival on the Alban mount, **The Latins.** when an ox was sacrificed to Jupiter as the god of the Latins, and cattle, milk, and cheese were contributed by various communities to a joint festival. It is impossible now to trace accurately the constituents which combined to form the Roman religion, but at least three tribes took part in it very early, and the oldest religious bodies consisted of a number divisible by three; and the earliest festivals, derived from times before the existence of towns, show the people as being pastoral and agricultural. We will not recite the familiar legend of Romulus, but we may note that it was on the Palatine Hill that various supernatural events connected with the founding of Rome were believed to have occurred; and there the priest of Jupiter lived, there was the sanctuary of Lupercus, and the meeting-place of the Leaping Priests of Mars; but there were no temples in early times. It is probable that the Quirinal Hill was at first the seat of a distinct community, later incorporated with the Palatine; and in its stronghold or Capitol was a sanctuary of Jupiter, Juno, and Minerva, and of the goddess of Fidelity (later replaced by the new Capitol and its temples). Mars and Lupercus too had their bodies of priests on the Quirinal. Within recent years a discovery has been made of pre-historic remains on the Esquiline—tombs of the most primitive type, going back at least to the fifth century B.C.; this, then, was doubtless the seat of a third settlement.

At a later period, but still early as regards authentic history, the Romans incorporated much that had been Etruscan, or identified the gods they already **Etruscan** had with Etruscan gods. We will not attempt **religion.** to discuss the racial connection of the Etruscans; but there is little in their religious remains to negative their being Aryans like the Romans. They recognised two classes of gods—those who directly managed the affairs of the world (Dii consentes), and others who were nameless—but controlled the rest. The former included Tinia (identified with Jupiter by the Romans), Uni (Juno), Meurfa (Minerva); but we find that their functions differed in some respects from those of the corresponding Roman gods. Jupiter was their god of war, though he ruled over all during peace, and caused the fertility of the earth. Minerva was winged as well as armed, represented Fate, and was symbolised by a serpent. Venus was known as Turan, Bacchus as Phuphluns, Mercury as Turms, and many other Greek gods were adopted by the Etruscans. They had also Janus, Saturnus, Silvanus, Mantus, Voltumna among nature deities; and the Lares, Penates, etc., which figure prominently at Rome, appear to have been Etruscan. No doubt the reigns of the Tarquins had much to do with establishing these at Rome. We have no remains of their temples, but they appear to have approached a square shape. Many of their tombs have, however, been preserved, and the sculptures, inscriptions and paintings on them constitute our most important source of information as to their religious as well as other customs. Their religious rites, which were gloomy and fantastic, and abounded in repulsive practices, were described in certain lost books. Divination, from animals' entrails, from natural phenomena and lightning, was much practised under fixed rules. There were families charged with the interpretation of them, and constituting a priesthood. The Etruscans undoubtedly had a vast influence on Roman religion—in augury, teleology, and even the architecture of their temples.

Commencing with Jupiter, we will now give an account of the Roman gods, and more particularly of those which are special to the Romans. The word Jupiter stands for *Jeu piter*, *Dieu piter*—the first part of the word being identical in root with divus and dyaus, heaven. Thus Jupiter means the heavenly father; and in keeping with this the Romans ascribed to him all changes in the heavens, rain, storms, thunder, etc., and indeed gave him a special name for each, as Jupiter Pluvius (Rainer), Fulgurator (Lightener), Tonans (Thun-

TEMPLE OF JUPITER CAPITOLINUS, ROME (RESTORED).

derer). He is termed best (*optimus*) and highest (*maximus*), Capitolinus from his dwelling on the Capitol, Imperator, Victor, Triumphator, etc., and he had temples under many of these distinctive names. His enthronement on the Capitoline Hill dates from the time of Tarquin; but long afterwards he continued to be the object of separate worship at various other shrines. One marked peculiarity of Jupiter was that of revealing his will by portents, which he sends to all who diligently seek them, especially by signs in the heavens and the flight of birds.

JUPITER.

He was originally the god both of the dead and the living; but, as in Greece, the former character dropped out of recognition. Jupiter was the patron and protector of human society, guarding the sanctity of oaths, the rights of strangers, the unity of the State, etc. Jupiter also led the people to war as Victor; and to him thanks and sacrifice were offered by the general on returning from battle. In concluding a treaty, the Romans took the symbols of Jupiter, a flint stone and a sceptre and some grass from his temple. The consuls sacrificed to

Jupiter on taking office, and young men did the same when they put on the *toga virilis*—the man's gown. He was invoked at the beginning of every undertaking.

The principal festivals to Jupiter were the Roman and the Great, the Capitoline and the Plebeian: all of these included a feast of the magistrates and senators in the Capitol. At these feasts seats were left for Jupiter, Juno and Minerva, as though they were family feasts of a tribe and its gods. There were numerous peculiar features attaching to the worship of Jupiter, which were derived from the Etruscans. The priest of Jupiter (called Flamen Dialis) was forbidden to touch a corpse; and if his wife died, he lost his office. He was the subject of many taboos; thus he must not see an army, nor leave the city for a night, nor take off his cap of office, nor touch a dog, etc.

*Festivals.*

As the god of light, the colour white was sacred to Jupiter; and white animals were sacrificed to him. The consuls wore white when they sacrificed to him, and his priests wore white caps. The god was represented as seated on an ivory throne, with a bundle of thunderbolts in his right hand and a sceptre in his left, an eagle standing beside his throne. We need not enlarge on the Greek aspect given to the god after the introduction of Greek learning to Rome.

Juno, identified later with the Greek Hera, was originally very unlike the wife of Zeus. She was introduced to Rome from Etruscan cities, where she was the goddess of the State and of society, and had no naturalistic functions. At Rome she was to the female sex what Jupiter was to the male, and was especially the goddess of everything connected with marriage, as well as of young girls; hence she was known as Juno Virginalis and Matrona, and also as Lucina, from the help she afforded in childbirth. A variety of other names, often associated with distinct shrines, were given to her. At her great festival, the Matronalia, on the Kalends of March, a grand procession of wives and maidens of spotless character was made to the temple of Lucina on the Esquiline Hill.

*Juno.*

It is probable that at an early period Mars was the chief god of at least one of the States which combined to form Rome. He was worshipped under the name of Marspiter (father Mars), or Maspiter, also Mavors or Maurs. Mamers was his name among the Sabines. It is questionable whether he was not at first purely an agricultural divinity, the god of spring, overcoming the evil effects of winter; but the necessity of war to preserve the fruits of agriculture no doubt aided in the transformation of Mars into the god of war, without his losing all his old characters. He was still god of heaven, giver of light, hurling thunder and sending rain.

MARS.

In olden times, there were propitiatory ceremonies to Mars, to ward off drought, pestilence, etc. At one festival a sheep and a reddish dog were sacrificed by the flamen of Mars, to avert mildew from the crops. In times of calamity a "sacred spring" (*ver sacrum*) was consecrated to Mars, all things born then being sacrificed to him. Like Jupiter, he gave oracles and portents, and was a god of the dead and of death.

The Palatine-priests of Mars, for many days after the first of March, were accustomed to dance in armour through parts of Rome, singing a certain song, mentioning all the gods of the city, but especially referring to Mamurius or Mamers. The name Quirinus (a Sabine word) was also applied to Mars, as reputed father of Romulus and Remus; and his sacred wolf was their foster-mother. The old goddess Bellona, goddess of war, was said to be sister, or daughter, or wife of Mars. As going to battle with his people, Mars was known as Gradivus; as an agricultural god, he was termed Silvanus. In late time the attributes of the Greek Ares were ascribed to Mars.

JANUS.

With regard to Janus, undoubtedly one of the oldest of the Roman divinities, there is much doubt, both as to his origin and his true character. He is variously represented as a dual-god, personifying the sun and moon, and as simply a god of opening and beginning, typified in the old beginning of the year with January, and by the opening of the gates of Janus at the beginning of war, and closing them when peace prevailed. The earliest representations of the god were simply two-faced heads; later complete statues of him were made with four faces. Such a statue was placed under a double covered gateway, known as the temple of Janus: the open gates in war signified that the god had gone out with the people to battle. But Janus was also regarded as the god of the beginning of all occupations and actions; and it was a marked feature of the Romans to attribute ill-success to an ill-beginning, necessitating recommencement. As Jupiter by favourable augury gave his sanction and Janus blessed the beginning, these two gods were invoked first in every undertaking. New Year's Day was the special festival of Janus, on which the people were anxious that every word and action should be pure and favourable. Consequently they gave presents to one another, abstained from cursing and quarrelling, began some of their work for the year, etc. His appropriate sacrifices were cakes, barley, incense, and wine, which were offered to him at the beginning of every month. His name was always invoked, and a libation was poured out to him before sacrificing to the other gods. Possibly Janus represents a very early ruler of one of the Italian tribes, who showed such powers of memory and foresight that he came to be credited with full knowledge both of the past and the future, and was deified after death. This is confirmed by the story that the Greek Kronos, whom they identified with Saturnus, one of their own agricultural gods, took refuge, after his defeat by the Titans, with Janus, king of Italy, who shared his throne with him, and so introduced a golden age of prosperity. Saturnus had a temple at the bottom of the Capitoline Hill, in which the State laws and the public treasures were preserved. The name Saturnus is really derived from the word for sowing (*sero, sevi, satum*), and probably represents the introducer of agriculture, his character resembling that of Demeter rather than Kronos. His wife was Ops, goddess of plenty, afterwards identified with Rhea, wife of Kronos.

Minerva. Minerva, the third of the early Roman triad (Jupiter, Juno, and Minerva—derived from the same root as *mens*, mind), is the impersonation of thought and invention, or even, according to Varro, of all ideas. She is said to have invented numbers, and was the patroness of all arts and trades. She specially, as a virgin goddess, protected women, to whom she gave skill in sewing, spinning, weaving, etc. But she was also a war goddess, supplying the mental qualities,—cunning, prudence, courage, and perseverance,—needed for success; consequently she wore a helmet, shield, and coat of mail. As the inventor of musical instruments, especially of wind, she was of great importance to festival celebrations; and the instruments used in them were purified on the last day of Minerva's festival in March. She was the guardian of schools; and during her festival boys had holiday, and brought a special gift to their master, known as the Minerval.

Vesta, the goddess of the hearth, an early divinity at Rome, was very like the Greek Hestia in attributes. She was honoured at every Roman family meal, together with the Penates; but her great sanctuary was between the Capitoline and Palatine Hills, where, instead of a statue, there burned an eternal fire, kept up by her virgin priestesses, the Vestals. A great festival, the Vestalia, was celebrated in her honour on the 9th of June. *Vesta.*

Numerous other gods may be mentioned as among the early objects of Roman worship, principally connected with agriculture; such as Flora, the goddess of flowers, represented as a beautiful girl decked with flowers, and honoured at a mirthful festival at the end of April; Pomona, the goddess of fruit-trees and representative of autumn; Vertumnus, god of garden and field produce, to whom gardeners offered the first produce, with garlands of budding flowers; he was also connected with various circumstances of change (*verto*, I turn), the change of seasons, purchase and sale, the return of rivers to their beds after floods; Pales, a god of flocks and shepherds, and also of husbandry. The name of the Palatine Hill is connected with this god. During his festival, on April 21st, shepherds ignited a quantity of straw and drove *Flora. Pomona. Vertumnus. Pales.*

their flocks through it, themselves following, as a purification from sin.

Terminus, the god of boundaries and landmarks; Consus, the god of secret counsel and of the infernal regions;

SACRIFICING TO THE LARES, OR GODS OF THE HEARTH.

**Terminus, Silvanus, etc.** Silvanus, the god of plantations and forests; Picus, the son of Saturnus, another divinity of the woods, possessing prophetic gifts; Comus, who presided over banquets and gay festivities generally; Libitina, the goddess of funerals, are other peculiarly

## THE PENATES, OR HOUSEHOLD GODS. 265

Roman divinities. The temple of Libitina at Rome contained all necessaries for burials, and these could either be bought or hired there. Terminus was probably an appellation of Jupiter in his capacity of protector of property. Picumnus and Pilumnus were two brother deities protecting marriage and newborn children. Pilumnus warded off sufferings, while Picumnus gave the infant health and prosperity. It does not tend to raise our idea of the Roman character when we learn that an altar was suffered to exist at Rome to Laverna, the goddess of thieves and impostors, as well as a grove on the Salernian road. Robigus, the antagonist of Flora, is more intelligible. As he destroyed young plants by mildew, he was appropriately propitiated by prayers and sacrifices. The Camenæ were four prophetic nymphs, analogous to the Greek Muses. Carmenta, one of them, was also a healing divinity, with a temple at the foot of the Capitoline Hill. Egeria was the nymph who is said to have taught Numa Pompilius the form of public worship. We shall not detail the various beliefs introduced into Rome from Greece in the later ages of the Republic and the early time of the Empire. Ceres, Venus, Apollo, Neptune, Diana, Vulcan, Mercury, Bacchus, and other gods besides those we have mentioned were considerably recognised and worshipped in this later period; and the characteristics of their Greek representatives were ascribed to them.

*[margin: Comus and Libitina. Other gods. Prophetic Nymphs. The Greek gods Romanised.]*

The Penates, or household gods of the Romans, were connected with inner or private matters (*penus*), and perhaps originally were gods of the hearth and kitchen. They were always spoken of as plural, and two images of them were placed on the hearth, but no specific name was given to them. In late times they were identified with various gods; but they are more probably derived from primitive animism, resembling the early Teutonic household gods, and the Chinese god of the kitchen. The close connection of the Penates with domestic life is evident from the fact that their name became synonymous with "home." The old

*[margin: The Penates, or household gods.]*

Romans used to have a morning family gathering (including the slaves), to offer sacrifice and prayer to the Penates. Their blessing was asked before meals, and after the meal part of the food was burned upon the hearth. Sometimes the images were brought in and set upon the table. On the Kalends (1st), Nones (5th or 7th), and Ides (13th or 15th) of the month a special family worship took place, when the images were decorated and crowned, and offerings of cakes, honey, wine, and incense were made to them; and birthdays, marriages and safe returnings from journeys were similarly celebrated. There were also public or national Penates, with a temple at Lavinium and another at Rome, in which were two images of youths holding spears.

**The Lares.** The Lares were the ancestral spirits of the family, regarded as still capable of protecting it and giving its inmates prosperity. One special Lar, the founder of the family, was worshipped in each house, and honoured by an image beside those of the Penates. A part of every meal was offered to it; and on every important occasion the head and members of the household saluted these images; and a bride's first duty on entering her husband's house was to sacrifice to the Lar. The name *Lar*, which is possibly Etruscan, signifies lord, king, or hero. There were public Lares, with temples and public worship at Rome and in all Roman towns; and there were also Lares of the country, the high roads, and the sea.

**The Manes.** The Lares were but special instances of the Manes or spirits of the departed. The tendency to think of the departed as good and favourable, led to the frequent interchange of the words; they are also spoken of as the *Dii Manes* and worshipped with divine honours. At certain seasons sacrifices were offered to the spirits of the departed, and there was an annual festival to them.

**The Lemures.** The Larvæ, or Lemures, were the shades of the dead considered as unfavourable, and as wandering upon earth in hideous shapes, seeking to harm their relatives. On three nights in May the Lemuralia were observed, in order to propitiate the

## THE LEMURES. 267

Lemures. At midnight the head of the family went outside the door of the house, making signs with his hand, which were supposed to keep the Lemures away. After three times washing his hands in spring water, he turned

VESTALS OFFERING SACRIFICE.

round, and placed some black beans in his mouth, which he afterwards threw behind him. It was believed that the spectres collected these beans. After some further ablutions, the father cried out nine times, " Begone, you spectres of the house!" and then they were harmless.

Associated in thought with the Lares and Penates, and sometimes confused with them, were the Genii, or protecting spirits; indeed, they were supposed to preside at the origin of, or to produce each living creature, and to accompany it through life. As to mankind, the genius was supposed to stimulate each person to noble deeds, to comfort him in sorrow, and generally to act as guide and guardian angel. Some held the belief that the genius could change character, and now be a good and now an evil genius; while another belief was, that an evil as well as a good genius accompanied each soul and struggled together for mastery. On various occasions, as birthdays, sacrifices of wine, cakes, and incense were offered to a man's genius; and merry meetings were regarded as pleasures given to the genius. Each State and town was supposed to have its peculiar genius. They are generally represented as winged beings.

JANUS.

While the Romans borrowed much of their architecture from the Greeks, they added to the elements thence derived, one of first-class importance, namely the round arch; yet they had not sufficient skill to make with the aid of the latter graceful buildings; and it was not till after the conquest of Greece that fine temples were built by the Romans. Then, however, they built them on a splendid scale, and with some new developments, but never reached the perfection of Greece. In early times there were but few and small temples in Rome; and the altar was the earlier and more important structure. Usually the temples were built facing the west, with the images of the god similarly placed, so that worshippers entering faced the east. The temples were also as far as possible so arranged that passers-by could readily look into them and salute the god.

Owing to the absence or fragmentary nature of the remains of Roman temples, it is difficult to give a satisfactory account of them. There are no remains by which we can certainly reconstruct the temple of the Capitoline Jove. The great Pantheon, with its magnificent dome, is the finest example of Roman originality in architecture; but it dates from the time of the early emperors, and it is not certain that it was ever used for public worship.

The earliest distinct mention of a priest at Rome is in connection with Mars—the flamen Martialis, accompanied by twelve leapers (the *salii*) who danced and sang at the annual festival of Mars. The organisation of early Roman worship seems to have included in some cases single priests of certain gods, and in others colleges of priests, often twelve in number, to celebrate worship on behalf of the people.

VESTA.

The priest of Jupiter (flamen Dialis) with the flamen Martialis and the flamen Quirinalis, formed the chief trio of priests. The **Roman priests.** worship of Vesta, attended to by the six vestal virgins, was possibly the most sacred of all. The virgins were chosen between the ages of six and ten years, and were of perfect form and intelligence and honourable family. They were compelled to serve for thirty years, ten of which were the novitiate; but mostly the vestals remained priestesses for life. Neglect to watch and maintain the sacred fire being deemed a heinous **The vestal virgins.** offence, endangering the existence of the city, the priestess in fault was severely scourged. The vestals had also to present offerings to the goddess, to cleanse and purify the shrine, to assist at all the great public festivals, and to guard the supposed sacred pledge and guarantee of the permanence of Roman power, which was kept in the inmost sanctum, and the nature of which is not known. If a vestal broke her vow of chastity, death was the penalty, at first by stoning, but later by burial alive with many of the ceremonies of a funeral. The Vestals were maintained at the public cost, and endowed with considerable funds, and they received many honours. The construction of the House of the Vestals shows many arrangements suited rather to a cold climate than to Italy—which may be survivals from the practices of the Romans' ancestors.

CASTOR AND POLLUX.

There were altogether fifteen flamens, who held office for life, unless they committed a breach of duty. They wore a special woollen cloak, and a round or conical cap called the apex, fastened by strings, and terminated by a pointed piece of olive-wood, the base of which was surrounded by a lock of wool.

*The flamens.*

The flamen Dialis, though highly honoured, was subject to many restrictions. He might never be absent from the city for one night; the legs of his bed were smeared with earth, perhaps an indication that he once slept on the ground; he might not touch a horse, a dog, a she-goat, ivy, beans, or raw flesh; in early times he could not hold a magistracy, though this was relaxed later. Thus he was compelled to be always devoted to his duties. His wife, called *flaminica*, gave essential service in certain ceremonies, and had a special costume.

## THE PONTIFFS.

The priestly colleges were more important than the individual priests. The pontiffs (*pontifices*) formed an order or college to which supreme religious authority was given by the State. They were originally five in number, including their chief, the *pontifex maximus;* but the number was raised to nine in B.C. 300, and in 81 B.C. to fifteen. They were elected by different methods at different periods; but on the whole they were pretty successful in retaining the right to nominate their own candidates when vacancies occurred. They had control over all the flamens of particular deities, and directed all State ceremonies. They kept the books which laid down the order of public and private worship, and they were bound to give information to any one who consulted them about religious matters. They determined the proper forms for burials and for appeasing the Manes. When any deficiency was observed in regulations already existing, they made new ones, generally, however, being guided by what was in accordance with established custom. Without being responsible to the Senate or to any court of law, they had the power of punishing any one who disobeyed their commands. They arranged and proclaimed the State calendar, containing the dates of the various festivals, of new and full moon, etc., and thus undoubtedly we must regard them as embodying much of the historical and scientific knowledge of the time; in fact, they themselves described their sphere as "the science of things divine and human." In general the Pontifex Maximus was a distinguished person; and in the later years of the republic he was often at the same time consul, though the pontifex never left Italy till the time of Crassus. Under the emperors their power was greatly

FLORA.

weakened, the emperors exercising the right to nominate any persons pontiffs when they liked, and always appointing themselves chief pontiffs.

Divination, or the ascertainment of the will of the gods, was represented at Rome by the augurs, a word at first **Divination.** applied to men skilled only in divining by birds, but later extended very considerably. Their art was known as augury or *auspicium;* and our use of the words auspicious and inauguration testifies to the deep impress which this mode of divination has left. According to Livy, at Rome everything was done according to auspices. The Romans were distinguished from numerous other nations by their small regard to astrology, prophecy, and oracles (excepting under Greek **The augurs.** influence); but they paid great attention to unusual natural events, especially unfavourable ones, which they termed prodigies—to thunder and lightning, the flight of birds, the feeding of chickens, etc. A remarkable account of divination is given by Cicero, who was himself an augur, in his two books on that subject. The regard given to the flight of birds at Rome was founded on the belief that birds were the messengers of Jove; they derived from studying them intimations of what they were to do or not to do. Thus, whenever it was reported by an augur that Jupiter thundered or lightened, the public comitia could not be held.

Birds gave auguries by flight or by voice. The eagle (known especially as Jove's bird) and vulture were among the chief birds whose flight was studied, while the raven, crow, hen, and owl afforded signs by voice, a special meaning being given to every sound they uttered, varying according to the circumstances, the time of the year, etc. The feeding of special chickens, especially on military expeditions, was noted; if they ate greedily, it was a favourable sign; if they refused their food, and beat their wings, etc., the omen was unfavourable. Auspices from quadrupeds were only used in private divination; a fox, wolf, dog, horse, or any quadruped unexpectedly crossing any one's path, gave an indication, varying according to circumstances. Sneezing, stumbling, and

# THE AUGURS.

other personal matters were also considered to be means whereby the gods indicated their will.

In taking the auspices, the augur first marked off with a wand a certain portion of the heavens which he was to observe for the flight of birds and other phenomena, and set up a tent with an opening in that direction. Then he watched from this observatory, amid silence and quiet, until some indication appeared by which he could interpret the will of the gods.

Originally the augurs were persons appointed to assist the king or chief magistrate, and for a long period only patricians were eligible for the office. Any patrician could take private auspices. The chief magistrates continued to be the possessors of the right to take and declare the auspices; but the augurs were the continuous representatives of the art of augury; and as they acquired the right of pronouncing whether the indications were favourable or unfavourable, they really had a veto upon all important public business. Up to B.C. 300 there were four augurs; then they were increased to nine. Sulla added six more, and Julius Cæsar made the number sixteen. New members were elected by the surviving augurs, till B.C. 103, when they were elected by popular vote, after which there were variations of law. Finally the emperors assumed the right of appointing augurs at pleasure. By this time augury had become a mere farce. *[margin: Relation to the magistrates.]*

We have little knowledge of early Roman marriage. In the later Republic the only form of marriage celebrated with religious rites was that known as *confarreatio*, when a sheep was sacrificed, and the bride and bridegroom sat down upon its skin, spread over two chairs. Then a solemn prayer was pronounced, followed by another sacrifice. Many of the other forms observed are of great significance in anthropology.

Roman funeral ceremonies were not specially religious in character; but a coin was placed in the mouth of the corpse to pay Charon, as in Greece. In early times burial was in vogue; in the later Republic burning took its place, and continued in general use till Christianity had gained great influence. In early times captives and slaves were killed at the funeral pile; later, animals took their place, and gladiators fought around the burning **Funeral cere-** pile. The ashes were deposited in funeral urns, **monies.** which, in the case of rich people, were placed in fine monuments of different forms, which occupied long distances by the side of public roads, such as the Via Appia. All persons who attended a funeral were rendered impure, and required purifying by a priest, who sprinkled them with pure water from an olive or laurel branch. Tombs were held sacred, and those who violated them were liable to heavy punishment. The mourning and various ceremonies after a funeral lasted for nine days, after which another sacrifice was offered, and a feast was given in honour of the dead. The tombs were visited at certain periods, and sacrifices and gifts were offered to the dead. In particular there was an annual festival (*Feralia*) at which food was carried to the tombs.

We gain considerable insight into early Roman religion from the very early calendar of public festivals which **The calendar** has come down to us. There we see Jupiter, **of festivals.** Mars, and Quirinus in the leading places. Jupiter was celebrated on all the days of full moon (Ides) and on various wine festivals and other days; Mars on the 1st of March and the great festivals of March, as well as in autumn after campaigns were over. In April there were festivals to Telusl, the earth, to Ceres, to Pales, goddess of flocks, and Jupiter as protector of vines, and to Robigus, the enemy of the crops. Consus and Ops were celebrated in harvest time and in December, in which month also the Saturnalia took place as a festival of seed-sowing. In February took place the wolf festival of the shepherds (*Lupercalia*), and the boundary festival of the husbandmen. Vulcan's was almost the only handicraft festival, in August; but there was a second festival to him in May, the consecration of trumpets. The *Neptunalia* in July, the *Portunalia* (the harbour festival), and that of the Tiber in August, represented sea divinities. Vesta and the Penates were honoured in June; the *Matralia* in the same month celebrated the goddess of birth, and the *Liberalia* was a festival of childbirth. Departed spirits were honoured on February 21st, and the ghosts or Lemures had a three days' festival in May. The flight of King Tarquin was kept in mind on February 29th, while the peoples' flight was noted on July 5th, though it is doubtful what event it commemorated. Several other festival days seem scarcely intelligible.

The abstractness of Roman worship is one of its most noteworthy features. Unlike the Greeks, with their warm imaginations, they did not give elaborate per- **Abstract** sonal histories to their gods; they were rather **deities.** names for qualities or ideals. Their festivals had reference mainly to practical wants and considerations. The frugal, legal, and commercial spirit of the people is well seen in their early religion. They were particularly interested in the departed spirits because of the benefits they thought they could render to the living; and no doubt many of their gods, like those of the Greeks, represented deified heroes who had conferred great benefits on the people. In all things the kings or magistrates were supreme. The priests never acquired the supremacy the Brahmans gained in India; and when the magistrates were priests also, it was rather a sign of the temporal power controlling the spiritual than the reverse.

We have received no verbal ritual, no celebrated sacred book from the Romans; and clearly their genius did not go in this direction. Mommsen says that their **Essence of the** religion depended only in a minor degree on **religion.** fear of natural forces, and consisted especially in songs of joy, in games and dances, and in banquets. Yet all extravagant expense was strictly forbidden. "At the very core of the Latin religion," he says, "there lay that profound moral impulse which leads men to bring earthly guilt and earthly punishment into relation with the world of the gods. . . . The execution of the criminal was as much an expiatory sacrifice offered to the divinity as was the killing of an enemy in just war. . . . The profound and fearful idea of substitution also meets us here; when the gods of the community were angry, and nobody could be laid hold of as definitely guilty,

THE EMPEROR CALIGULA WORSHIPPED BEFORE THE STATUES OF CASTOR AND POLLUX.

they might be appeased by one who voluntarily gave himself up; noxious chasms in the ground were closed, and battles half lost were converted into victories, when a brave burgess threw himself as an expiatory offering into the abyss or upon the foe. The sacred spring was based on a similar view; all the offspring, whether of cattle or of men, within a specified period were presented to the gods." This was no doubt a sacrifice in view of the removal of a calamity, and at first, no doubt, all infants born within the assigned periods (March and April) were sacrificed. In later times the infants were allowed to grow up to the age of twenty, and then were marched out of the State, to go where they would. Thus, no doubt, many colonies were formed; and the Mamertines of Sicily in particular derived their descent from such an exodus.

Such a religion, in the hands of a commercial and legal people, became very formal. "The gods confronted man just as a creditor confronted his debtor—each of them had a right to certain performances and payments; and as the number of the gods was as great as the number of the incidents in earthly life, and the neglect or wrong performance of the worship of each god revenged itself in the corresponding incident, it was a laborious and difficult task even to gain a knowledge of one's religious obligations," and the priests gained a corresponding influence. Yet the individual man had to discharge his religious obligations himself; and no doubt through this there came to be various ceremonies in which a sham or a literal fulfilment of an obligation at little expense was substituted for something more genuine. "They presented to the lord of the sky heads of onions and poppies, that he might launch his lightnings at these rather than at the heads of men. In payment of the offering annually demanded by father Tiber, thirty puppets plaited of rushes were annually thrown into the stream." Legality, not genuine devotion, zeal for the State and its progress, not for the righteousness of the individual, were the keynotes of Roman religion. It was on the whole a religion easy to understand; it powerfully aided the State in its growth and in maintaining its stability; but it did not tend to give rise to great works of imagination, of poetry, of art, or even to great religious books. Hence it died, while Hinduism and Buddhism have lived.

Greek influence may be credited with the origin of the third college at Rome, of men skilled in interpreting oracles, originally the keepers and interpreters of the Sibylline books, which contained prophetic utterances and oracles in Greek. At first two men were charged with this function, who had two slaves skilled in Greek; later there were ten and then fifteen members in this college, who consulted the books only by special command of the Senate. The books were destroyed when the temple of Capitoline Jove was burnt, in B.C. 82; but new ones were collected and compiled in later times. The Delphian Apollo was also consulted by the Romans in comparatively early days of the Republic; and Hercules was adopted into current conceptions as a god of gain by special adventure or good fortune. Generals gave a tenth of their spoil, and merchants a tenth of their property, to Hercules at the altar in the cattle market, and business agreements were confirmed at the same altar. His altars were everywhere to be seen in the streets and on country roads. Castor and Pollux, Hermes as Mercury, and Æsculapius were also among the Greek gods early adopted by the Romans.

*Keepers of the Sibylline books.*

We must view the moral character of the Romans by the light of the conquests they achieved as well as the religion they believed in. Justice to equals, sternness to inferiors, to women, to children, were among its characters. The religion was certainly a binding force, but not one of affection. Morals were cherished, such at least as could be seen to affect the welfare of the State; but any questions of conduct which did not affect the State or the father's rule were most probably decided on selfish principles; and the aristocrat and the rich man did largely as they liked, within the limits of State welfare. Extravagance was sternly repressed, however; rich men were heavily taxed; and we

*Moral character of early Romans.*

may view Roman morals under the earlier Republic as the most advanced the world had yet seen in general practice. A more than Chinese rule of the father over his family gave him power to kill or to sell his son; and this discipline, loveless and stern, carried out in State and army, enabled the Romans to conquer the world.

In the third and second centuries B.C. the State religion, Hellenised, became more expensive; and in 196 B.C. a new college of three banquet masters was added to the other three. The priests gained more privileges, and were more highly endowed; and it was rare for an estate to descend without a heavy sacrificial obligation as a perpetual charge. A tenth of a man's property was often given to religion, and with the proceeds a public feast was given twice a month at Rome. More money was spent, and more pedantry was displayed in every department of religion, and insensibly the old beliefs were being undermined. The consuls began to arrange the auguries to suit their own views; and poets and philosophers began to explain away the gods, leading to belief in no gods. Then superstitions, conjuring, charms, and astrology from the East began to make way. In B.C. 204 the Phrygian goddess Cybele, mother of the gods, was publicly admitted among the Roman divinities, and a rough stone was imported as the real Mother Cybele with great rejoicing; and her eunuch priests in Oriental costume marched through the streets with foreign music and begged from door to door. A few years afterwards Bacchus worship was introduced, and corrupt orgies were celebrated, leading rapidly to widespread crime and immorality. Though many thousands were sentenced to death for these crimes, the evil was not suppressed. Against it the pure, well-governed life of the type of Cato the Elder had little chance of permanence. With him may be said to have disappeared that grand morality which was a reality in ancient Rome, that zealous industry for State and family which made Rome great. Crime, immorality, and luxury spread, as vividly described in Mommsen (Book iii. chap. xiii.); and the festivals of the gods were made the occasion for extravagant banquets and display, women taking a more and more prominent part. Grand spectacles and gladiatorial games became common. Money and pleasure were the new gods. "All shifts seemed allowable to attain rapidly to riches—plundering and begging, cheating on the part of contractors and swindling on the part of speculators, usurious trading in money and in grain, even the turning of purely moral relations such as friendship and marriage to economic account. Marriage especially became on both sides a matter of mercantile speculation; marriages for money were common."

*Degradation of morals.*

Are we reading the description of rich Rome only? Cannot the same things be said to a large extent of England in the nineteenth century; and if so, are we so much better than the Romans?

Later still, from 150 to 100 B.C., extravagance and immorality increased at Rome to a frightful extent. Luxury and Hellenism, with scepticism about the national gods, were almost universal among the educated classes, though there are signs that the uneducated were not so bad, at any rate in many parts of Italy outside Rome. Yet the example of the leaders was most evil in its effects. There was in progress a combination of Greek and Roman civilisation in which the old faith and the stern morality were largely lost. Instead there were unbelief, state-ceremonial, and the Greek gods, popular superstition, and the introduction of Asiatic and Egyptian sects. Not being original in philosophy, the Romans became bad imitators only; and the schools we described in the last chapter gave their names if not their thoughts to those Romans who cared to think at all seriously on such subjects. The Stoics were the most influential, for their toleration of popular and State religion, their view of every phenomenon as in its degree divine, their honour for deceased heroes, their casuistical morality, suited the intelligent Roman very well. Many said, that while the intelligent had no need of religion, the populace must be fed and controlled by signs and wonders; and religious rites and

*The later Republic.*

*Decay of religion.*

grand festivals were kept up more than ever. Indeed, the providing of expensive sacrifices and games came to be a qualification for magistracy, which none but the rich could afford. We need not detail the foreign elements which found their way to Rome; it must suffice to say that they were abundant, varied, and not in any way an improvement on the beliefs which Rome had now laid aside.

These evils grew, and were exaggerated up to the time of the Cæsars. Julius Cæsar, at least in some respects, endeavoured to stem the torrent of evil, making regulations against extravagance, and, to a considerable extent, enforced them. Morality and virtue had almost become unknown; crimes of all kinds, including murder, were frequent. Cæsar's police at least checked this open licence. As he tolerated the Egyptian gods in Rome, so he permitted the Jews to worship freely there, and so established at Rome the germ of the mighty Christian revolution. But the spirit of the people is shown by the introduction at the gladiatorial games of the practice of deciding as to the fate of the vanquished by the will of the spectators. Men of strength and courage were so far without a field for their labour, that free men were known to sell themselves to be gladiators. Nothing new arose in Rome itself to purify morals and religion, except so far as the rise of imperialism led to the adoption of measures needed to secure military unity. The Epicureans and Cynics extended their influence. *Julius Cæsar.*

Under the Empire some renewal of life came to the old religion, with its Greek transformation. The Emperor Augustus discerned that religion might be made use of to strengthen his empire; and his superstition about many things is well established. His very title embodied an idea of sacredness allied to divinity. He rebuilt old temples and restored ancient customs; and he added three important new worships and temples, those of Venus Genitrix, Mars Ultor (the avenger), and Apollo Palatinus. The latter he particularly affected, often wearing the attributes of his favourite deity. He also endeavoured to reform public *The Empire.* *Augustus.*

morals as to expenses, marriage, and the behaviour of women. He restored (in B.C. 16) the "secular games," which had previously included expiatory sacrifices to the deities of the lower world, Pluto and Proserpine, but which he replaced by Apollo and Diana. It was for this occasion that Horace's "Carmen Sæculare" was composed, in magnification of Rome and Augustus. The Emperor was made a member of all the priestly colleges, and supreme pontiff; the latter title was held by the Emperors up to the reign of Gratian, that is, for nearly four centuries. The Emperors were supreme in matters of religion. This supremacy was recognised in many quarters of the Roman Empire by the introduction of the Emperor's name into the old festivals, and the celebration of many new ones in his honour. Augustus, in the latter part of his life, built a new temple to Vesta adjoining his temple of Apollo; and his own palace assumed many of the characters of a temple. The people, who had already acquiesced in the deification of Julius Cæsar, made Augustus a god during his lifetime; and we can trace in the history of early Roman Emperors the process by which many at least of the ancient gods came to be worshipped. Temples of Augustus, of Rome, and of the living Roman Emperor were rapidly built in many cities, served by priests of Augustus and of Rome. These became in each province the heads of the national religion, and, as such, played a great part in endeavouring to put down Christianity. Space does not permit us to follow here the history of the downfall of the Roman religion before the advance of Christianity. We can but note the singular accord between some of the teachings and beliefs of Seneca (died A.D. 65) and several of the Christian doctrines, such as the forgiveness of injuries and the overcoming of evil with good; and the lofty moral tone of the Emperor Marcus Aurelius (121–180), whose practical wisdom, control of bodily passions, and belief in the necessity of obeying conscience, make him very remarkable among Roman Emperors.

Seneca, though far from offering a bright example of moral conduct,—for he was the confidential adviser of the notorious Agrippina, and his having been the tutor of Nero does not redound to his credit as a successful inculcator of moral precepts,—must be judged in the light of his evil surroundings. Though he made happiness the main object of life, his statement of his aim is not an ignoble one: "True happiness is to be free from perturbations, to understand our duties toward God and man; to enjoy the present, without any anxious dependence upon the future; not to amuse ourselves with either hopes or fears, but to rest satisfied with what we have, which is abundantly sufficient; for he that is so wants nothing." But, he adds, there is no condition of life that excludes a wise man from discharging his duty: and in everything a man is to be honest and conscientious. Seneca has a comfortable belief in Providence, saying that God deals with us as a good father does by his children; tries us, hardens us, fits us for Himself; chastises some under the appearance of blessing, and blesses some when appearing to chastise them. He teaches that men ought to live for others, and be kind to slaves; and that the mind ought to rule the body. He strenuously denounced gladiatorial exhibitions. Marcus Aurelius, as Emperor, was an upholder of the Roman State religion and a persecutor of the Christians who denied it, and who especially denied the deity of the Roman Emperor. Yet he did many noble acts, and regarded mankind as a brotherhood, bound to strive for the common good. "No man," he says, "can do me a real injury, because no man can force me to misbehave myself; nor can I find it in my heart to hate or be angry with one of my own nature and family." He had not such a particular belief in Providence as Seneca, though he thought the gods directed all for the best; and neither he nor Seneca had a very confident faith in a future life.

[Mommsen's "Rome"; Boissier's "Roman Religion from Augustus to the Antonines"; Smith's Dictionaries; "Encyclopædia Britannica," under names of gods.]

# CHAPTER XII.

## The Religion of the Teutons (including Scandinavians).

Imperfect materials—Grimm's Teutonic mythology—Animism and ancestor worship—Woden, or Odin—His attributes—Frigg, or Frigga—Thor, or Donar—His hammer—His worship in Norway—Tiu, or Ziu—Fro, or Frey—His temple at Trondheim—Freyja—Njord—Æger—Balder—His death—Explanations of the Balder myth—Heimdal—Bragi—Goddesses—Erda, or Nerthus—Loki—Hel and her domain—The Teuton cosmogony—Origin of the gods—Valhalla—Its influence—The ash-tree Ygdrasil—The Supreme Deity—Prayer and sacrifice—Human and animal victims—Fruit and drink offerings—Worship in woods—The temple Tanfana—Images of the gods—Destruction of Irminsul—The priests—Beliefs in spirits, etc.—Ragnarok, or the end of the world—Doubtful points—Moral condition.

ALTHOUGH the native religion of the Teutons,—including in that name Scandinavians and Anglo-Saxons, as well as Germans,—was practised much later than that of the Greeks and Romans, we know far less about it, because the Teutons were less literary and cultivated than the Mediterranean peoples, and because, apparently, the northern religion was less fully and definitely developed. Yet we have in the collections of old myths known as the Eddas,—the older believed to have been compiled in the twelfth century in the Orkney or Shetland Islands by an Icelander, the younger in the thirteenth, by Snorre Sturlason, the Icelandic historian,—and in the writings of Are, an Icelandic priest who wrote in the early part of the twelfth century,

*Imperfect materials.*

in the "Historia Danica" of Saxo Grammaticus, written in Latin, and in various writings of Tacitus, Dis, Marullinus, etc., extremely valuable materials for study.[1]

But it remained for the nineteenth century to furnish us with a most important contribution to the elucidation of Teutonic religion in the gigantic work of Jacob Grimm (1785–1863), "Teutonic Mythology,"[2] in which philosophy, folk-tales, old customs, and antiquarian remains were combined with the old literature to reconstruct a system of ideas and practices which had long vanished from general recognition. He demonstrated the close affinity of speech and mythology between the Scandinavian and the German divisions of the Teuton race, the joint possession by all Teutonic languages of many terms relating to religious worship, and similar changes of gods into devils, of old festivals into Christian ones, and the remains of old beliefs about the gods in folk-tales and common phrases. Consequently Grimm is a great source from which knowledge on the subject must be drawn, although there is still much to be done in tracing the relations between the Teutonic and other Aryan mythologies. *Grimm's "Teutonic Mythology."*

Mr. York Powell ascribes to the Teutons animistic and anthropomorphic beliefs, as well as ancestor worship. They believed that all inanimate objects and animate beings had spirits akin to their own. The wizard and medicine-man flourished among them, and dreams were greatly regarded. Thus all the main primitive elements or types of religion existed among them. In addition, certain gods had attained prominence under cognate names in many tribes; but each had more or less its own special gods and observances. Consequently we find many variations of the same myths, and many tales related of different personages in different *Animism and ancestor worship.*

---

[1] See the works of Are (ed. Vigfusson and F. York Powell); the Elder and the Younger Edda; Saxo's "Historia Danica"; Jacob Grimm, "Teutonic Mythology"; Rydberg's "Teutonic Mythology"; Rasmus B. Anderson's "Norse Mythology."

[2] First published in 1835; now obtainable in an excellent English translation.

localities; but on the whole the general cast of the religion of the Teutonic peoples was the same.

The highest deity, by general consent, among the Teutons, was Woden, Wodan, or Wuotan, otherwise Odin (the Norse form). The word means all-powerful, all-penetrating; Woden bestows shape and beauty on man and things, gives song, victory in war, the fertility of soil, and the highest blessings. With such a warlike people, he was prominently the arranger of wars and battles, and thus he was sometimes confused with Tiu, the god of war. He is sometimes described as looking down on the earth through a window, and having Frigga sitting by his side. He took up the heroes who fell in fight into his heavenly dwelling. In the North, faring to Odin, visiting Odin, meant simply dying.

*Woden, or Odin.*

The Norse Odin is represented as one-eyed, wearing a broad hat and wide mantle. He has a wonderful spear, which he lent to heroes. To him were attached two wolves and two ravens, following the fight and seizing on corpses.

Just as in Gaulish mythology there is a god who represents several Greek and Roman types, so we find Woden also as a water-spirit or god, answering to Neptune. Others of his attributes are more like Hermes and Apollo. Severe pestilences spring from him, and also their cure. There are multitudinous details about the wanderings and journeys of Woden, or Odin, and his visits to giants and men. The sun is his eye. To him are traced up all the races of heroes and kings. The number of place-names in various countries compounded with his name shows the extent over which places were sacred to him or named after him. In England may be named Wednesbury and Wednesfield. The association of the name with Wednesday ( = Woden's-day) is another evidence of his importance. In Southern Germany his worship died out sooner than in the North, while the Gotlanders and Danes worshipped him more than the Swedes and Norwegians. In the Norse sagas Thor usually took precedence of Odin. The so-called historical Odin, the leader of the migration of the original

*His attributes.*

## ODIN WELCOMING A WARRIOR TO VALHALLA. 287

ODIN AND THE VALKYRIES WELCOMING A WARRIOR TO VALHALLA.

Teutons or Asas from a land near the Black Sea a century before Christ, appears to be mythical.

Frigg (Frigga) is the wife of Odin (distinct from Freyja, the sister of Freyr), and represents the inhabited earth, free, beautiful, lovable. It is doubtful which of the two gives the name to Friday. Frigg, as consort of Odin, takes highest rank among the goddesses; she knows the fates of men, is consulted by Odin, presides over marriages, and is prayed to by the childless. Balder is her son, whose fate she and Odin mourn together.

*Frigg, or Frigga.*

Returning to the great gods, Thor, Thunar, or Donar occupies the chief place after Odin. He rules over clouds and rain, lightning and thunder; yet he is a fatherly god, though a punishing one, and frequently angry. This conception answers well to that of Jupiter Tonans. Inasmuch as crops are greatly influenced by rains and thunderstorms, the control of them is attributed to Thor; so also Thor, like Odin, presides over the events of war, and receives his share of the spoils. Indeed, in the Norse mythology the warlike exploits of Thor greatly predominate over his peaceful achievements.

*Thor, or Donar.*

Thor is represented as enormously strong, with a long red beard, fiery eyes, girt with a belt of strength, swinging a hammer in his hand, wearing a crown of stars on his head. He rides in a chariot drawn by two goats. He is terrible when angry, but naturally good-natured. His hammer (mjolner) can split the mountains; the belt of strength redoubles his divine strength; he always wears an iron gauntlet when wielding the hammer. Longfellow, in his "Tales of a Wayside Inn," has vigorously represented some of the characteristics of Thor:—

*His hammer.*

> "The light thou beholdest
> Stream through the heavens,
> In flashes of crimson,
> Is but my red beard
> Blown by the night-wind,
> Affrighting the nations.

\* \* \* \* \* \*
Mine eyes are the lightning;
The wheels of my chariot
Roll in the thunder,
The blows of my hammer
Ring in the earthquake."

Thor's wife, Sif, is a symbol of the earth, and gold is termed her hair, Loki having cut off her hair and having caused dwarfs to make golden hair for her.

Thor is the true national god of the Norwegians; and his temples and statues were the most numerous in Norway and Sweden. Even into comparatively modern times there was special observance of Thursday or Thorsday; and the Esthonians thought Thursday more sacred than Sunday. According to Grimm, his sturdy strength recommended him specially to certain peoples; and "prayers, oaths, curses retained his memory oftener and longer than that of any other god." The numerous adventures and achievements recorded of him in the myths we have not space to refer to. <small>His worship in Norway.</small>

As showing how intensely the old Teutons valued military prowess, we find their third great god, Tiu, Tyr, or Ziu, associated with warlike deeds, though his sphere is wider than that; and it is here that we find a name as well as a signification closely like that of Zeus and Dyaus, the cases of which word are very parallel with the Gothic forms of Tiu. Although represented in the Edda as Odin's son, he becomes equal with him as a war god. He is the god of martial honour, the most daring of all gods, the giver of valour. The Romans identified Tiu with their Mars from the prominence of the martial character. The name Tuesday, wide-spread among the Teutonic peoples, is paralleled by the Latin *Martis dies*, French, *mardi*. <small>Tiu, or Ziu.</small>

Fro, or Frey, was a divine being (son of Njord) presiding over rain and sunshine and the fruits of the earth, and dispensing wealth and good harvests. He had a ship Skidbladner, made by the dwarfs, and capable of containing all the gods, with their weapons and war stores. Grimm connects him with the <small>Fro, or Frey.</small>

U

Roman Liber. The Edda ascribes to him a sword of surpassing powers, which could put itself in motion against the giants.

In Trondheim, during the reign of Olaf Tryggvason (king 995–1000 A.D.) there still existed a temple of Frey, in which he was zealously worshipped. The king overthrew the wooden statue of the god, and scolded the peasants for their foolish idolatry; where-

THOR.

upon they replied that Frey had often talked with them, foretold them the future, and given them good seasons and peace. There are numerous records of temples of Frey, sanctioned by wonders and miracles, in Iceland and Scandinavia. At Upsala, Frey was worshipped in conjunction with Odin and Thor.

Freyja, sister of Frey, as a goddess ranks next to

*His temple at Trondheim.*

Frigg, already mentioned. She is the Teuton Venus, and was invoked by lovers. The elder Edda thus describes Freyja and her abode in heaven:— *Freyja.*

> "Folkvang 'tis called
> Where Freyja has right
> To dispose of the hall-seats.
> Every day of the slain
> She chooses the half
> And leaves half to Odin."

Her husband, Oder, left her, and travelled into far countries, since which Freyja continually seeks him, weeping tears of pure gold. Hence gold is in poetry termed Freyja's tears. Women after death go to Freyja. All the varied emotions of love are exemplified by her. The name of her abode, "Folkvang," signifies the human dwellings, since no human being escapes her influence.

The father of Frey or Freyja, Njord, is a water deity, ruling over the winds and controlling the sea, in its relation to man. Hence he was invoked by fishermen and sailors. Over the raging ocean outside, Æger (the terrible) reigns, far from land. He is rather a giant than a god. He marries Rau, who has a net that catches those who venture out to sea. The nine daughters of Æger and Rau represent the varying aspects of the waves. *Njord.* *Æger.*

The story of Balder (Paltar), though there are fewer traces of his worship than of that of the superior gods, is perhaps the most attractive in Scandinavian mythology. Balder is the son of Odin and Frigg, and is the favourite of gods and men. He is rich in physical beauty, and rays of light issue from him. He is mild, wise, and eloquent; and his judgments, once pronounced, are unchangeable. Into his heavenly mansion nothing unclean can enter. The critical point in his history is reached when he has terrible dreams threatening his life. On his relating them to the gods, Frigg took an oath from everything not to harm Balder, but forgot the mistletoe. Then the gods wrestled with and struck Balder with darts and stones, but nothing could *Balder.*

harm him. But the evil spirit Loki found out the power of the mistletoe, and guided the hand of blind Other (a god of war) to throw it at Balder, who was pierced to the heart and died. The gods were smitten with utter grief, and at last besought Hermod the nimble to ride into the lower world to ask Hel, the goddess of the grave, to release Balder. Meanwhile Balder's dead body was burned on a great ship, amid great commotions of the elements; and Nanna, Balder's wife, died on the same pyre. This is told with great elaboration in the Eddas. Finally Hermod found Balder occupying the most distinguished seat in Hel's kingdom. Hel granted Balder the right to return to the gods, if all things living as well as lifeless would weep for him. Everything wept except the witch-giantess Thok, the step-daughter of Loki. The general explanation of this myth is, that Balder represents summer, which is finally overcome by darkness which long pervades all nature, till the thaw after frosts makes everything weep, and then summer returns. But a still deeper significance is read in it by some. So long as Balder, the best and wisest of the gods, lived, evil could not prevail. Loki, and the powers of evil, at last, after fierce contests, kill Balder, and it is only after this that the world can be renovated and purified, and Balder can return to the upper world to recommence a reign of happiness and peace. He is believed to represent also the heavenly light of the soul and the mind, purity, innocence, and piety.

*His death.*

*Explanations of the Balder myth.*

Most of the gods treated of after this are peculiar, or almost so, to the Scandinavian mythology. Heimdal, a son of Odin, is a bright and gracious god, and a powerful deity of strange origin, of whom the elder Edda says,—

*Heimdal.*

> "Born was I of mothers nine,
> Son am I of sisters nine."

He is watchman of the gods, with a powerful horn; and one of his functions is to keep the gods from forcing their way out of heaven. No sound escapes him; he sees by night as well as by day, etc., etc.

## BRAGI.

Bragi is another son of Odin, and the god of wisdom, poetry, and eloquence. At the Scandinavian sacrificial feasts a horn consecrated to Bragi was often drunk from by the guests, who at the same

Bragi.

THE GODDESS FREYA.

time promised to perform some great deed, to furnish matter for song.

Several of the goddesses have already been mentioned, together with their husbands or sisters. "They are,"

says Grimm, "thought of chiefly as divine mothers,
**Goddesses.** who travel round and visit houses, from whom the human race learns the occupations and arts of housekeeping and husbandry, spinning, weaving, tending the hearth, sowing, and reaping. These labours bring with them peace and quiet in the land; and the memory of them abides in charming traditions."

Erda, the earth, appears under many appellations among the Teutons as the fruitful, teeming mother. Tacitus **Erda, or Nerthus.** relates that numerous Teutonic peoples worshipped Nerthus, who was mother Earth. She was said to be worshipped in an island at a great festival, during which the priest communed with the goddess, and then performed a secret bathing of the goddess and her vestments and vehicle in a lake. The other goddesses, numerous enough, are too indistinct, or too considerably derived from Roman sources, to be dealt with at length here.

Loke, or Loki, the spirit of evil, appears among the gods in various seductive guises, and he pervades all **Loki.** nature as a corrupting influence. Originally he appears as the companion and relative of Odin, and in the Elder Edda he says,—

> "Do thou mind, Odin,
> That we in time's morning
> Mixed blood together!
> Then thou pretendedst
> That thou never wouldst ask a drink
> Unless it was offered to both of us."

He was fabled to have taken part in the creation of man, contributing the senses and passions, the sources of evil desires. He became sly and treacherous, beautiful in appearance, but inconstant and evil, the slanderer of the gods and the contriver of deceit and fraud. Thus nobody honours him as a god. His name is variously derived from air and flame. In union with a giantess he begot the wolf Fenrer; Hel, who presides over the land of death, is his daughter. He is represented as leading the gods into all kinds of predicaments and calamities, though often extricating them by his artifices. Through his devices gold was cursed and became the source of many calamities to mortals, as related in the Edda, in the songs about Sigurd, Brynhild, Gudrun. The whole constitutes in effect a great epic, which may be read in the Volsunga Saga, as translated by Eirikr Magnusson and William Morris.

The goddess or giantess Hel has a gloomy domain under one of the roots of Ygdrasil, surrounded by a fence, and watered by rivers. A dog stands outside of a cave and loudly howls. Hel binds the dying man with chains which cannot be broken. She has a nethermost place for the wicked, with a palace named Anguish, a table, Famine, and a bed, Care. *(Hel and her domain.)*

We must now turn to the cosmogony current among the Teutons. Originally there existed nothing where the world is; there was simply a space or gap between the two poles, cloud and fire. In the cloud was a spring, out of which twelve rivers flowed. *(The Teuton cosmogony.)* By a mysterious process, by the might of him who sent the heat (i.e. the Supreme Being), out of thawing drops of water Ymer was formed, a giant and evil principle: from him arose the race of the giants. Later a cow arose, from whose milk Ymer was nourished. The cow fed by licking stones, and after much licking there was born from the spot a man, Bor or Buri, who became the father of Odin, Vili, and Ve, the gods and rulers of heaven and earth. There is much more of this fanciful mythology, which we cannot go into; and moreover, it is by no means certain how far it was believed in by the people as a part of their religion. The giant Ymer being killed, his huge body supplied material out of which the gods formed all the world, while mankind were formed out of two trees on the seashore, to which the gods gave breath. In this mythology the gods, *ass* (plural *œsir*), appear as a higher product, after an imperfect first creation. They dwell together in Asgard, with higher heavens above them. Twelve gods were reckoned, and twenty-six goddesses. Odin dwelt in a great hall, Valhal or Valhalla, its ceiling supported by spears, its roof formed of shields. To it Odin *(Origin of the gods.)* *(Valhalla.)*

invited all those who were wounded or fell in battle; there they were fetched and waited upon by the Valkyries, Odin's waiting-maids. Similarly distinct abodes are assigned to the gods and goddesses.

The belief in Valhalla exercised a great influence on the Norsemen. The warrior was cheered when dying by the thought that the Valkyries had been sent to invite him to Valhalla; only by true courage could he win Odin's welcome. The cowards he would despise and drive away, and thus it was misery to the Norseman not to die valiantly in battle. In Valhalla there is a perpetual food, a miraculous boar, cooked every day, but becoming whole again every night; and perpetual supplies of mead and water furnish them with drink.

*Influence of Valhalla.*

One of the most interesting Norse conceptions was that of the ash-tree Ygdrasil, whose branches furnish bodies for mankind, whose roots extend through all worlds, whose branches reach through the heavens, and which fosters all living things. One of the three great roots of Ygdrasil stretches to the giants, and under this is Mimer's fountain, in which wisdom and wit are hidden. Under the root which extended to the asa-gods is a holy fountain, where the gods sit in judgment. By this fountain there dwell three maidens, Urd, Verdande, and Skuld (Present, Past, and Future), called norns, who fix the lifetime of men, and dispense good destinies; while other evil norns give men bad destinies or misfortunes.

*The ash-tree Ygdrasil.*

The Supreme Deity cannot be identified with any of the Norse gods, but rather with that "him who sent it," who was before the beginning of creation. And the word "God," which is a very old Teutonic word, is not identified with any particular named god, whence we may possibly derive the conclusion that the named gods are mainly ancestors or hero gods, or personifications of powers or departments of nature.

*The Supreme Deity.*

Both prayer and sacrifice to the gods date from the earliest times we can discern among the Teutonic peoples. Sacrifices were not necessarily, though frequently, of animals. The gods were invited to take their share of human food, and later, separate offerings were made to them. They were frequently thank-offerings, a share of the gift or gifts bestowed by a god being offered to him. Other sacrifices were expiatory, and offered on occasions of disaster, famine, pestilence, etc. Human victims were, no doubt, occasionally offered, in circumstances of special gravity; frequently they were captured enemies, or slaves, or criminals. Horses were favourite animals for sacrifice, horseflesh being very generally eaten by the Teutons. The head was not eaten, but specially consecrated to the gods. Oxen, boars, pigs, rams, and goats were also offered; white being a favourite colour for sacrificial animals. Among the Norse peoples the animal was killed on a sacrificial stone, and the blood caught in a trench or in vessels; with it the sacred vessels were smeared and the worshippers were sprinkled. A great part of the meat was eaten by the priests and people. *Prayer and sacrifice. Human and animal victims.*

Fruit offerings occupy but a small space in the Teutonic records; but drink is more prominent. On any festal occasion some of the food would be laid aside for the household spirits, and some drink would be poured out to the gods; and at great festivals and sacrifices the gods were separately honoured, and horns drunk to them. This was called drinking their *minne*, or memorial draught; it was also the custom to bemoan absent or deceased friends in this way. *Fruit and drink offerings.*

The old Teuton words for temple also mean "wood," indicating that primitive Teuton worship was conducted in woods or groves. "There dwelt the deity," says Grimm, "veiling his form in the foliage; there the hunter must present to him the game he has killed, and the herdsman his horses and oxen and rams." There are scantier traces of worship of the gods on hill-tops, in caves, or by the river side. In the groves no images are mentioned as being set up, and no temple walls appear to have enclosed the sacred space. But altars and sacred vessels were erected there, and heads of animals were hung from boughs. The proper name of Holy Wood, *Worship in woods.*

common in many parts of Germany, probably is a relic of this ancient worship.

There are, however, traces of the existence of built temples among the Teutons. Tacitus gives an account of the destruction of a celebrated temple of the Marsi called Tanfana, in A.D. 14; and he also describes a worship of Mother Earth, the carrying about of her image, and its return to the "temple." But descriptions of these temples are very scanty and imperfect. As soon as Christianity gained headway, we have records of their burning and destroying both sacred groves and temples, and often of the Christians building a church on the same sites. We hear of an important temple of Frey, at Upsala, where was a famous oracle and place of sacrifice. Heligoland was once a noted Teuton place of assembly, with a temple. The temples had the usual sacred character, and no improper action (that is, censured by the god or his priests,) must be done within their precincts.

*The temple Tanfana.*

Images of the gods, of some kind, were no doubt made; they were of wood, stone, and metal, but to what extent they were made in human forms we do not know, as none have come down to us. They may often have been but rude symbols, bearing some form associated with the gods. In some cases they had covered carriages, analogous to the Hindu idol-cars, in which the images were dragged about over the fields, to give them fertility. Sometimes we hear of three images of gods seated side by side; that of Thor was the most common in Norway.

*Images of the gods.*

From the Frankish annals we learn that Charlemagne destroyed a principal seat of Saxon heathendom in Westphalia, called Irminsal, or Ermensul; and the accounts give us to understand that there was a celebrated worshipped pillar designated by this name. It appears to have been a great wooden pillar in the open air, as a symbol of the supreme god.

*Destruction of Irminsal.*

The early German priests were generally chiefs or leaders as well, and exercised a powerful influence, being judges as well as priests, controlling discipline in war, to which they carried such images of the gods as they possessed. But details about them are very scanty, and the same is the case as regards the Norse priesthood. **The priests.** They no doubt exercised the functions of divination, as well as of sacrifice and prayer. Prophetesses were in high repute among the Teutons, and they were much occupied in divination.

We have not space to describe the crowds of spirits of various kinds, heroes, giants, elves, dwarfs, etc., with which the Teutons peopled the unseen world. **Belief in** They belong to the domain of animism, which **spirits, etc.** can be studied abundantly in the pages of Grimm, and in the folklore of the Teutonic peoples, but which cannot be framed into any body of doctrine definitely taught as a religion. There is a vast body of mythology too, relating to magic, ghosts, devils, animals, and plants, which it is impossible to enter on here, which would be of great importance if we were endeavouring to trace the nature, or growth, or varied forms of the religious sentiment.

We must briefly refer, in conclusion, to the ideas associated with the name Ragnarok, which signifies the final catastrophe of the world, and the death of the **Ragnarok, or** gods. Throughout the mythology, events hap- **the end of** pening to the gods foreshadow their final des- **the world.** truction. The growing depravity of the world precedes this, attended with frightful calamities, akin to those described in the Christian Apocalypse. Strange miracles and phenomena will abound. The great contests between the evil spirits and the good, and the final destruction of all are grandly described in the elder Edda; but it is difficult to be certain that parts of it are not a reflection from the Apocalypse, and therefore we do not go into details. When the earth and the heavens have all been consumed by flames, a new heaven and a new earth arise. "The fields unsown yield their growth. All ills cease: Balder comes." There are halls for the good and virtuous, in some of which all who delight in drinking good drink will find plenty. A terrible hell also is imagined for the evil, built entirely of the backs of serpents, with heads turned inwards, vomiting venom.

> "Then comes the Mighty One
> To the great judgment;
> From heaven he comes,
> He who guides all things:
> Judgments he utters;
> Strifes he appeases,
> Laws he ordains
> To flourish for ever."

It should be borne in mind, as a qualification of any too confident conclusion on the Teutonic religion, that **Doubtful points.** scholars vary in their estimate as to the degree in which Christianity influenced what we know of the religions it superseded in the North. But in this account the elaborations found in the later Edda are very largely omitted. We have made no attempt, also, to trace the influence of totemism in Teuton countries, which was no doubt considerable.

The moral principles of the Teutons may be summed up briefly thus: honour and kindness among kin and **Moral condition.** tribesmen, deceit, violence, and enmity to all outside. Bravery was a cardinal virtue, and sincerity and generosity were appreciated towards kinsfolk and friends. Reverence certainly existed both towards gods, superiors, and the old, but was liable to be overborne by passion and self-seeking. Great cruelty was often shown towards slaves, strangers, and enemies; and the witchcraft and superstitions believed in indicated a comparatively low intellectual elevation.

## CHAPTER XIII.
### The Religion of the Slavonians.

**Nature and ancestor worship—Svarog—Dazhbog—Perun, or Perkunos—His great image at Kief—Its destruction—The sacred oak—Other gods—Svantovit—Temple at Rügen—Four-headed image—Great expense of service—The horse of Svantovit—Great harvest festival—The horn of mead—Zernabog—Lado and Lada—Inferior spirits—The journey after death—Heaven and hell—Haunting spirits—The house spirit—Witches, charms, and spells—Priesthoods and temples—Imperfect remains.**

AS the latest race to enter into civilised ranks, it is not to be wondered at that the religion of the Slavs[1] was less elaborate than that of the Teutons. It is doubtful whether there ever existed a Slavonic collection of poems at all comparable to the Eddas, still less to the Vedas; but there still remain isolated songs and fragments, which illustrate the popular ideas, even if they fall far short of what we might desire. We find reason to believe that they combined, like other Aryan peoples, worship of the forces of nature with that of the spirits of deceased ancestors. While they worshipped the sun, moon, stars, and elements, or their spiritual governors or actuating powers, they most deeply reverenced the forces producing storms, and had a thunder-god Perun, who may be compared with the

*Nature and ancestor worship.*

---

[1] W. R. S. Ralston: "Songs of the Russian People," and "Russian Folk-Tales;" G. F. Maclear: "The Slavs" (Conversion of the West).

Teutonic Thor, and who ultimately became the supreme god.

There appears, however, as in the Vedic religion, to have been a gradual transference of the supremacy from one to another series of gods. Thus it is believed that the earliest great god was Svarog, said to mean "shining one," and to correspond to the Vedic god Varuna, and the Greek Ouranos. Both the sun (Dazhbog) and fire (Ogon) are described as his children, to whom he deputes the work of creation, and the actual rule over creation. The word Dazhbog appears to mean Day-god, the last syllable signifying god.

*Svarog.*

*Dazhbog.*

Perun, or Perkunos, who afterwards became the chief deity, has been identified with the Vedic god Parganja (supposed by some to be another name for Indra), the thunderer, the showerer, the beautiful. In Lithuania we read of a statue of him, which held in its hand "a precious stone like fire, shaped in the image of the lightning." Before it a fire of oak-wood was constantly kept burning. His name still lingers in popular expressions about thunder. The following is said to be a prayer formerly said in Livonia at a feast in the beginning of spring, " Perkons! Father! thy children lead this faultless victim to thy altar. Bestow, O father, thy blessing on the plough and on the corn. May golden straw, with great well-filled ears, rise abundantly as rushes. Drive away all black, haily clouds to the great moors, forests, and large deserts, where they will not frighten mankind, and give sunshine and rain, gentle falling rain, in order that the crops may thrive." In one of the Lettish songs we are told that "Father Perkons has nine sons; three strike, three thunder, three lighten." Among the White Russians Perun is described as tall and well-shaped, with black hair, and a long golden beard. He rides in a flaming car, grasping in his left hand a quiver full of arrows, and in his right a fiery bow, and sometimes he flies abroad on a great millstone, which is supported by the mountain spirits who are in subjection to him, and who by their flight give rise to

*Perun, or Perkunos.*

storms. In the spring Perun goes forth in his fiery car, and crushes with his blazing darts the demons, from whose wounds the blood is sometimes described as streaming forth. (Ralston.)

The great image of Perun at Kief, set up on rising ground, had a trunk of wood, a head of silver, and moustaches of gold, and held a mace. Near the end of the tenth century this was still worshipped until Vladimir, who reigned over the Russians at Kief, was converted to Christianity, and had the statue pulled down, dragged across the hills at a horse's tail, flogged all the while, and finally flung into the Dnieper. The people called on their god to show his power, but nothing happened, and the conversion of the Russians was rapid. Similarly the image of Perun at Novgorod was thrown into the Volga. *His great image at Kief. Its destruction.*

Perun's bow has been identified with the rainbow, and his flaming dart has been represented as a golden key, with which he unlocked the earth, brought to light its concealed treasures, and locked away fugitives from the reach of wizards. His golden key is also interpreted as the lightning with which he breaks up the frost-bound earth in spring, or pierces the clouds and lets loose the rains.

As among numerous other Aryan peoples, the oak was a sacred tree among the Slavonians; and it was connected with the worship of Perkunos by the oak-fire already mentioned. *The sacred oak.*

Together with the statue of Perun at Kief, there were the images of other gods. Khors and Dazhbog, probably different forms of the Sun-god Stribog, god of the winds, Simargla and Mokosh, the latter two being otherwise unknown. *Other gods.*

Svantovit is the name given to the chief god of the Baltic Slavonians within the historic period. This as well as Radegast, the god of war, and Yarovil have been interpreted as forms of the Sun-god. *Svantovit.*

At Arcona, the capital of the island of Rügen, the Danish Christian missionaries, as related by Saxo Grammaticus, found a beautiful wooden temple with inner and outer

304   *THE RELIGION OF THE SLAVONIANS.*

**Temple at Rügen.** courts, the latter with a roof painted red. The inner court was draped with tapestry, and contained numerous paintings. But the image itself was of Oriental strangeness. It had four heads and necks,

HERTHA LAKE, ISLAND OF RÜGEN.

**Four-headed image.** two chests, and two backs, but only two arms, it would seem. The great right hand held a horn of several metals, which was once a year filled with mead. The left arm was bent in the shape of a bow, and the lower limbs were covered. Beside the statue lay a bridle and a sword with silver hilt and scabbard.

In honour of the deity thus represented, expensive worship was maintained, partly devoted to the priests and partly to the ornamentation of the temple. Besides the proceeds of a yearly tax, one-third of the booty taken in war was given to the temple; and in addition it received large offerings from the chiefs. A special body of horse-soldiers, said to number three hundred, fought in the name of the god and gave all their spoils of war to the priests for the ornamentation of the temple. *Great expense of service.*

The white horse of Svantovit was an animal sacred to the god, on which he was believed to accompany his people to war, of course invisibly. Only priests might feed him or ride upon him, and it was a serious offence to do the slightest injury to him. The horse was regarded as an oracle in case of war. He was led out, after prayer to the god, to step over three rows of spears; and if, in stepping, he lifted his right foreleg first, that was regarded as a favourable omen for the success of the war: any other proceeding was unfavourable. *The horse of Svantovit.*

A grand harvest festival was held at the close of the harvest in Rügen. Considerable sacrifices of cattle were first offered, followed by a feast. An old priest, with hair and beard uncut, then entered the innermost sacred enclosure of the temple, to sweep it carefully. During this operation he was strictly required to hold his breath, in order not to defile the presence of the god; each time when he was compelled to breathe he must emerge from the temple precincts. When this was over, he took the horn of mead from the hand of the image and carried it out to the assembly, proclaiming whether it had decreased or increased since the last festival. If the former, scarcity was imminent; if the latter, plenty was in store. It was then poured out as a libation to the god, and the horn was refilled by the priest, with a prayer for a prosperous year *Great harvest festival.* *The horn of mead.*

X

and for success in war. This horn-full was next drunk by himself at a draught, and the horn again filled, to remain untouched (it was supposed) till the succeeding year. Offerings of sweet cakes made of honey and flour were then presented, and finally the priest, representing the god, blessed the people, exhorting them to sacrifice continually to the god, who in that case would give them victory over their enemies. An abundant feast followed. It appears that there were other images of gods in Rügen, one, named Porenut, presided over the seasons, and had five faces, one being upon his chest. Another, Rhugevit, had seven faces and eight swords; possibly he is identical with Radegast, already mentioned. Triglav was another god, whose image was destroyed at Stettin, and the triple head sent to the Pope.

*Zernabog.* Among the evil or cruel deities feared by the Slavonians must be included Zernabog, to whom human sacrifices were offered with frightful rites.

Lado and Lada are two names of gods about whom there is some doubt. They have been compared to Frey *Lado and* and Freyja, and Lada is called the goddess of *Lada.* love and pleasure. Lithuanian songs are quoted, in which Lada appears as "our great goddess," and Lado is coupled with the sun. An old chronicle describes Lado as the god of marriage, of mirth, of pleasure, and of general happiness, to whom intending brides and bridegrooms offered sacrifices, to secure prosperity in their married life. In Russian songs *lado* and *lada* are commonly used as equivalents for bridegroom, lover, husband, and bride, mistress, wife. Kupala was a god of the fruits of the earth, and Koleda, a god of festivals. The name Koleda has been transferred to Christmas in various parts of Russia; while in some districts the midsummer festival of St. John's eve is called St. John Kupala.

Besides gods, the Slavonians peopled their outer world *Inferior* with numerous inferior spirits, such as dwarfs, *Spirits.* wood-spirits, water-sprites, house-spirits, etc.; and beliefs about them are still common among the Russian peasants. In fact, animism, combined with reverence for the spirits of deceased ancestors, was in full vogue among them, and it still lingers.

The Slavs thought that after death the soul had to begin a long journey, either in a boat across a sea, or on foot. One view was, that a steep hillside had to be climbed, at the top of which paradise was situated. One word for the abode of the dead, Rai, meant the abode of the sun, in the East, always warm and light. Similarly, another name for it, Peklo, means a place of warmth; but it is now used as a name for hell. But there are other views which consider the grave itself as the abode of the spirits of the dead. The old Slavs seem to have had no idea of a future state of reward and punishment, of redress or compensation for evils suffered in this life. Rather did they consider death only the preliminary to a similar life to the present. *The journey after death. Heaven and hell.*

Before burial, the spirit was supposed to remain near the body, sometimes haunting the old home for six weeks, during which they watch the behaviour of the bereaved. No doubt it was a very general belief, that the souls of parents watched over their children and grandchildren, and that ancestors ought always to be reverenced. How this belief came to be associated with the domestic fire, and how the stove became associated with the house-spirit is not clear. The house-spirit is believed to live behind the stove; formerly he was more closely connected with the fire. Even now Russian families are known, when removing from one house to another, to rake out the fire from the old stove into a jar and carry it to the new house, the words "Welcome, grandfather, to the new home!" being pronounced when it arrives there. On the 28th of January, Afanasief says, the Russian peasants after supper leave out a pot of stewed grain, for the house-spirit. This pot is placed on the hearth in front of the stove, and surrounded with hot embers. Very generally the hearths are believed to be haunted by the spirits of deceased ancestors. There are many superstitions connected with beliefs or fears as to these household spirits, which are *Haunting spirits. The House-spirit.*

often believed to be at times malicious or mischievous.

**Witches, charms, and spells.** It is scarcely necessary to say that the old Slavonians had their witches and wizards, and believed in charms and spells, were-wolves and vampires; to a considerable extent their descendants do so still.

There are many other features of Slavonian belief and custom that it would be interesting to dwell upon; but it is so doubtful to what extent they belonged to the developed Slavonic religion, or to previous states of belief, and to what extent they have originated or been transformed in Christian times, that we must not venture farther into regions of hypothesis and doubt.

We know comparatively little, too, about the priesthoods and administration of the Slavonian religion. The **Priesthoods and temples.** Eastern Slavs, indeed, appear to have had no regular priesthood, religious rites and ceremonies being performed by the heads of families or communities; and no doubt the chief of a community or tribe was also its priest. Sacrifices were simply offered under a tree, preferably an oak, or beside a stream, and regular temples were not built. Among the Western Slavonians the priesthood assumed a more definite character, though even here associated largely with civil or warlike functions; and references to temples have already been several times made. On the whole, the Slavonic religion appears to have been as little developed as that of any Aryan **Imperfect remains.** people, though its beliefs were firmly held, and have left marked traces even to the present day. But the lack of anything like Scriptures, or even a mythology of distinct and elevated type, diminishes its general interest and value very considerably.

## CHAPTER XIV.

### Celtic Religion.

Rhys's Hibbert Lectures—Julius Cæsar—Roman names of Celtic gods—Ogmios, the Gaulish Mercury—Maponos, the Gaulish Apollo—Caturix, the Gaulish Mars—Camulos—Baginates and Esus—The Welsh duw—Nodens—Stonehenge—The mistletoe—Aryan affinity of myths—The Druids probably pre-Aryan in origin—Cæsar's account.

WE are extraordinarily ignorant as to the religious ideas of the early Celts, and their origin. We have but scanty or unsatisfactory literary or other remains to help us, and their decipherment and reconstruction have only recently been undertaken. Professor Rhys, in his "Celtic Heathendom" (Hibbert Lectures, 1886), has made by far the most important contribution to the question; but much that he puts forward is merely tentative, and thus it will not be profitable to dwell at any great length on the subject. Rhys's Hibbert Lectures.

Julius Cæsar, as on so many other subjects, has left us the most important information as to the religion of the Gallic Celts ("De Bello Gallico," vi. 17). He learned much from the Druid Divitiacus; and although he identifies and names the chief Gallic gods in accordance with Roman beliefs, at any rate we are in contact with an authority contemporary with the actual existence of the religious ideas set down. Julius Cæsar.

Cæsar tells us that a god he names Mercury was worshipped above all others, and under many images. He was regarded as the inventor of the arts, the patron of roads and journeys, of commerce and money-making. Apollo was regarded as driving away diseases, Minerva as the teacher of various trades and arts, Jupiter as the ruler of the sky, and Mars as the director of wars, to whom all spoils of battle were dedicated, the animals being sacrificed and the other booty being collected and dedicated in sacred places. Most of our information from inscriptions dates from Gaulo-Roman days, when the Romans following Augustus had taken the Celtic gods into their pantheon, and included the Gaulish divinities among the Roman Lares and Penates, as Lares Augusti; and thus the evidence is imperfect.

*Roman names of Celtic gods.*

In a single district like that of the Allobroges (mostly east of the Rhone and south of Lake Geneva, with Vienne as capital) there were twenty-six temples dedicated to the Gaulish "Mercury;" and there were many others in the department of the Puy de Dôme, on the summit of which was a great temple of the Arverni, which Pliny describes as having an image of Mercury 120 feet high, which was not destroyed till the middle of the third century A.D. The native name of this god appears to have been Ogmios (also represented as Hercules), god of speech, eloquence, and wisdom; and this name, Ogmios, Professor Rhys identifies with the Welsh ovyd or ofydd, a teacher or leader; while in Irish Ogma is one of the gods, the inventor of writing and of the Ogam alphabet, to provide for secret speech known only to the learned.

*Ogmios, the Gaulish Mercury.*

The Gaulish "Apollo" bore among others the names, Maponos, Grannos, and Toutiorix. The first name has been found in three inscriptions in the north of England; it means boy, or male child. Grannus, the name used among the Belgæ, suggests "shining," "glow," "sunshine." Several of his inscriptions are found near medicinal springs, as those of Aix-la-Chapelle, Granheim, etc. A female divinity associated with this Apollo Grannus was Sirona, represented

*Maponos, the Gaulish Apollo.*

as a matron holding in one hand a bunch of fruit, in another some ears of corn.

The Roman Mars was identified with a Gaulish god Caturix, meaning king of war, or lord of battle. Other names assigned to him are Segomo and Dunates. The Mars Vintios is yet another name, suggesting the wind as associated with the war-god. Again, the name Camulos is met with in association with the war-god; it is the name found in Camulodunum (Colchester); and Camulos is supposed to mean the sky, and he has been compared to Jupiter as god of the heavens. And numerous facts point to the war-god having been in early times the supreme Celtic divinity, though reckoned lower in Cæsar's time. *Caturix, the Gaulish Mars.* *Camulos.*

A god named Baginates has been identified with Jupiter, but very little is known about him. Esus, or Hesus, who may possibly be connected with this god, was identified by the Gauls with the Roman Silvanus; and he is represented as felling a tree with an axe, and probably presided over woodlands and the interests of shepherds. But all these gods are very dim and shadowy as yet. There appears to be more certainty about the ascription of a genius or divinity to each locality, to whom libations were annually made; and about the worship of matron goddesses, or matres, who enjoyed a large share of Gaulish worship; besides which the land was regarded as having an indefinite number of evil spirits, goblins, witches, etc. They, as well as the good spirits, are often represented in threes. *Baginates and Esus.*

Coming to the gods of the insular Celts, while the Sanskrit *deva* and the Greek Zeus are represented by the Welsh *duw*, the latter means any god, and the word never appears to have become used of one supreme god by the early Celts. There are facts which suggest that the Irish Nuada of the Silver Hand represented Zeus and Jupiter. He was said to have been the king of the mythical colony that took possession of Erin more than 3000 years B.C. In Wales we find this name Nodens, remains of whose temple have been found at Lydney, on the west bank of the Severn, in the coun- *The Welsh duw.*

STONEHENGE, SALISBURY PLAIN, A SUPPOSED CELTIC TEMPLE.

try of the Silures. In both countries he appears to have been a leader in war, and there are symptoms of his being the king of the gods, giver of wealth and lord both of land and sea; he appears to be a relic of a time when the sharing of domains among the gods was by no means so far advanced as among classic Greeks and Romans. Other gods are even less definite, and we can gain more vivid notions about the demigods or deified heroes of the Celts than about the nature-gods. According to Mr. Rhys, Stonehenge was believed to be the work of Merlin the enchanter working under the orders of the Celtic Zeus, and thus it would be a temple of this god; but we have no evidence as to the precise way in which it was used for worship. Merlin, though an enchanter, was believed to be immortal; and even when his body is killed, his living spirit abides with it, though no longer able to render it active. *Nodens.* *Stonehenge.*

Leaving till a little later such descriptions of the Druids as we can find, what can we say of the god they worshipped? What is the meaning of the intimate association of the Druids with the oak? This is, in fact, a part of the common heritage of the Aryans, who associated the grand growth of the oak with their supreme god. Pliny says the Gaulish Druids hold nothing more sacred than the mistletoe and the tree it grows on, provided it be an oak. They selected groves of oak, and performed no sacred rites without its leaves. Maximus Tyrius says the Celts worshipped Zeus under the image of a lofty oak. *The mistletoe.*

Prof. Rhys infers that the early mythology and beliefs of the Celts were substantially similar to those of the Greeks and Hindus, but that the form in which we have the narratives handed down to us is so modified by the influence of Christianity, that it is difficult to disentangle the ancient elements. He lays stress upon the traces of a sun hero, a culture-hero, and dawn goddesses; but the precise conclusions which should be drawn are very uncertain. *Aryan affinity of myths.*

We must place the Druids here, though no doubt their occupation dated from pre-Aryan times, and perhaps was more rooted in pre-Aryan than in Aryan thought. Cæsar gives the fullest and apparently the most authentic description of the Druids, though of course allowance must be made for his Roman education. We quote the following from the "Gallic War" (Book vi., c. 13, etc.): "They attend to sacred things, perform public and private sacrifices, and interpret all matters of religion. A great number of youths resort to them for the sake of instruction, and they enjoy the highest honour in that nation; for nearly all public and private quarrels come under their jurisdiction; and when any crime has been committed, when a murder has been perpetrated, when a controversy arises about an inheritance or about landmarks, they are the judges too. They decree rewards and punishments; and should any one, whether a private individual or a public man, disobey the decrees, then they exclude him from their sacrifices. This is with them the severest punishment. The persons who are thus laid under interdict are regarded as injurious and wicked people; everybody recoils from them, and shuns their society and conversation, lest he should be injured by associating with them; nor is justice administered to them when seeking it, nor is any dignity bestowed on them.

"All these Druids have one chief, who enjoys the highest authority among them. When he dies, he is succeeded by the member of the order who is most prominent; . . . if there are many equal, the successor is elected by the Druids. Sometimes they even contend in arms for the supremacy. At a certain time of the year, the Druids assemble on the territory of the Carnutes, which is believed to be the centre of all Gaul, in a sacred place. To that spot are gathered from everywhere all persons that have quarrels, and they abide by their judgments and decrees. It is believed that this institution was founded in Britannia, and thence transplanted into Gaul. Even now-a-days, those who wish to become more intimately acquainted with the institution generally go to Britannia for instruction's sake.

"The Druids take no part in war; nor do they pay

tribute like the rest of the people; they are exempt from

DRUID.

military service, and from all public burdens. Attracted

by such advantages, many come to be instructed by their own choice, while others are sent by their parents. They are reported to learn in the school a great number of verses, so that some remain there twenty years. . .
Beyond all things, they are desirous to inspire a belief that men's souls do not become extinct, but pass after death from one body to another; and they hold that people are thereby more strongly urged to bravery, the fear of death being disregarded. Besides, they hold a great many discourses about the stars and their motion, about the size of the world and of various countries, about the nature of things, about the power and might of the immortal gods; and they instruct the youths in these subjects."

"The nation of all the Gauls is extremely devoted to superstitious rites; and on that account they who are troubled with unusually severe diseases, and they who are engaged in battles and dangers, either sacrifice men as victims, or vow that they will sacrifice them, and employ the Druids as the performers of those sacrifices; because they think that unless the life of a man be offered for the life of a man, the mind of the immortal gods cannot be rendered propitious, and they have sacrifices of that kind ordained for national purposes. Others have figures of vast size, the limbs of which, formed of osiers, they fill with living men, which being set on fire, the men perish enveloped in the flames. They consider that the oblation of such as have been taken in theft, or in robbery, or any other offence, is more acceptable to the immortal gods; but when a supply of that class is wanting, they have recourse to the oblation of even the innocent."

Nothing really more satisfactory than this can be ascertained about the Druids; and we must leave readers to derive from it what notions they can. To us it appears that the Druids were the descendants of old magicians and medicine-men, who adopted to a great extent the ideas about the gods which the invading Celts introduced: but at best this is conjecture.

# INDEX.

## A.

Abadites, 169.
Abbaside caliphs, 116.
Ablutions, Mahometan, 131.
Abu Bekr, 76, 90, 92, 93, 94.
Acaba, Pledge of, 73, 74.
Adar, 36.
Adonis, 53.
Æger, 291.
African Mohammedans, 178.
Akala, 174.
Ali, "the Bab," 168.
Allah, 60.
Altar, Greek, 222.
Amen-ra, Hymn to, 4.
Amun-ra, 11.
Ana, 32.
Ancestor worship, 184, 186, 285, 301.
Angels, 99.
Animal Worship, 11.
Animism, 12, 285.
Anubis, 10.
Aphrodite, 200.
Apis, 8.
Apollo, 195.
"Apology" of Plato, 242.
Arabian, early religion, 57.
Arabs, 58, 60.
Ares, 206.
Aristotle, 248.
Artemis, 198.
Aryan myths, 313.
Ashtoreth, 52.
Assur, 41.
Assyrian religion, 31.
Astrology, 20, 45.
Athēnē, 193.
Augurs, 272.
Augustus, The Emperor, 281.
Aurelius, The Emperor Marcus, 282.

## B.

Baal, 52, 54.
Babel, Tower of, 47.
Babism, 167.

Babylonian religion, 31.
Bacchus, 207, 279.
Bagdad, Fall of, 118.
Baginates, 311.
Bairam festival, 153.
Baker, Sir S., Conversation with African chief, 24.
Balder, 291.
Banquets, Egyptian customs at, 30.
Bel and the Dragon, 47.
Bel-merodach, 38.
Books, Ancient Egyptian, 22, 24.
Bragi, 293.
Burial, Ancient Greek, 231.
  Egyptian, 21, 26.
  Mahometan, 136.
  Roman, 274.

## C.

Cæsar, Julius, 281, 309, 314.
Cairo, Mosque at, 149.
Calendar,
  of Roman festivals, 274.
Caliphs, The first, 114.
  in Spain, 116.
Camulos, 311.
Caturix, 311.
Celtic Religion, 309.
Chaldæan sacred literature, 32.
  tablets, 46.
Charms, 308.
Chemosh, 55.
Christians, Influence of, on Arabs, 62.
Circumcision, 135.
Comus, 264.
Concubinage, 107, 135.
Cordova, Mosque at, 149.
Cosmogony, Early, 45, 187.
  The Teuton, 295.
Cox, Sir G. W., on Myths, 187.
Creation, Account of, in Koran, 98.
Crusades, 117.
Cybele, 279.
Cynics, 249.
Cyrenaics, 249.

## D.

Dagon, 55.
Damascus, Mosque at, 149.
Dancing dervishes, 158.
Darazi, 173.
Dav-kina, 34.
Day of Judgment, 102.
  of Sacrifice, 81.
Days, Sacred, 49.
Dazhbog, 302.
Dead, Book of, the, 22.
  Egyptian idea of, 21.
  Immediate fate of, 187.
  Recitals for the, 23.
Death, Early Greek idea of, 230.
  Mahometan idea of, 136.
  Slavonian idea of, 307.
Deified kings, 299.
Deities, Abstract, of Rome, 275.
Delphian Oracle, 198, 223.
Dēmētēr, 201.
Dervishes, 157, 158, 161, 166.
Devil, 99.
Dionysos, 207.
Divination, 272.
Divorce, 107, 135.
Dome of the Rock, 148.
Donaldson, Dr., on the Greek Theatre, 227.
Donar (or Thor), 288.
Dósch, 160.
Drama, The Greek, 227.
Druids, 314.
Druses, 172.
Duw, The Welsh, 311.

## E.

Ea, 33, 35.
Eddas, The, 284.
Egyptian religion, 1–30.
El, 52.
Eleusinian mysteries, 227.
Epic of Izdubar, 47.
Epicurus, 250.
Erda, 294.
Esus, 311.
Etruscan religion, 255.
European Aryan religion, 183.
Exorcism, 32.

## F.

Fakirs, 157.
Fasts, 81, 105, 154, 156.
Fatimite dynasty, 116.
Festivals of modern Islam, 156.
  Ancient Greek, 211, 218, 226.
  Bairam, 153.

Festivals, Chaldæan, 49.
  Egyptian, 18.
  Harvest, 305.
  Roman, 259.
  Roman Calendar of, 274.
Filial piety, Egyptian, 27.
Fire-god, Egyptian, 38.
Flamens, 270.
Flora, 263.
Freyja, 290.
Frigg (Frigga), 288.
Fro (or Frey), 289.
Future life—
  Heathen idea of, 20, 44, 99, 230, 244.
  Socrates on, 244.

## G.

Games, Ancient Greek, 226.
  Olympic, 226.
  Pythian, 226.
Genii, 268.
God, Arab idea of, 60, 62.
  of the Koran, 97.
  Moslem idea of, 127.
Gods of—
  Ancient Greece, 183, 186, 210.
  Celtic, 310.
  Egyptian, 3.
  Local, 2, 184.
  Philistines, 55.
  Roman household, 265.
  Slavonian, 302.
  Teuton, 291, 293.
  Tribal, 57, 188.
Goddesses, Teutonic, 294.
Greek morals, 232, 234, 247.
  philosophers, 236.
  religion, Ancient, 183.
Grimm Jacob, on Teuton mythology, 285.
Grote, Mr., on Greek myths, 188.

## H.

Hades, 209.
Hajj, 142.
Hakim, 173.
Hamza, 173.
Hanbalites, 121.
Hanifites, 121.
Harun-al-Raschid, 116.
Harvest festival, Slavonic, 305.
Hathor, 10.
Haunting spirits, 307.
Heaven and earth as creative powers, 82.
  Moslem idea of, 99.
  Slavonian idea of, 307.

INDEX. 319

Heimdal, 292.
Hel and her domain, 295.
Helios, 195.
Hell, Mahometan, 101.
   Slavonian, 307.
   Teutonic, 299.
Hellenism, 279.
Hephaistos, 203.
Hera, 192.
Heraclius, 74.
Hermes, 207.
Hestia, 203.
Holy War, 156.
Horus, 10.
Hosain, 115.
House-Spirit, Slavonian, 307.
Hymns, Babylonian, 43.

### I.

Iblis, 99.
Ibrahim, 170.
Idolatry, 104.
Idols, Arab, 60.
Images, Babylonian, 50.
   of Peruu, 303.
   Slavonic, 303.
   Teutonic, 298.
Imams, 126.
India, Mahommedans of, 177.
Indian Mosques, 151.
Intermediate state, 102.
Invocation of the Nile, 18.
Irminsal, 298.
Isis, 9.
Islam, 104.
   Modern, 114, 153.
Israelites, 28, 31.
Istar, 37.
Izdubar, 47.

### J.

Jabarites, 119.
Jackson, Dr. H., on Socrates, 238.
Janus, 261.
Jesus and the Koran, 103.
Jews and Mahomet, 80, 84.
Jinn, 58.
Judgment, Day of, 102.
Jummoo Musjid, 152.
Juno, 259.
Jupiter, 185, 256.

### K.

Kaaba, Rebuilding of, 64.
Kabiri, 54.
Kerbela, 176.

Khadijah, 63, 72.
Kharijites, 121.
King-deification, 298.
Kisweh, 156.
Koran, 96–113, 126.
Koreish, 76, 83, 84.
Kronos, 185.

### L.

Lada, 306.
Lado, 306.
Lake, Sacred, of the Egyptians, 24.
Lares, 226.
Latius, The, 255.
Lemures, 226.
Libitina, 265.
Local gods, 184, 188.
   religion, Egyptian, 33.
Loki, 294.

### M.

Magic, 32.
Magistrates and augurs, 272.
Mahmal, 156.
Mahometanism, 56–181.
Mahomet, Life of, 56–95.
   Family of, 63.
   birth and early life, 63.
   his marriage, 63, 73, 84.
   the awakening of his spirit, 65.
   and the vision of Gabriel, 66.
   receives the command to preach, 66.
   his nervous disorders, 66.
   his early adherents, 66.
   and the first pledge of Acaba, 73.
   his vision of Jerusalem and heaven, 74.
   and the second pledge of Acaba, 76.
   leaves Mecca, 77.
   at Medina, 77, 78.
   his later life, 82.
   his wars and politics, 82, 83.
   fights at the battle of Badr, 83.
   visits Mecca, 86.
   marches on Mecca, 86.
   destroys the Meccan idols, 88.
   Mecca submits to, 88.
   wins battle of Honein, 88.
   and the Coptic maid, 89.
   his dominion, 89.
   proclaims ban against unbelievers, 90.
   his last pilgrimage, 90.
   his last illness, 92.
   his death and burial, 93.
   Personal characteristics of, 93.
   his frailties, 95.
   his character and influence, 95.

Malikites, 121.
Manes, 226.
Maponos, 310.
Marduk, 36.
Marriages, 107, 135, 229, 273.
Mars, 260.
Matu, 38.
Mecca, 62, 67, 74, 77, 80, 81, 83, 91, 138, 141, 170.
Medina, 76-80, 86, 138, 170.
Megarians, 249.
Mehemet-Ali, 170.
Melkarth, 52.
Merodach, 36.
Meshed, 176.
Mesopotamians, 51.
Minerva, 262.
Miracles, 112.
Mistletoe, 313.
Moharram, 156.
Mollahs, 166.
Moloch, 54.
Mommsen on Roman religion, 283.
Monotheism, 2, 51.
Moon-god of Ur, 36.
Mos'em hell, 101.
   paradise, 99.
Mosques, Indian, 151.
   Mahometan, 79, 137, 139, 151, 152.
Motazilites, 119.
Muir, Dr., 79, 81.
Müller, Prof. A., on modern Islam, 164.
Mul-lil, 32, 36.
Mysteries, Eleusinian, 227.
Myths, Aryan, 313.
   Growth of, 187.

## N.

Nature gods, 54.
Nature-personification, 184.
Nature-religions, 4.
Nature-worship, 184, 301.
Nebo, 40.
Negroes and Mahometanism, 179.
Neith, 10.
Nergal, 38, 42.
Nerthus, 294.
Nile, Invocation of, 18.
Nin, 42.
Njord, 291.
Nodens, 313.
Noldeke, Dr., on Koran, 112.
Norwegian worship of Thor, 238.
Nymphs, Prophetic, 263.

## O.

Oak, Sacred, 303.
Oaths, 129.
Odin, 286.
Offerings, Fruit and drink, 297.
   Votive, 212.
Ogmios, 310.
Olympic festival, 226.
Omar, Mosque of, 147.
Ommyads, 115.
On, 6.
Oracles, 19, 397.
Orders of Modern Islam, 158.
Osiris, 6, 21-26.

## P.

Pales, 263.
Pallas Athēnē, 193.
Pantheism, 164.
Paradise, 99, 137.
Passion plays, 167
Pelasgians, 184.
Penates, 265.
Penitential psalm, Egyptian, 33.
Personification of Nature, 184.
Perun (or Perkunos), 302.
Philistines, The gods of, 55.
Philosophers, Greek, 236.
Phœbus, 195.
Phœnician religion, 52.
Pilgrimages, 58, 106, 142.
Plato, 236, 246, 247.
Pluto, 209.
Polybius, 252.
Pomona, 263.
Pontiffs, 271.
Poseidon, 208.
Prayers, Mahometan, 97, 105, 131, 158.
   Teuton, 297.
Predestination, 103.
Priests, Ancient Grecian, 211, 214, 216.
   Chaldæan, 49.
   Egyptian, 16.
   Roman, 269.
   Slavonic, 308.
   Teuton, 299.
Processions, 18.
Prophetic nymphs, 263.
   of Koran, 103.
Ptah, 10.
Pyrrho, 251.

## R.

Ra, 4.
Ragnarok, 299.

Ramadan fast, 81, 105, 154.
Ramanand, 222.
Republic of Plato, 247.
Rhys, Prof., on Celtic Heathendom, 309.
Rifayeh, 158.
Rimmon, 43.
Ritual, 23, 160, 305.
Roman,
  Early Empire, 281.
  Early Republic, 278.
  names of Celtic gods, 310.
Romanisation of Greek gods, 265.
Rome, ancient, Religion of, 253-283.

S.

Sacred days of Chaldæans, 49.
  lake of the Egyptians, 24.
  places of the Arabs, 59.
  tree, 303.
Sacrifices, 212, 213.
  Animal, 19, 50, 54, 59, 81, 297.
  Human, 19, 50, 54, 59.
Sacrificial gifts, 60.
Saints, Worship of, 162.
Saladin, 118.
Samas, 37.
Scandinavian religion, 284.
Schuyler, Mr. Eugène, on Turkestan, 158.
Scriptures, Moslem, 96.
Sculpture, Greek, 221.
Seneca, 282.
Sepharvaim, 37.
Serapis, 9.
Shafiites, 121.
Shiites, 118.
Shu, 5.
Sibylline books, 278.
Sidgwick, Prof., on Socrates, 241.
Silvanus, 264.
Sin, Ancient Greek idea of, 214.
  Moslem idea of, 129.
Slaves, Mahometan, 135.
Slavonian religion, 301, 303, 305.
Smith, Mr. George, his discoveries, 46.
Socrates, 237.
  his mode of life, 237.
  his discharge of religious duties, 238.
  his sign or dæmon, 238.
  not a sceptic, 239.
  and the Deity, 239.
  his view of Providence, 240.
  a moral teacher, 241.
  his ardour for knowledge, 242.
  personal appearance, 242.
  and his judges, 242.
  his condemnation, 243.

Socrates, his death, 245.
  on the future life, 244.
Spirit, House, Slavonian, 307.
Spirits, Haunting, 307.
  Inferior Slavonian, 306.
Star-worship, 45.
Stoics, 250.
Stonehenge, 313.
Sufism, 162, 164.
Sun god, 37.
Sunnites, 118.
Svantovit, 303, 305.
Svarog, 302.

T.

Tablets, Chaldaic, 46.
Taj Mehal, 152.
Tammuz, 37.
Tashkend, 158.
Tefnut, 5.
Temple, Delphian, 197.
  of Frey at Trondheim, 290.
  of Merodach, 40
  at Rugen, 304.
  Tanfana, 298.
Temples, of ancient Greece, 212, 218-222.
  Egyptian, 301.
  Private, of ancient Greece, 218.
  Roman, 268.
  Slavonian, 308.
  Teuton, 290, 298.
Teutonic cosmogony, 295.
  goddesses, 294.
  gods, 295.
  mythology, 285.
  religion, 284.
Themis, 195.
Thor, 288.
Thoth, 10.
Tiu, 289.
Tombs at Cairo, 149.
  Indian, 151.
Tower of Babel, 47.
Tree worship, 303.
Trinity, Doctrine of, 103.
Turkey, 176.

U.

Ulema, 123-126.
Ur, 36.

V.

Valhalla, 295.
Vertumnus, 263.
Vesta, 203, 263.

Vestal virgins, 269.
Votive offerings, 212.
Vulcan, 202.

### W.

Wahhabis, 169, 172.
War, The Holy, 156.
Witchcraft, 308.
Woden, 286.
Woman, Egyptian, 27.
   Mahometan, 108.
Woods. Worship in, 297.

### Y.

Ygdrasil, 296.

### Z.

Zeidites, 169.
Zernabog, 306.
Zeus, 190, 191, 193.
Ziu, 289.

www.ingramcontent.com/pod-product-compliance
Lightning Source LLC
Chambersburg PA
CBHW021207230426
43667CB00006B/594